To Piermont
Library

Letters describing
the life under soviet
occupation in
Lithuania from
1923 to 1965

Nijolė Paronetto

October 31, 2008

JUST ONE MOMENT MORE...
THE STORY OF ONE WOMAN'S RETURN FROM SIBERIAN EXILE

The letters of Konstancija Braženienė and Mindaugas Braženienė
written from Lithuania, East Germany and Siberia, 1944-1966

Konstancija Braženienė

Translated by Laima Sruoginis
Introduction by Laima Sruoginis

EAST EUROPEAN MONOGRAPHS, BOULDER, CO
DISTRIBUTED BY COLUMBIA UNIVERSITY PRESS, NEW YORK
2007

East European Monographs, No. DCCX

Printed in the United States of America

Table of Contents

Dedication	1
A Brief Overview of Twentieth Century Lithuanian History By Laima Sruoginis	3
A Silent Genocide By Laima Sruoginis	5
Bibliography	13
Introduction	15
Remembering Mama and our Brother	17
Letters from 1943 – 1947	23
Letters from 1956	53
Letters from 1957	75
Letters from 1958	97
Letters from 1959	113
Letters from 1960	129
Letters from 1961	139
Letters from 1962	159
Letters from 1963	173
Letters from 1964	191
Letters from 1965	205
Letters from 1966	229
Afterword	247
How Mama's Release Really Happened	249
Appendix	*251*

A Brief Overview of Twentieth Century Lithuanian History

Lithuania's post-World War Two experiences have shaped the national consciousness of that country, one can say, even up to the present. After being oppressed by the Tsar of Russia for over a century, Lithuania became an independent nation on February 16, 1918. In 1939 that independence was threatened with the secret signing of the Molotov-Ribbentrop pact between Hitler and Stalin, which divided the territories of Eastern and Central Europe under Nazi and Soviet rule. In 1940 the Soviet army invaded Lithuania. During that first occupation, which lasted from 1940 to 1941, roughly 185,000 Lithuanians were deported to concentration camps in the far reaches of Siberia. This number is a rough estimate because the deportations were kept secret from the outside world and solid records were not kept. The deportees were intellectuals, teachers, wealthy farmers, and government officials. These people were removed from their homes in the dead of night and placed into crowded cattle cars headed for Siberia. Family members were separated and in most cases never reunited. This wave of deportations came to an abrupt end in 1941 when the Nazis broke the Molotov-Ribbentrop pact and occupied Lithuania, causing the Soviet army to flee. During the German occupation from 1941 to 1944 roughly 200,000 Lithuanian Jews were murdered by the Nazis, wiping out almost the entire Jewish population of Lithuania. Jews had resided in Lithuania since the Middle Ages and Vilnius was called the Jerusalem of the North. The destruction of the Jewish community in Lithuania was a major blow to both cultures.

On July 7, 1944 the Soviet army invaded Lithuania a second time and this time remained there until 1992. During the second Soviet occupation roughly 118,000 more Lithuanians were deported to Siberia. Intellectuals who suspected they were on the deportation lists fled. This group of people made up the foundation of the Lithuanian émigré community that exists to this day in the United States, Canada, Australia, South America, and Europe. From 1944 through 1956 Lithuanian partisans, known as the "Brotherhood of the Forest" waged guerilla warfare against the Soviet regime. Within a decade roughly 20,000

Lithuanian young men and women died fighting for Lithuania's freedom.

Despite over four decades of Russification and Sovietization, Lithuania did not lose its national identity. On the fifty-year anniversary of the signing of the Molotov-Ribbentrop pact on August 23, 1989 roughly one million Balts joined hands, forming a human chain that stretched 600 kilometers from Tallinn, Estonia, to Riga, Latvia, to Vilnius, Lithuania. This massive event, organized by the three Baltic grassroots resistance movements, sent a clear message to Moscow and the West that Gorbachev's reforms alone would not satisfy the Baltic nations; that the people would not rest until those three countries were independent from the Soviet Union. On March 11, 1990 Lithuania declared its independence from the Soviet Union. Moscow imposed an economic blockade on Lithuania, creating shortages of gasoline, medicine, food, and heating oil. On January 13, 1991 Gorbachev sent Special Forces to take over the Vilnius Television Tower, Radio, and the first democratically elected Lithuanian Parliament. As a result of attacks on peaceful demonstrators fourteen people were killed and roughly 700 were injured. Only after the coup that toppled Soviet power in August 1991 was Lithuania officially recognized as an independent nation by the world.

Laima Sruoginis

A Silent Genocide

Ours was a silent genocide. Silent, complex, far-reaching, lasting more than a decade from its beginnings in June, 1940 when the Soviet Union violated the terms of its secret Molotov-Ribbentrop pact with Nazi Germany, to its resumption in 1944 when the Soviet army invaded and occupied the Baltics a second time, continuing through 1953. Only since the collapse of the Soviet Union in 1991 and the reinstatement of Lithuanian independence have the mass deportations of Lithuanians, Latvians, and Estonians been documented and studied in any formal way. Previous to 1991 the mass genocide that took place in the Baltics was kept silent by the KGB. The survivors of Siberian exile who managed to return to Lithuania after Stalin's death lived marginalized lives, stripped of the most basic rights. They could not register as permanent residents as required by Soviet law in order to seek employment and enjoy the basic benefits of civic life, and in that manner were forced to seek shelter with relatives or friends, if they had them. They could not obtain passports and therefore could not travel, much less join their relatives in the West. They could not receive packages or mail in their own names at a time when the Soviet economy was so dire that people subsisted by either selling or consuming the contents of packages mailed from relatives in the West.

This was because the exiles were considered enemies of the state, although they'd never been tried. L. Latkvoskis of the Latgale Research Center describes the manner in which exiles were tried in his article *Baltic Prisoners in the Gulag Revolts of 1953:*

There was a conspicuous lack of legality to these arrests, imprisonments, and deportations. The basic problem was the application of Soviet Law to occupied countries and the refusal of both the occupied peoples and the international community to recognize their incorporation. Under international law, deportation of a population in an occupied territory is forbidden. But even aside from this issue, there was a lack of regular judicial process or proof of guilt beyond the assertion of the secret police. Some prisoners, like the Latvian Miervaldi Ravis, were actually put on trial in the place of deportation itself. The trial took place before a special three-person military tribunal in the trial hall in Vorkuta. Ravis had no lawyer because "criminals under Article 58 are not expected to have lawyers represent them." Ravis reported: "the Vorkuta military prosecutor had authorized my arrest, based on the USSR criminal code Article 58, for 'military betrayal of the fatherland.'" (Miervaldis, Ravis, "Smagie gadi Vorkuta," *Latvijas Arhivi,* No. 2, 1995, 56.) The Latvian Valentins Ozolins, sentenced to 25 years when he was a 19-year-old soldier in the Latvian military, said that he was tried on the basis of testimony by someone who had never met him. Many of the imprisoned were sentenced without any trial or legal proceeding other than an MVD directive or tribunal decision made *in absentia.* (12)

Although the mass deportations of the Balts and the GULAG slave labor infrastructure created by Stalin were clandestine in the Soviet Union, during the course of the Cold War the Lithuanian, Latvian, and Estonian émigré communities compiled whatever fragmented information they could get from survivors of deportation to Siberia who had managed to join their families in the West. During the Cold War period a few books published eye-witness accounts of the mass deportations describing the inhumane conditions in the forced labor camps. One of the most significant of these publications is *Lithuanians in Siberia (Lietuviai Sibire)* published in 1981 by the Lithuanian Library Press. It is worth noting that even as late as 1981 the editor of this book found it necessary to add the following comment to the end of his Lithuanian introduction:

While working on this book I received threats: A postcard depicting a lonely path with my photo superimposed on top of it, showing me that following this path carried with it the threat of never returning; a magazine clipping with my name crossed out in red, as though dripping with blood; and then a photograph of an open, empty, coffin, supposedly waiting for me if I carried on with this project. However, all of us love the victims of our nation's genocide and Lithuania more than we love our own lives, and therefore these types of threats were not able to deter me from my work. (Prunskis 29)

Almost thirty years after the system of deporting Lithuanians in crowded cattle cars to Siberia had ceased, in Chicago, an editor documenting the stories of survivors had to fear for his own life. This type of fear was very real and it was pervasive both in Soviet occupied Lithuania and in the émigré communities abroad.

The Webster's New World College Dictionary defines genocide as "the systematic killing of, or a program of action intended to destroy a whole nation or ethnic group." Although accurate records of the numbers of Lithuanians deported were not kept by the NKVD, enough rough estimates exist to tell us that approximately one third of the Lithuanian, Latvian, and Estonian nations were exiled to their deaths in Siberia. Deportees were taken from all walks of life, but mostly educators, government officials, former military personnel and their families, and university faculty and students were deported. Infants, young children, and the elderly were deported along with adults.

In her article "The Legal Situation of Exile's," which appears in *Lithuanians in Siberia*, Elena Juciūtė, a former deportee, describes how people deported to Siberia were divided into two groups: exiles and prisoners. Juciūtė writes:

In Russian exiles were called "volnoje poselenie"—freely relocated. Although the exiled person arrived like the prisoner in a locked cattle car guarded by armed soldiers, once they were brought to their destination they were not kept behind barbed wire and were not escorted to their assigned work by armed guards like the prisoners.

The entire family would be exiled together. Only before the war, in 1941, were the heads of the families (the men) separated and placed in prisons. Women and children remained together...

A captured family would be taken away without any trial or interrogation and brought to a sparsely populated place, where they would have to start their lives over again in the most primitive conditions. They had to built themselves a shelter and find food on their own. They could walk freely in the area without being guarded, but they were required to register on time for the day's work quota. They had no passports and so they could not leave.

The second type of deportee—the prisoner—flowed in an endless stream through the Vilnius transit point to Siberia. Prisoners were taken from their homes without their families. Often the families would be deported later as exiles. The prisoner would be brought first to an interrogation center. There he would be held for two to three months or longer. He would be interrogated using various forms of torture. Once a case had been made it would be sent to Moscow for trial in absentia...

After the case had been made the prisoner would be held in jail, mostly the Vilnius Lukiškis jail, where he'd wait for the sentence from

Moscow—for how many years would he be given. Once the sentence was sent the prisoner would listen to the sentence, would be told how many years he was receiving and under what article, and would be told to sign. After this "trial" the prisoner would be placed in a cell to await deportation to Siberia…

In the place of exile the prisoner would be escorted back and forth to his work place under armed guard. (Prunskis 18 – 19)

Aleksandr Solzhenistsyn writes of the Baltic inmates at Ekibastuz in the Karaganda province where he was a prisoner: "I found the Estonians and Lithuanians particularly congenial. Although I was no better off than they were, they made me feel ashamed, as though I were the one who had put them inside. Unspoiled, hard-working, true to their word, unassuming—what had they done to be ground in the same mill as ourselves? They had harmed no one, lived a quiet, orderly life and a much more moral life than ours—and now they were to blame because we were hungry, because they lived cheek by jowl with us and stood in our path to the sea" (Vol. III. 43.)

Konstancija Bražėnienė was deported to Siberia in 1949. She was never told the reason for her deportation, but later learned that it was because her two deceased brothers had been priests, because her brother-in-law had been a member of the pre-war Christian Democratic Party, and because her deceased husband had been a member of independent Lithuania's first freely elected parliament, and also because her three children had gone to the West to study during World War Two and had not returned to live in Soviet occupied Lithuania. At the time of her deportation she was fifty seven years old.

In transit to Siberia Konstancija Bražėnienė found herself in good company. In the cattle car in which she ended up, among the throngs of people packed tightly together, there were a group of young newly ordained Catholic priests and seminarians from the Kaunas Seminary. One of the newly ordained priests, Vincas Algirdas Pranckietis, wrote a memoir in 1988 titled *Baikalo Žvejys (The Fisherman of Baikal)* in which he documents the trip to Siberia and his memories of Konstancija Bražėnienė who was assigned as Pranckietis's work brigade's house keeper. Father Pranckietis remembers Konstancija Bražėnienė in this way:

> For us lonely exiles Mrs. Konstancija Bražėnienė was truly a gift
> from God. She washed our clothes, mended them, and patched

them. We fishermen would go to her first when we needed help. Mrs. Bražėnienė often talked to me about her children, about how proud she was of them. But then she'd take a deep breath and wonder out loud if she'd ever see them again. She reminded me of my own mother—she was as pleasant, as sincere, as good, and just about the same age. I trusted this woman. When I'd go out on the lake fishing (with the fishing brigade) I would leave anything I had of value with her for safekeeping. (Pranckietis 58)

Pranckietis documents the long, crowded train journey north and reports how the priests even managed to hold mass in the cattle car using an over-turned suitcase as an altar. To keep their spirits up the people in the cattle car, young and old alike, would recite poems together or sing Lithuanian songs. One conservatory student had even managed to lug her most prized possession with her—an accordion.

However, not everyone made the journey in such relatively good spirits. Often infants, children under five, and the elderly would die during the long trip north. When the train stopped along the way at stations, soldiers would open the wagon doors, rip the dead from their relative's arms, and dump them alongside the tracks.

Pranckietis describes how on April 16th, after a journey of three weeks' duration, the train stopped in Irkutsk. The exiles were brought to a large hall where other Lithuanian exiles from Vilnius had already been brought. Every few hours new trainloads of people would arrive from various regions in Lithuania. The exiles were separated into work brigades and displayed to local Russian directors of factories, coal mines, logging camps, etc. in a type of twentieth century slave auction. The potential "employers" would walk the hall around examining each group and bartering with the KGB agents to get for themselves the youngest and healthiest work brigade (Pranckietis 51). Pranckietis recalls the moment when his group of thirteen priests and seminarians and six lay men and Konstancija Bražėnienė were handed over to be fishermen on Lake Baikal:

Everyone wants exile labor. They look over all the groups and go off to barter with the KGB agents, asking that they be given this or that group. They are looking for people who can work. They come and look us over. They like our group and that's why they want us for the coal mines, for the gold mines, for arctic expeditions, for logging.

We are quiet. After all, we do not care where they take us. We don't understand much of what is going on. We don't know anything. But a Jewish man from the canneries takes a look at us, sees that many young men together in one group, and decides: "You are coming to Lake Baikal to fish."

Lake Baikal… Fishing… It was unheard of! But we were interested in this lake. It seems that he too was able to quickly cut a deal with the KGB. By that evening we received one salted fish each. (Pranckietis 52)

In this manner Konstancija Braženienė found herself living on an island on Lake Baikal where she became the housekeeper for the men's fishing brigade. She was responsible for keeping house for a brigade of twenty fishermen. Her duties included cooking in the most primitive conditions with little food, cleaning, washing the men's clothes by hand, gathering wood from the forest and chopping it into firewood, and lugging water uphill from Lake Baikal back to the barracks. All of these duties had to be performed despite the weather, and often outdoors during blizzards. She lived on the island of Chuzhyr in the Olchonsky region until she was granted permission to return to Lithuania in 1956 because of extreme poor health.

Daina Parulskienė, in her introduction to the Lithuanian publication of *ir dar valandelė… (Just One Moment More…)* writes:

When Konstancija Braženienė unexpectedly receives a letter from her children while still in exile in Siberia, whom she'd had no news of for seven years, she writes to them, "I believe that you have remained my same three darling children, jut as I have remained your same mother, and I believe that the tides of life did not wash away from you those high ideals, and I believe that you have not brought shame onto my gray head, just as I have not brought shame onto you…" This simple Lithuanian woman, who'd suffered so much, who'd had no news of her children's whereabouts for seven years, does not ask about her children's material well-being, security, careers, but asks about their souls, about their humanity. Can there be any better evidence that suffering purifies? That it strips one of all that is unnecessary? It is my belief that this book has not only historical value, but also spiritual value. Konstancija Braženienė's experience bears witness to the fact that it is not external wealth that creates quality of life. A woman who has lost her son, her health, her stature in society, all her wealth, who is separated from her children, who after exile in Siberia is sleeping on a couch in her relative's home, writes, "Now, thank God, I want for nothing. I am living in my homeland, I receive news from you, what else do I need? Just to live and to give thanks to God." Even about her suffering in Siberia she writes the following, "I've brought home many treasures for my soul and for my mind." (Parulskienė 1)

Just One Moment More... documents the life of Konstancija Bražėnienė through her letters written to her children from 1944 to 1966, when after numerous unsuccessful attempts to obtain an exit visa from the Soviet Union, and aided only by a bribe delivered by a Lithuanian-American journalist to a Soviet government board in Vilnius, Konstancija Bražėnienė is finally reunited with her children after a twenty-two year separation.

It is important to remember while reading these letters that they were written under censorship. The early letters from 1944 were written during the Nazi occupation of Lithuania. At the time Konstancija Bražėnienė was hiding two Jewish children—Alexander Gringauz and Sarah Shilingovsky—in her home. She refers to these children in her letters simply as "the children." Konstancija Bražėnienė arranged to have the children brought to her from the Jewish ghetto in Kaunas by sending her son, Mindaugas, who'd been conscripted into the German army, to escort the children out of the ghetto and to her home wearing his German soldier's uniform. Konstancija Bražėnienė knew clearly that by hiding the children and other Jewish adults in her home she was risking not only her own life, but the lives of her four children as well. Her act was one of pure Christian belief as she believed that God would watch over her.

After the Soviet army invaded Lithuania a second time in 1944 censorship was once again imposed. Until 1966 Konstancija Bražėnienė wrote her letters under the watchful gaze of the Soviet authorities, especially since, unbeknownst to her, her daughter, Nijolė, had married the famous resistance leader Juozas Lukša-Daumantas.

And yet, despite the overbearing shadow of censorship, Konstancija Bražėnienė manages to speak her mind. In her letters she chronicles how the old Lithuania of the pre-war era gives way to a new Soviet Lithuania—one in which religious worship is a punishable crime, one in which young people are indoctrinated to unquestioningly internalize communist ideology, one in which Lithuania is cut off from the world and the only news available is Soviet propaganda, one in which people are encouraged to veer away from introspection, especially the type of introspection that comes from religious training, and instead to embrace a life of superficialities, drinking, parties. Konstancija Bražėnienė documents how the bureaucratic machinery of the Soviet Union grinds on, obfuscating any attempt to hold onto one's dignity.

This book is a tribute to the memory of Konstancija Bražėnienė. May her spirit of generosity, selflessness, and her example of courage in the face of tyranny live on.

Laima Sruoginis

Bibliography

Bražėnienė, Konstancija. *ir dar valandėlė...* Vilnius: Dialogo Kultūros institutes, 2004.

Gross, Kate Elizabeth and Rozentals, Darien Jane. *Lithuanian Children in the Gulag. Deportations, Ethnicity, and Identity.* Chicago: Lituanus, Volume 51:3 (2005)

Latvokskis, L. I. *Baltic Prisoners in the Gulag Revolts of 1953.* Chicago: Lituanus, Volume 51:3 (2005).

Pranckietis, Vincas Algirdas. *Baikalo Žvejys.* Vilnius: Vilniaus Dailės Akademijos Leidykla, 1998.

Prunskis, Juozas. *Lietuviai Sibire.* Chicago: Lithuanian Library Press, Inc., 1981.

Solzhenitsyn, Aleksandr. I. *The Gulag Archipelago.* New York: Harper and Row, 1973.

Introduction

It is likely that these letters would never have been published if it hadn't been for the persistence and the curiosity of our mother's grandchildren. They wouldn't let up asking us about who their grandmother was, why people talked about her so much, and what had happened to her. They asked us to tape record our memories of her. But it wasn't so easy to describe her the way we would have liked. All three of us, Algimantas, Vida, and Nijolė, had saved the letters our mother, whom we called Mama, and our youngest brother, Mindaugas, had written to us during our long separation—one that lasted twenty-two years (1944 – 1966). Mindaugas's letters ended in 1944 when he died an early death as a result of his imprisonment in a Soviet Prisoner of War Camp. Mindaugas's heroic act of saving two Jewish children from the Kaunas ghetto is described in Mama's letters. As adults both of these children described their rescue in letters that appear in the appendix of this book. For his heroism, many years after his death, Mindaugas was awarded The Life Savior's Cross by the President of a free and independent Lithuania.

These letters were written from Nazi-occupied Lithuania, from Siberia, and after 1956 onwards from Soviet-occupied Lithuania. We decided to gather all the letters together in one place. First we brought them to New York where Nijolė lives, and then later, when Vida became gravely ill, to Melbourne, Australia, where Vida lived. In 2001 and 2003 Nijolė spent weeks with Vida, nursing her through her illness. At that time Nijolė got the idea to transcribe all the letters written to us into the computer, so that they could be accessed more easily and be available to the grandchildren. We thought that eventually we'd translate them into English. The three of us had held onto all of the letters written to us by Mama. Most of the letters had yellowed and were disintegrating. They were fragile to the touch. Because the letters were written to the three of us at the same time, there was a lot of repetition. Finally, working between two continents, Nijolė and Vida were able to copy all the letters, removing sections that were repetitious.

For a long time we couldn't decide what to do with the letters. It seemed to us that Mama's descriptions of life in Lithuania, in Siberia, and again in Lithuania, in addition to the documentation of the ten years' struggle we engaged in to give Mama a peaceful place to live by pulling her out of the manacles of the Soviet Union, was worth much more than just something to be held onto as a memento for us and the grandchildren. Especially, since the letters revealed the inner workings of the Soviet system.

In Mama's letters you can feel how painfully she pined for us, how passionately she cared for us, and her indescribable desire to see us. It seems as though only her belief in the divine Lord helped her hold on with her poor health, without any rights, reduced to seeking shelter with relatives. Many of her sentences end with exclamation points. Especially in those instances when she wanted to tell truth about the communist system, but knows she must hold back because of censorship. In some places in her letters she fearlessly shares her thoughts on how communism undermined people's morals.

The title of this book, "Just One Moment More..." comes from the final words she wrote to Nijolė in her last letter, before her trip to America. By writing these words she was telling us that she would see us in a matter of moments.

Algimantas, Vida, and Nijolė

Remembering Mama and Our Brother

Our mother, Konstancija Bakšytė-Bražėnienė, was born February 10, 1892 in the village of Paraudė in the Utena region. Her parents, Jurgis and Konstancija Bakšys, were farmers and had eight children. Four died in childhood and the four that remained—Konstancija, Juozas, Pranas, and Veronika pursued higher education. Juozas and Pranas became priests. Father Juozas completed his doctoral degree in theology at Innsbruck University in Austria. He was very good with languages and according to family lore, spoke eleven languages fluently. He returned to Lithuania and was assigned the directorship of the Merkinė Gymnasium located on the border with Poland, which at the time occupied a third of Lithuania's territory. He was known there for his Lithuanian nationalist activities, particularly for helping Lithuanian young people escape out of Lithuanian areas occupied by Poland and into Lithuania. He was shot by the Poles for his activities in 1924. Pranas died in 1919 of typhus. Veronika also earned her doctorate at the University of Munich. Later she married Dr. Petras Karvelis and they had one daughter, Ugnė.

Konstancija was the least educated in the family. She completed elementary school and a well-known home economics school in Zakopane, Poland. She was a wonderful housewife and at one time, before Lithuania became independent in 1918, she was the manageress of a Lithuanian student dorm in Voronezh, Russia. She remembered those times fondly and with warmth and love recalled the names and surnames of the Lithuanian students who'd studied there. Many of them worked hard and went on to make meaningful contributions to the rebuilding of a free and independent Lithuania. Mama always mentioned them in her letters and those of them who later ended up in the West often remembered her with just as much love and admiration. They'd want to read her letters, written to us from Siberia and from Nazi and Soviet occupied Lithuania. They'd ask us if they could borrow them so that they could retype them and hold onto the copies. Dr. Domas Jasaitis and Ambassador Edvardas Turauskas especially treasured Mama's letters.

In 1920 Mama married Konstantinas Bražėnas and started a lovely family. They had two sets of twins: Vida and Nijolė and Mindaugas and Liucija. Only Algimantas, the eldest, was born a singleton. Liucija died when she was only a few days old.

I remember our carefree childhood days on the Jasonys manor between Leliūnai and Utena. At first Father taught at the Saulė Gymnasium in Utena, while he studied law. He belonged to the Christian Democratic Party and was a member of the first Founding Parliament of independent Lithuania. Later he worked as a notary in Utena, but during the Smetona government years he was transferred to Panevėžys. Mama raised us with devotion, paying special attention to our education and to bringing us up as well-rounded individuals. From our earliest childhoods she instilled in us a respect for learning, maybe because she herself didn't get much schooling in her youth. Mama liked to dress my sister and me in identical outfits. We were as alike as two drops of water and no one could tell us apart except for her.

Mama had an especially big heart and she was always ready to help anyone in need. She was very sensitive to the needs of poor farmers in the area and helped them quite a bit, especially when their children were sick or if there was an accident. She took a very young orphan girl in to live with us. Father knew a lot about law, and would give advice to the local farmers. His office door was almost never closed—so many people came to him for consultation.

I have vivid memories of our family's trips on Sundays to the Utena Church in the wagon or in the winter with the horse drawn sled. Father had a beautiful baritone and always sang in church. When Mama's friend, Vincė Jonuškaitė-Zaunienė, from her days in Voronezh came to visit, he'd sometimes sing with her. The duets they sang together in Jasonys still ring in my ears today.

Our idyllic life in Jasonys ended suddenly when on January 6, 1933 Father died suddenly of a heart attack. Mama was left alone with four young children and two grandmothers to care for—her mother and Father's mother. Algimantas was ten at the time. Vida and I were nine, and Mindaugas was five. Mama's sister, Veronika's husband, Dr. Petras Karvelis, whom we called "Uncle," helped Mama liquidate her home in Jasonys and move in with them at the Noreikiškės manor near Kaunas. He and my aunt took care of not only our family, but also six children orphaned when his brother died. He helped Mama buy some land and part of a house on Laisvės Alėja in Kaunas. The rent from the land provided us with food and the rent from the house in Kaunas paid for our educations. Four of the boys attended the Jesuit Gymnasium. Vida and I attended the Kaunas Aušra Gymnasium for girls. The two older girls living with us were students already. Mama adored her niece, Ugnė, who was the youngest of us all. She mentioned her in almost every single one of her letters. Unfortunately, because of the Soviet occupation life was turned upside down and Mama did not have the opportunity to follow Ugnė on her path through life. She never was able to see how well Ugnė did for herself, how later, after Lithuania regained its independence, Ugnė became ambassador to UNESCO. Mama would have been very proud of her achievements.

After a few years our family of seven moved into our own house in the Kaunas Aleksotas neighborhood. Mama was able to support us and focus all of her energy on our educations. During our summer vacations she'd hire foreign language teachers, sharing them with other families. We almost never had a vacation; we studied and studied. Mama was literally obsessed with our studies, and wouldn't even let us help her out with household chores; she'd send us off to our books. She probably had a premonition that her efforts to get us to learn languages would pay off. It so happened that we were forced to leave Lithuania and travel into the unknown. Notwithstanding the difficulties of providing for a family of seven, Mama opened her big heart to any friends and relatives who grew ill or were touched by misfortune. Among them was a girl who was born with dislocated hips. Mama helped to find adequate medical care for her and took care of her for many months in our home because it would have been impossible to care for her in the village.

This idyllic life in Aleksotas was cut short by the Soviet and the Nazi occupations of Lithuania, which tore apart our family unit. Already at the end of the first year of Soviet occupation Mama clearly saw that life under this regime would be impossible. She, like everyone else, lost all her material wealth, which had given her the opportunity to support us and to educate us. All of us (at the time Vincė Jonuškaitė-Zaunienė and her son Saulius and daughter Giedrė were hiding in our house to evade arrest because her late husband was prime minister in the independent Lithuanian government) saw how on June 14, 1941 at three o'clock in the morning our neighbors, the General Raštikis's wife's parents and their three young daughters, were shoved into a truck and taken off to the train station to be sent to Siberia. That was the very beginning of those horrible days of exile to Siberia, just days before the Nazis invaded. This occupation caused even more heartache and trouble for Mama. During the 1941 Lithuanian uprising against the Soviets our house became the resistance movement's headquarters. Our shed was crammed full of weapons, and Algimantas joined the resistance. Mama's courage and her belief in eventual freedom, and especially her faith in God, gave her the strength to take such an incredible chance. She knew that Vida and I were involved in the resistance movement's activities. We helped print leaflets that appealed to the nation.

Mindaugas, and later Algimantas, ended up in the German army by force. Under the Nazi occupation Lithuanian men from 18 to 35 years old were forced to choose between forced labor or service in a Lithuanian Unit formed by General Plechavičius to fight against the Soviets. In 1943 when the Nazis closed down the universities, through Mama's efforts and with the help of Jesuit Father Gruodis, Vida and I, together with a group of other Lithuanian students, were sent off to Germany to continue our studies. Mama was left alone with our two grandmothers. I'll never forget how she, just before we left for Germany, called Vida and I back as we were leaving, and said: "I feel as though I'm pushing the two of you into your graves, but there's no other alternative… I want you to complete your studies." I don't know if there are many such mothers who'd rather send their children off into the unknown than to hold them close during such uncertain times. Mama, though it broke her heart, wanted a better life for us. That is how our long separation began, a separation that lasted twenty-two years. This time, up until 1966, is filled with her letters, written from Nazi-occupied Lithuania, from Siberia, and from Soviet-occupied Lithuania.

In 1943 the Nazis decided to liquidate the Kaunas ghetto and transport all the Jews to concentration camps or shoot them. Since the interwar period Mama had known Bella Baronienė. Bella would sometimes slip away from the Nazi supervised work brigade, when they were forced to labor at the Aleksotas airport, and come visit with Mama. Bella told Mama about two children whose parents were desperately searching for a means of saving them from a certain death. One of them was nine-year-old Aleksander Gringauz, and the other was a little girl who was almost five—Sarah Shilingovsky. Mama agreed to help save them, only they had to come up with a way to sneak them out of the ghetto and bring them to her. At the time Mindaugas was still at home and was awaiting his assignment in the German army. He already had his German soldier's uniform. His role in saving these children is described in the letters in the appendix, written almost 60 years later. Sarah had to cross the Aleksotas Bridge by herself, to the appointed place where Mindaugas would come to take her to Mama, covered with a blanket, so no one would suspect anything. He succeeded and carried her home to Mama. With Mindaugas's help Mama found a way to bring Sarah's mother to her, so that she could see her for one last time before she was brought to a concentration camp in Stutthof. Dina Steinberg, Bella Baronienė's daughter, also wrote her memories of Mama, which are with the documents in the appendix.

When someone would ask Mama if she wasn't afraid of bringing disaster onto her entire family, she'd answer that she would not have been able to live with herself if she hadn't helped these children, who'd been sentenced to death. Mama was very religious and believed that the divine Lord would assist her. And really, no one turned her in. Mindaugas was just 18 at the time. He understood very well the dangers of what he was doing, but he also suffered very much over being forced into serving in the German army. And so, this young Lithuanian man, wearing a German uniform, saved Jewish children.

At the end of the war in Prussia Mindaugas was taken by the Russians as a prisoner of war. The prisoners were forced to cross the whole of Lithuania on foot to Gardin, Byelorussia and were kept in horrific conditions, doomed to exile in Siberia. Eventually, Mama was able to arrange for Mindaugas's release and he returned to Kaunas. However, his health had been so severely destroyed by the conditions of his imprisonment—by starvation and exhaustion—that he died soon afterwards at the age of 22. Algimantas ended up a prisoner of war with the French. He died in America at the age of 77.

During the Nazi occupation Mama acquired a cow to help her provide for her family and the two Jewish children whom she was hiding. She could feed the children with milk and cheese and sell the milk and thus was able to increase her meager income.

Both children never forgot Mama, especially Sarah, whom Mama renamed Kotrynėlė to hide her identity. Sarah loved Mama very much and did everything she could so that the Israeli government would recognize Mama's bravery and self-sacrifice. In 1985, fifteen years after

Mama's death, she was awarded the Yad Vashem Medal of the Righteous of the Nations of the World posthumously along with an honorary certificate. In her memory trees were planted in the Yad Vashem Memorial Garden in Jerusalem.

Vida and I always maintained close ties with Alexander and Sarah. Alexander, who has now retired, became a professor of pharmacology and chemistry. He'd earned his PhD and taught at Stoneybrook University in New York. He wrote an extensive work on pharmacology and is a passionate photographer and traveler. Sarah also earned her PhD and is a professor as well as a neural development therapist. She works with brain damaged children in Israel. Valdas Adamkus, President of Lithuania, awarded Mama and Mindaugas posthumously the Life Savior's Cross.

Mama will remain always for us a symbol of deep patriotism, belief in the divine, tremendous courage, self-sacrificing love, and the stubbornness, notwithstanding huge difficulties, to make it possible for us to better ourselves. Whether we fulfilled all her wishes is hard to say; all I can say is that we tried. She was pleased that Algimantas acquired a Bachelors of Business Administration, and that I completed a degree in medicine, and became a pathologist. Only Vida, who struggled with tuberculosis for many years, and raised five children, was not able to complete her studies in the humanities. Mama's memory always was and will remain with us. Often we've asked ourselves—what would we have done if we'd been in her shoes?

Dr. Nijolė Bražėnaitė-Paranetto

1943 – 1947
Excerpts from Konstancija and Mindaugas Bražėnas's letters written to Berlin, Giessen, Marburg, and Innsbruck.

The German occupying forces closed down all the universities in Lithuania because they suspected Lithuanian students of being involved in anti-Nazi activities. Nijolė and Vida left Lithuania at Mama's insistence to continue their studies in Germany.

Near the end of the war major German cities were bombarded by allied forces, and therefore Vida and Nijole had to move from Berlin to Giessen to Innsbruck, registering as students in each location in order to continue their studies without losing a semester. In this manner Nijole completed her medical studies in 1947 in Innsbruck and become a medical doctor.

In 1944 Vida became gravely ill with pulmonary tuberculosis. Nijole had to practically carry Vida on her arms from location to location as the allied bombs fell on the major German cities. Mama's and Mindaugas's letters followed them.

Between the Russian and Nazi occupations of 1941 the Lithuanian underground organized a revolt and declared their independence. The Bražėnas family was involved in this revolt and their house became headquarters for the underground movement. Nijole and Vida helped print proclamations to the nation.

In 1944 under the Nazi occupation Lithuanians managed to create the Plechavičius Unit to defend Lithuania against Russian attack and in order to avoid the Nazi demand that Lithuania create a SS battalion. Unfortunately, the Lithuanians were deceived and the Unit was absorbed into the German Army and mobilized. The other choice for Lithuanian youth at the time was to complete six months of forced labor. Mama and Uncle Karvelis decided that it would be best for Mindaugas to complete his six months of forced labor, so that he would gain the right to study. However, as the war drew on, the men from forced labor brigades and from the Plechavičius Unit were coerced into the German Army, mainly as units in the Luftwaffe that guarded the airports. In this

23

manner, Mindaugas was transferred from forced labor to the German Navy. Mindaugas was devastated by being forced to live through the irony of serving within enemy ranks, however, unfortunately there was no way out for him. He, like many of his generation, was in fact, a prisoner of the Germans and was taken by force.

Kaunas, date unknown
(This letter was sent to Berlin)

My dearest Nijolė,

I received a few of your letters. I never seem to find a moment to write to you, although I have nothing good to report. From early morning until late at night I am busy with work and worry. Life is hard, and my leg is hurting me badly, and my nerves are out of sorts. Besides me, nobody moves a finger around here; no one bothers to provide even a crumb. The cow is a big problem. It's hard to buy feed and she's practically dry. So much for that. Nothing seems to be working out the way it should for you either. It seems as though that's our fate. Father Gruodis called me and asked about you and your sister. Write to him. People here are talking a lot about mobilizing all troops. I can't wait for Christmas. You promised to visit. With an uneasy heart I wait for news from Berlin. Is everything all right with Vida? I await your letters. Love and kisses.

Mama

Kaunas, January 8, 1944

...I'll meet my end in the midst of all this trouble. But that doesn't matter at all. If only the two of you are happy and can finish your studies and never have to live a hard life like mine. Mindaugas is good and takes care of me, but he has so much work to do and he's growing weak. *(Mindaugas has a congenital heart condition)* He needs a rest, but how could he possibly have a rest during these difficult times? The children *(the Jewish children Mama had rescued from the ghetto)* are healthy and are doing well, but they need a lot of care. Maybe that's how fate has ordained it? I received your packages. The coffee was delicious. If you can get more, send some. Grandmother thanks you for the dry toast. Please send me some vitamins for the children. Grandmother sends her best. She is weaker this year.

Mama

Kaunas, February 3, 1944

...I received letters from both of you. Thank God you are alive and that you are all right. Only, I worry that life is hard for you. I'm very concerned about Nijolė's exams. Will she be able to take them in March? I am eagerly awaiting your visit. When you come to Lithuania take everything you have with you because it's likely that you will not have the opportunity to go abroad again. I've heard that your dean is saying that all the students from Lithuania will be sent home from Germany. I'm not sure what to believe. I'll be waiting for you.

Mama

Kaunas, February 14, 1944

...In the mean time, nothing bad has happened. Grandmother is growing weaker. There's the threat that Mindaugas will have to go to forced labor. The children are doing well. *(The Jewish children Mama was taking care of)* I took care of business with Laisvės Alėja 11. I am exhausted. Algimantas wrote a few letters, but he hasn't been able to visit. If you can, send me some face cream... Kisses.

Mama

Kaunas, February 25, 1944

...I think you won't complain anymore that I don't write, but you won't be happy either because I have nothing good to say. Today Mindaugas signed himself up for forced labor. He'll be leaving in either May or June. I thought about it for a long time. I tormented myself over it, but in the end, after discussing it with Uncle *(Karvelis)* and a few serious people, we all decided that he should join, so that he wouldn't end up a drifter without any rights. Besides, once he serves his time he'll be able to apply for the university. Right now forced labor has been shortened to six months, so it shouldn't be all that bad for him, only I'm very worried about his health. On the 4th there will be physical exams. They might not take him after all. The young people are all signing up for the Plechavičius Special Unit. They say there will be military training.

...You should not give up your studies, even if the house collapsed and I broke down. You must continue your studies in Germany and you must finish them there, because here it will soon no longer be possible to study. You must take advantage of the opportunity to study while you have the chance. Uncle *(Karvelis)* is of the same opinion. Your class-mates are upset that you went abroad, but older people, who see it all through more serious eyes, are angry with the young people who don't take advantage of the opportunity to go abroad while they have it, who instead spend their time at parties and dances. These young people waste their precious time sitting at tables piled high with food and drink, at dances, and what do they have in the end? Nothing.

I visited with Father Gruodis. He'd like to see more students going abroad to study in Germany, so that we'd have a better-educated popu-lace. I think that you should thank the Lord that you are able to continue your studies in the middle of wartime. It would be a sin to let go of your studies, even for more important things.

....My health is not so bad. Recent events have cost me my nerves. If Mindaugas leaves for forced labor, I think the two of you will be able to visit with him, or maybe he can visit you. In Lithuania right now they are requiring that all men between the ages of 18 and 35 join the Plechavičius unit. The people agree and are joining up. These are the more important things I needed to tell you.

Mama

Kaunas, March 22, 1944
Mindaugas Bražėnas, Kaunen, Ostland, Darius-Girėnas Street 26

Dear Nijolė,

Nothing new with me. It's still not clear when I'll be leaving for forced labor. They say some time in the beginning of June. I want to get an official certificate. I definitely want to have the opportunity to take exams. Many students from my high school and other area high schools have joined the local troops.

Mindaugas

Kaunas, March 23, 1944

Dear Vida,

I am sending you Malishka's letter, which he'd sent to me and asked me to send on to you. The poor thing is suffering over the loss of his brother. Write to him. As you can see, there is nothing but tears and suffering here. The best people keep on disappearing and disappearing... Aunt Veronika *(Mama's sister Veronika Karvelienė)* has been granted the right to live in Lithuania for three months, but Uncle *(Karvelis—her husband)* has been given only three weeks. After their time is up, they'll have to go to Germany unless that decision is changed.

While you still have the chance, study and then study some more. Earlier people condemned you for going abroad, but now they are jealous. In a short while Mindaugas will be able to join you, and then he'll be safe.

Mama

Kaunas, May 28, 1944

...I know that you are waiting for a letter from me. Believe me that I want to write to you, but I have so precious little time and I get so tired that sometimes nothing is dear to me anymore. When you never get a free moment you become like some kind of a wind-up toy—you go and go, plotting, planning, and there's no end to it. The cow takes up a lot of my time. Veriutė *(Mama's relative)* and I take care of her and take her to pasture. The cow is trouble, but there is no other way, because she is our only source of sustenance. We get over twenty liters of milk out of her. I earn quite a bit of money from the milk and have some left over for us.

...I wonder what you know about your homeland? We have lived through painful moments. Our future is uncertain...

Mama

Kaunas, June 2, 1944

Dear Nijolė,

Since the day you left so much has changed here. The most important event, as you probably already know, is that the Plechavičius Special Unit has been liquidated. In its place is a mobilization headquarters, whose commander is Colonel Birontas. We keep on working, but not for the local units, but for a police state.

...Life is as always. I work from 7 am to 4pm with no break, and then almost every Sunday from 9 am to 1 pm. The work is tedious and I'm bored with it. If they'll accept it, I'm going to hand in my resignation, mostly because our soldier's identification booklet is decorated with a German eagle. The local unit has disappeared as though it were a dream. I don't know if I've had a better day than at headquarters when soldiers ran one behind the other, and their spurs rang. Now it is quiet, depressing. The mood we had earlier is gone. Now I sit and wait for the clock in front of the Museum of War to strike four o'clock.

...I need to tell you some sad news. Our teacher died, the one I'd told you so much about so often—Mr. Lelešius. He died in his sleep, quietly, with his eyes closed. Our best teacher has left us... The police determined that it was a heart attack.

Mindaugas

Kaunas, June 15, 1944

Dear Vida and Nijolė,

Soon I will begin sending you and your hosts some lard. I ask only one thing—that you set some aside as a precaution. I will do the same. My intuition tells me that life will only get harder. We need to take care that we don't end up on starvation's door. You can feel the heat of war everywhere. God only knows how everything will change... We didn't die of starvation before and we don't die of starvation now either. That only you may remain alive and well. Until now God has protected our family. I believe in His divine will and that he will keep us free from danger throughout the war. Here people are uneasy, unsettled, we're expecting something terrible to happen. June brings much pain and tears, and it seems that there's more to come... The weather is bad. It's been raining and raining... The wind is blowing to the West. I've heard that the house on the corner of Mickevičius and Kęstutis Streets has been emptied and prepared for new occupants *(Russians)*.

Today Aunt Veronica called often; she was very upset. Uncle Petras must leave Kaunas. I don't know what will happen to Aunt. Most of the residents of Kaunas are planning to leave for the countryside, because June is usually hot and humid. There are no air raids here as of yet. In some places bandits are causing havoc. While the days are long it's not so much of a problem, but when the days grow shorter in autumn it will be dangerous to walk around again. It's all too much for me. Our nation has suffered so much and has been driven to such poverty and on top of all that it has to suffer at the hands of those who are supposed to be friends... The two of you shouldn't worry about a thing. It is the will of the Lord. He will do as He sees fit. However, pray as much you can that the Lord would have mercy on our nation.

While it is still possible, take advantage of the opportunity to study. It probably will be impossible to study here. Take care of your health, because without it you cannot live.

Mama

Giessen, July 3, 1944
(Nijolė's letter written to Mama from Giessen that was returned)

My dearest Mama,

We are so grateful to you for writing to us so often. These days let-ters, even those bearing the worst news, are eagerly awaited.

Today I received a letter from Father Gruodis. It turns out that he was in Utena and wrote to me from there. He wanted to spend time in the province to improve his health, which recently has been very bad. Maybe the Lord will give him renewed energy, because otherwise it would be very sad. He writes that he goes to the cemetery to say the ro-sary and always stops at our family's graves. How dear those letters are! They are like a balm that heals wounds and brightens our gloomy days. Mama, I don't believe it will be as bad as you write, that we won't see each other again. That type of a finale would be too cruel. You shouldn't think that way!

Now we are waiting for Uncle Petras. Dear God, what a blow it is for him! You wrote once that Mindaugas might come to visit us. If that were at all possible, we'd be so happy because we miss that child so much. But I don't believe that they'll let him out so easily.

My internship in Salzburg did not work out because the hospitals were already overfilled with students. I was offered the opportunity to stay here and work in the surgery clinic. I'm even happy for that because I'll learn more than I would have somewhere else and I won't need to move. I especially am not in the mood for that right now.

The semester will end in a month. It'll pass by in a flash. And now I don't feel the time because one day chases the next, and each week chases the next. If time flies that quickly we won't even notice and we'll soon end up at home outside the door, waiting for you, Mama, to open it...

I cannot think about the people who probably are no longer with us... We were both shocked by the news. It was totally unexpected.

Poor Vida has a lot of studying to do. And after all these "sur-prises" that's really not that easy. Maybe, God willing, she'll manage to pass her exams. I am especially happy with my studies. Right now everything is so interesting to me. The path of a true doctor is opening up to me. Really, the two of us should be happy that at least we have our studies, even though our loved ones are so far away... Send our greetings to everyone. Many kisses.

Your Nijolė

Kaunas, July 4, 1944

Dear Vida,

I had the opportunity to send you a letter by airplane through a certain good soldier. In exchange I gave him some fresh milk to drink. Uncle, Auntie, and Ugnė are already leaving for Germany. They'll probably live in Vienna. Mindaugas and Algimantas are in the same place. Algimantas will probably have to go into the army. It'll become more clear later. Yesterday we lived through some considerable danger from the East... Today we're feeling its ebb. Maybe, God willing, we'll hold out. Almost all the Lithuanians have fled Vilnius due to unrest with the Polish population and because the front is near. At night sirens awaken us, but for the moment the bombs aren't falling. Today they fell on Vilnius. Although it's dangerous, you're in the best situation possible. For that you should thank the good Lord. Pray for your homeland, so that God would keep tragedy away... There's a lot of activity in Kaunas, a lot of movement. For the moment I'm not going anywhere and don't have any intention of going anywhere, unless they evacuated me. Deep in my heart I feel that it will all end for the best... Maybe, God willing, you'll be able to come home for vacation. That would be a miracle.

Mama

Grieslienen, August 8, 1944
Kampfh. M. Bražėnas, 5b Grieslienen über Allenstein.

...For the third day we are located not far from Allenstein. Where Aviža is I don't know. I was separated from him in Tilžė. After that, it seems, he tried to go to Kőnigsberg. How it turned out, I don't know. I am in the Luftwaffe. We live well here. There's enough food. In a word, if things continue like this I'll be okay. I might leave here pretty quickly. Where to, I don't know. When we stop somewhere for a longer time, I'll send you my real Fieldpost number. For the moment, don't write me any letters because I probably won't get them.

Now—about home. These three words chase away any happier thoughts I might have had. Mama stayed in Kaunas. Our house is gone. Whether she remained alive or not is hard to tell. The way it looks now, if all this nonsense continues, things can get very bad for Mama. For certain they'll run out of food and then they'll be facing starvation. I don't know where Algimantas is. I was there in Kaunas a few days before it was occupied. No, maybe it was a little longer. I was taking my superior, the major, to his hometown of Marijampolė by motorcycle. At the time I still found Mama there. Algimantas was there too then. What happened after that, I don't know. Kaunas was already empty at the time; there were no radio towers left. In Tilžė I was able to buy the newspaper *Ateitis* and there I read that in Kaunas the more important buildings had been bombed and that the bridges had been bombed too.

That's enough for this letter. Wait for my next letter, or I'll tell you what, try to write me a letter, only, of course, the faster the better.

Mindaugas

Grieslienen, August 31, 1944

...I hadn't written to you because I'd left Grieslienen for a while, but I should be here another month. After that I'll be going to the place I've been assigned to. Life is not so bad here. I get plenty of food. Everything would be well enough, only that I'm very worried about home and that means Mama. All I know is that all the people from occupied regions are being relocated to Russia. What awaits people there you can decide for yourselves. In a word, sooner or later I will find out what hardship is. I don't have any civilian clothing with me, so things might be hard for me later, when the war ends. Do you know anything about Algimantas? I'm curious where he is now? I don't know Aunt or Uncle's address. I'd like to write Uncle a letter. I might be getting a few days leave soon, so I'll come and visit you.

Mindaugas

Grieslienen, September 25, 1944

Dear Nijolė,

I haven't received your answer, so I'm writing you both a short letter. Vida mentioned that she could knit me some mittens. I didn't say anything about them in my last letter. But I thought about it and decided that I would write to tell you that I think she should go ahead and knit the mittens. This Saturday they are taking us to Strahlsond for training. We'll be there for about three weeks. I'll write you a letter from there and give you my new address. Life is the same as always. Yesterday our entire unit went to church together. It's so beautiful when the entire unit prays together. It's just like back home in Kaunas. The only difference is that the hymns are in German. When we leave for our new destination we probably won't have the opportunity any more to attend Catholic mass anymore.

Mindaugas

Grieslienen, October 11, 1944

...Every day I wait eagerly for a letter from you and I can't wait. In all that time I've already written you two letters and now I'm writing the third. I started thinking all sorts of things when I didn't get a letter. I also haven't received any news from Algimantas.

Things are pretty quiet here in Grieslienen, but preparations are being made and I'm not altogether sure why so suddenly. You've probably heard about the Russians' strong attacks to the north and southwest from Šiauliai. In my opinion, the Russians are going to take over Lithuania. I'd like to write something else to you, but I doubt you'll get this letter. Last week we had a talent show. The entire unit participated, and the captain, and the commandant of Grieslienen. I played my accordion in the show. We didn't have much time to prepare for the evening, but it went very well. After the show and the party I had to stay and play for the officers, because they'd arrived with their dates. The next day some of our men left for Osterod to help finish building the airport. It appears that we'll be here until October 20th. Though that's not entirely certain.

This Sunday a few girls from Osterod came to visit. We partied all night. So what that we partied. What lies ahead? We're just lucky that they haven't sent us for training yet. Then our sad days will begin. We might not be sent to the front; we might be left behind to guard the airports, but that's not so great either. I'd rather be sent to the front in Lithuania. There at least I'd know what I was fighting for. It looks to me as though the end is not that far away. Only living here up until now we haven't felt a thing. It's eternally quiet. If you didn't listen to the radio, you'd think that you were living in peace times. I'm satisfied with everything being here. I don't need anything. I have enough food. In a word, as long as I live here my life will resemble the life I had in Kaunas. It's too bad that autumn has begun, that it rains almost every day. I'll wait for your letters.

Mindaugas

Grieslienen, October 18, 1944

...I happened upon a good opportunity to write you a letter, which should reach you quickly. Today I received two letters from you. One made me very happy, but the other, yours Nijolė, shocked me. I never thought that things could get so bad for Vida. Even now I can't believe it. But if it's really so... (*Vida was gravely ill with pulmonary tuberculosis*). I went to church to pray for Vida. Occasionally I can make it for evening mass. And everything is the same as in Lithuania. I'll probably have more time starting Monday, so I'll go to church every evening. Before I used to worry about saving myself, but now I don't care anymore. Where things are falling apart, that's where I'll go. Next week they'll be reorganizing us. It seems that we'll remain in the construction battalion at the front. We'll get weapons and it appears that we'll be in East Prussia. All sorts of movement and preparations are going on here each day because it seems more and more like the front is getting closer. Lithuania is as though it didn't exist. I think the Klaipėda region has not been evacuated yet. There are some fierce battles going on near Tauragė and Šilutė. Our regiment, it seems, is scattered. I cannot imagine why everything is happening this way. It can't be that those Russians are this powerful? We get newspapers and in them we read about the Russian army. Many of them are barefoot. Where do they get their strength?

I'm trying to arrange it so that I can get a few days of vacation and come to visit you. A few of us have already done it. I think it'll work for me, but of course, I need to have a good reason. And I have one. *(Vida's tuberculosis)* It would be wonderful if I could come. Next week I should know more about what our fate will be. Then I can write and tell you.

And so you see, how many things have changed for me. Give Vida my best and tell her from me to get well soon. Write to me immediately. I'll be waiting for your letter.

Mindaugas

Fliegerhorst, Lötzen, October (?), 1944

I'm writing letter after letter to you. You might be tired of reading them already. But you probably understand that those autumn nights are so long and so boring that you could hang yourself out of boredom. And in the evenings I mostly have to sit by the telephone. I'm so bored I don't know what to do with myself. I don't have any Lithuanian books with me. So I read German ones. What I'm saying is that my German must have improved immensely if they've assigned me telephone duty. Sitting here I begin daydreaming and only the ringing phone wakes me up. And every day it's the same. I'm so sick of that hopeless waiting that I don't know what to do with myself in the evenings. I'm lucky that I share a room with the commandant. His last name is Andriuška, his first name Antanas. He's completed three years at the University. It turns out that his wife and I were in the same class during the Russian occupation. In the evenings we talk about old times. Basically, you could say that's my only entertainment. Besides that I have a good accordion. It's mine but I haven't even paid a pfennig for it. As I've told you before, we've put together two evening programs and now we're putting together a third. The two first ones were a success.

And so you see how I live. What a shame that it takes so long for them to send over our letters from Grieslienen. How is Vida doing? Write quickly.

Mindaugas

P.S. By the way, Nijolė, if you have any books in English, send them to me.

Lötzen, 1944 (?)

Dear Nijolė,

I'm writing letter after letter. You might have received a pile of letters from me. There's nothing you can do about it. If there's time, I write. The matter is this: I can get vacation time, but I need to get a certificate for Vida, saying that she is very ill and that she wants to see me. You have to get the certificate from the hospital. You don't have to go out of your way to get it because Vida really is that sick. Nijolė, all you need is a head and a tongue. Tell the hospital director or the doctor who is treating Vida that you need this certificate. Ask nicely and everything will be okay. You can do anything, Nijolė, as long as you don't lose your head. The certificate should be mailed to: An Kompanie Chef, 3/1 Lw. Fest. Bau Batl. Fliegerhorst, Lötzen (5b).

So try to get it done if you want for us to meet. I'll take care of everything on my side. Just do your best, Nijolė, to get it done as quickly as you can and mail it registered. Naturally, you need to stress that this is serious. See you soon!

Mindaugas

Lötzen, October 26, 1944
Soldaten M. Bražėnas, 3/1 Lw. – Fest. – Baubatl.
Fliegerhorst Lötzen über Gensburg

Dear Vida and Nijolė,

I'm writing to you from a new location. On Tuesday they woke us up suddenly at 4:00 am and after brief preparations we left. We thought that we were going to the front, but it turned out that we weren't. We arrived much closer to the East. Life is livable here. The food we get here is better than in Grieslienen. We live in better barracks; only it's not so pleasant that they're often shaking. You can here the tanks shooting. But life is bearable. My job assignment is the same as it was last time—I'm assistant to the steward and I've been given one more assignment—to keep the offices clean. The work is easy and there isn't much of it. My boss and I have a separate room. Although it's small, it's enough for the both of us. In the corner there's a nice stove, which we use during the day because it's already cold here. Soon we should get the first snowfall of the year. We are about three kilometers away from the town of Lötzen. I haven't been there even once. Coming here we met many refugees who were heading for the center of Germany. Their journey was very hard. Lötzen is already half evacuated. Often "Ivans"—as we call the Russians—fly overhead, but they don't disturb our peace. The scenery around here is beautiful. Right here besides us is a lake and a forest. Too bad that it isn't summer anymore. Sitting in my room my thoughts often go back to Lithuania. Everything runs past my eyes. All my memories don't give me any peace and I can't get away from them. Often I think of Mama. Where is she now? If she is alive, how will she get through the winter? In a way I regret that I came here. It is easier to suffer together. I can't think about that too much because my eyes fill with tears. I lose all hope and all my thoughts are at home. Is there any hope of ever going back there? Maybe sometimes... But what would I find there? That which is most important won't be there anymore. I feel that. I might yet be able to see the two of you, but that's still unresolved. What will my fate be? It's good that I'm here in a decent place, but for how long? I can feel that our happy days will soon be over. But I don't care anymore.

The one comfort I have is that up until now Lithuanian girls came to visit us, girls who traveled often to Osterod. We had a show there. I played the accordion. I played for some more important guests too—the major and a few officers. The major liked my music very much. We're lucky that we have a good commandant who takes care of us.

We'll be here for about three weeks. I don't know where we'll go from here. How are things with Vida? Write back right away. Pass on my best wishes.

By the way, I am now a Soldat *(soldier)*.

Mindaugas

Lötzen, November 8, 1944

Dear Vida,

I received two letters from you addressed to Grieslienen. Later they resent them here. Our lives here are no different than in Grieslienen. The days are monotonous: Wake up at 5:30, breakfast at 6:30, parole at 7:00, work until 10:50, from 10:50 to 13:30 lunch break, from 14:00 to 16:00 work again. From now on my schedule will be different, because like in Grieslienen, I'll be working in the office here. Besides that work, they add on Streiffedienst in Lötzen a few days a week. There, at night, I have to catch our men who go out on the town without permission. I hate night duty; it exhausts me. The worst is that you can't go have a beer or go to the movies. You have to wander around the empty streets at night with a lamp. But it's all the same to me right now. The most important concern we have is with food, of which we have enough. Every morning, besides our food ration, which consists of 30 grams of butter, 95 grams of sausage or 100 grams of cheese, we get soup and pudding two times a week, and milk soup in the evenings. The food isn't bad, but some of us feel the lack of bread. We only get 600 grams of bread a day. That's enough for me. We also get white bread every day. They treat us well here. They don't make any distinction between us and the Germans. In some ways, we're treated better.

Like I mentioned earlier, we often have to go to the town of Lötzen, which is about as big as the part of Kaunas that goes from City Hall to Laisvės Alėja. And the main street looks so much like Vilnius Street that if someone dumped me here in the middle of the night and then asked me where I was, I'd say I was in Kaunas. But that is, of course, a daydream, to imagine Kaunas still standing. We don't meet Lithuanians here anymore. At first we could clearly hear the front, but now we don't hear anything anymore. There are some Germans here who speak Lithuanian, only they're not Lithuanians, and that's a shame. Somewhere here, in East Prussia, there is a Lithuanian unit, only we have no communication with them. The Germans who live with us ask a lot about Lithuania because most of them have been there.

Winter is coming. The local people tell us that it gets extremely cold here. But, I think we'll make it through somehow. I have five pairs of woolen soldier's socks and three pairs of warm leggings. I have good boots and shoes, and two soldier's sweaters. They're not that warm, but they'll do. We'll have to figure out a way of getting more warm clothing. If only we don't run out of food, we should be okay. There's just one piece of sad news that I received today. Instead of our old major, they've assigned some sort of an Oberleutenant. The major we had was like a father to us. He really would have given me the vacation time to come see you, but now I don't know. That's all that's new here, Vida. I wish you well and get better soon. I'll be waiting for your letters. Mindaugas

Mindaugas

1945

Lötzen, 1945 (?)

Dear Nijolė,

I'm writing to you one letter after another. You really must be getting tired of reading my letters by now. I wrote you a letter in which I asked you to organize sending me a certificate. But up until now I haven't received any reply. Maybe I'm asking the impossible? Write me and tell me how it is? It seems as though they'll keep us here until Christmas. Then we'll have training and they'll probably send us to the front. But that's not so important. Before that I definitely want to come and see you two. I received your package with letter writing paper, envelopes, and two books. By the way, write and tell me what your money situation is. I still have some.

It remains calm here by comparison, only yesterday evening was a mess. Our munitions warehouses blew up. It was probably the Russians. They're about one kilometer away from us. I mean the Russians and not the warehouses. Otherwise everything is okay enough. That's most important.

Nijolė, I'm asking you again, organize that certificate saying that Vida is seriously ill and that she wants to see me. After all, Vida is gravely ill. I think that you'll be able to do this. Send the certificate to this address: An Kompanie Chef, 3/1 Lw. Fest-Bau-Batl. Fliegerhorst, Lötzen. I'll be waiting for your letter then.

Mindaugas

Because of heavy bombing in Giessen, Nijolė and Vida had to evacuate. Nijolė and Vida, who could barely walk, arrived in Innsbruck, where Lithuanian student refugees were beginning to gather. They all had hopes of continuing the studies that they'd begun in Lithuania.

January 3, 1945
(This letter was written to Lans near Innsbruck, to the student dorm "Lansersee")

Dear Vida and Nijolė,

Every day I've been waiting for news of you and today I finally received your letter. I wrote many letters to you in Giessen, but you'd already left. I even sent you my photograph. It can't be that you didn't get it?

Don't worry about me at all. I could even send you food, but it's hard for us to mail anything, and, most importantly, I don't have anything to pack it in. As far as food is concerned, I'm okay—I eat better than I did in Lithuania, but I'm still not putting on any weight. We got all sorts of extras for the holidays. We had four days off. I had plenty of work over the holidays. I had to distribute all the extras, and like on usual days, the food rations. I had no inclination to celebrate, but I had to play at one party. I celebrated New Years in a village. We could celebrate in peace there, because the further away you are from the city the better. The Russians fly over us every day and every day we listen to the music of bombs. But it's all a joke. Only sometimes at night the thundering bombs toss me out of bed. We all handle it in our own way.

It is very cold here and it snows a lot. I have good gear though and I'll get through the winter. I was able to finagle leather gloves, and I have two sweaters, four pairs of woolen socks, etc.

There are only twenty Lithuanians left here. The rest have been transferred. We will stay here, as planned, until January 15. After that we'll go to Stettin or Chenstachava *(Poland)* for training. Whoever ends up in Chenstachav will have to fight the Polish guerillas; whoever ends up in Stettin will have to guard the airport. Of course, I'll put all the effort I can into ending up in the West, because in Poland you can quickly lose your mind.

You two are dreaming terrible dreams. *(Nijolė and Vida worried constantly over what Mindaugas's fate would be at the end of the war).* When I get through training, then you can start worrying about me. Right now I'm living a life as peaceful as the one I lived in Kaunas. There's no reason to be worrying about me.

I think that you two are having a harder time with money. I don't spend much here. I am mailing you 300 Reichsmarks. When you get it, write to me immediately. Anyway, try to write as soon as you can, because, as I said, we might be transported very soon. Goodbye for now!

Mindaugas

Innsbruck, January 19, 1945
(Nijolė's letter, which was returned)

My dearest Mindaugas,

Both of your letters arrived almost at the same time, although one of them was written on the 3rd. The mail is really messed up. The money came yesterday too. We are very moved by your kindness and we're proud of you. It would be a shame, if the money you sent to Giessen disappeared. You're probably thinking that we don't have any money left. In that regard, we're not doing too badly. Vida still gets her stipend, and the hospital doesn't cost her that much. But since you've sent it, we'll hold onto it for an emergency. Who knows, you might need it yourself one day.

Over the last few days, when we still hadn't heard from you, we were sad beyond belief. The Russian offensive has just begun and you're not very far from the front at all. We were both so worried that they'd shove you into the first fires of the oven.

Vida gained five kilograms. Her fever is gone completely and she's in a good mood. Everything would be fine, if we didn't know what kind of a horrible disease she's carrying around inside of her. You know, Mindaugas, that after all that worry, all the horrible things she saw, and that horrible trip here, that she's developed abscesses in her side. Now she has tubercular fistula. That's a disease that is incredibly difficult to cure if at all. Notwithstanding, I haven't given up hope and I firmly believe that she will get better. It would be too horrible to think otherwise. In a few weeks they will transfer her to a sanatorium thirteen kilometers away from Innsbruck, in a beautiful area, about a kilometer and a half up a mountain slope. The view is heavenly. *(Nijolė had to practically carry Vida in her arms across Germany as it was being bombed by Allied Forces. When they arrived in Austria, during a blizzard, Nijolė climbed a mountain slope to the tubercular clinic and begged the doctors there to admit Vida. Although the clinic was overfilled, the doctors agreed to treat Vida because of Nijolė's insistence.)*

Oh, if only you could come here! You could visit Vida and see Tirol. We would be so happy to have that opportunity and of course we'll do everything we can to get that certificate and send it to your superior. If you could really come, it would be more than perfect.

Right now there are three of us living in one room. It's almost better than Giessen here because there are more Lithuanians and not as many air raids. Besides all that, the mountains are such that I couldn't even describe them to you in writing.

If you could send us food, that would be very good. Vida has an incredible appetite and I really and truly want her to regain the weight she's lost and to gain some. Then she'll have more strength to battle this disease. But if it's hard for you or not convenient, or if you'd have to give up your own rations, of course you shouldn't.

We are so happy that everything is going well for you and that you are so good and for everything...

Write often. I believe that our plan will work, and so I'm waiting, expectantly, hoping that finally you'll be able to come.

Yours, Nijolė

Hall, January 22, 1945
(Vida's letter to Mindaugas, which was returned)

Dear Mindaugas,

You have no idea how dear your letters are to us. That word—ATTACK—stands before my eyes always, and all I can think about is how close you are to all that mess. The only thought that gives me some peace is that they might send you to Stettin. All in all, life is so idiotic, and it seems to me that all the horrors of war are yet to come. We haven't been through enough yet. I don't trust that it will all end as it is now. Every day I pray to God that he'd help you stay alive and keep you healthy.

Nijolė received the money you sent to Innsbruck. From your letter I understood that earlier you'd sent 300 Reichmarks to Giessen. If we get it, we'll hold onto it for you, because who knows, you might need it later. You are a wonderful person, Mindaugas, for thinking of such things at a time like this. You see, I receive a stipend of 250 Reichmarks a month. While I'm hospitalized it doesn't cost me anything to live, and as long as the student organization in Marburg pays for me, there's enough money. Besides that, Nijolė brought a lot with her from Lithuania. The only thing I'm uncertain about is how we'll pay for the sanatorium. But we have enough to get by for six more months. Aunt and Uncle *(Karvelis)* ask us in every letter if we have enough money. So you really shouldn't worry. You should buy yourself good things because you don't know how long you'll be able to eat well, and you'll need those layers of fat for the future.

Today I'll talk to the doctor about that certificate. Although I'm not in danger anymore, I think that she'll be able to write out the certificate for me. What a joy it would be if you could really come!!!

If you could manage to get us some lard that would be great because right now we're living from ration cards. Of course, only if you can get it easily and cheaply. I wouldn't want to owe you too much later for it. We will remain in Innsbruck until the war ends, if only there aren't any political events that get in our way.

And so, Mindaugas, live well, and for the love of God, take care of yourself! You can't even imagine how worried we are right now over your existence. I greet you and I kiss you. *Vida*

Vida and Nijolė received no more news about Mama or Mindaugas until 1947, when suddenly they began receiving letters from Mama, which at the time were difficult to decipher. As it turned out, Mama had found a way of writing to them through an unknown person, using an alias, and writing a type of invented history, in order to be able to get past censorship and write about what was going on in Lithuania at the time. Mama's letters were addressed to an imaginary person named Motiejus Moja, Glasmalerei Str. 6, Innsbruck and were delivered by hand to Nijolė by the landlady, who rented her a student's room.

1947

Kaunas, June 22, 1947

Dear Motejius,

I never expected for you to write to me. Although you are a distant relative to me, the letter you sent me was very pleasant.

I'm very happy to hear that you've found yourself a fiancée—someone named Nijolė Virginija. When you complete your required residency you must definitely bring her back home with you. I'd also like to get to know her sister, Veronika, and her brother Algimantas. It's wonderful that you are still able to continue your studies after such hardship, having spent a long time in a cruel German concentration camp. Here, in Soviet Lithuania, everyone can get an education. That's why the high schools and universities are packed with young people. The only ones who don't study are those who either don't want to or are lazy.

My little house is still standing, despite the war. Only during the bombings all the window glass shattered and in some places the roof caved in. Once the storm was over, I was able to renovate and I'm living in it now. Those cruel Germans bombed many cultural sights and beautiful buildings as they withdrew their forces. And that's why fate has punished them. They were defeated and we won't suffer at their hands anymore.

My mottled cow still feeds me. Last year I pastured her in No-reikiškės field. This year the Agricultural Academy has taken over the Noreikiškės property and they no longer allow other people's animals to pasture. They take very good care of the fields. This year I pastured my mottled cow on the slopes not far from Noreikiškės. It's a long walk to milk her, but then again, it's pleasant to walk along those lovely winding wooded roads.

I can't complain about my life. Though it's true, I'm beginning to feel my age. My feet are not as light, my knees won't bend, my heart is weak, and my hair has grown white. That's not surprising; after all, I'm 57 already. I lived through two wars. During the first war I was living in Russia, in Voronez. I have pleasant memories of my youth in Voronez. I remember well the revolution with all the passion of youth. Voronez left me with a deep impression. Those are my memories of youth, after all.

With all my heart I congratulate your fiancée and her brother and sister. I kiss you heartily and will be waiting for your letter or your visit.

Yours, K. Braženienė

Kaunas, July 6, 1947

Dear Motiejus,

This is my third letter to you. I don't know if you'll get it, but I'm writing any way. I wanted to share a few memories with you.

When the Germans withdrew, at my neighbor's house, I met a Russian major named Vladimir Antonovich Zherdiev. He was staying temporarily at my neighbor's house. He was a pleasant man, around fifty. We talked a lot. We reminisced on all the familiar places we both knew and loved in Russia—the theater, the movies, and so on. We remained good friends. After the Germans capitulated, many Lithuanians began returning from Germany—people who'd been sent there to do forced labor. Among them was my son Mindaugas. After some time, I remember, that was July 15, 1945, I received a letter from my beloved son, whom I no longer believed to be alive. He wrote: "My dearest Mama, I am in Gardin, in a concentration camp, I am coming home to my homeland. From a distance I can see you, worried, crying. Don't cry, my dearest Mother, I will come home. Algimantas, Vida, and Nijolė will come home too—we'll all come home. All those years of suffering will only have given us more strength to work towards reconstructing our homeland. And you, Mama, your old age will be filled with real joy and rest. Dearest Mama, I keep on writing and writing, because I miss you so much. The Nemunas flows right here, the church bells ring, reminding me of Kaunas, of the organ, the choir... Goodbye, dearest Mama. I kiss you a thousand times. Wait for me. Your Mindaugas."

I couldn't contain my joy. I wanted to see him right away. I ran to Vladimir Antonovich, who I knew was traveling to Gardin, and I begged him to bring me with him. What joy! He agreed. I quickly prepared for the journey and we left early. The good major brought me right to the prison gates where the friendly guards allowed me to see my son. What joy! I pressed him to my heart and for a whole hour we talked. After that they arranged my son's documents so that he could return home to his mother. And that's how I was able to bring him home, healthy, unharmed, simply tired. *(The real history of what happened to Mindaugas is in Aldona Marcinkutė's letter, which follows.)*

And so I'll end this letter because I have nothing else to write about. I'll write more in my next letter. Give my greetings to your fiancée, her sister, and her brother. I press you close to my heart.

Yours, K. Bražėnienė

Kaunas, October 11, 1995

This letter was written forty eight years later to Vida in Australia by Aldona Marcinkutė, who lives in Kaunas. In the letter she describes Mindaugas's final days spent in prison in Gardin while waiting to be exiled to Siberia. Stasė Mištautaitė, a classmate of Aldona, Vida, and Nijolė from the Aušra Gymnasium, told this story to Aldona.

...It was wonderful to hear your voice over the telephone last Sunday. I called Stasė Mištautaitė right away and we agreed to get together on a sunny day and talk in more detail about those long ago days in Gardin. Last Friday, October 6, I met her on Savanoris Street, I brought her home, we drank tea, and looked over your family photographs, and plunged into the past.

This is what she told me about that summer of 1944, about July. She was escaping to the West, but at the border the Russians caught her, arrested her, and brought her to Gardin, where they held prisoners until their deportation *(to Siberia)*. There they interrogated them and waited for the cattle wagons that would take them to the depths of Russia. You see, prisoners were allowed to walk in the prison yard, and so one day, after interrogations, while walking, she noticed your Mindaugas. She spoke to him and he immediately said her name and last name out loud because he remembered her well from when she visited your family in Noreikiškės.

That summer was very hot. The plumbing in Gardin did not work. The prisoners received only a little water to drink. They took away their belongings. Mindaugas somehow managed in the middle of the night to collect some dripping water in his canteen and brought it to Stasė, so that she could wash herself with it. He told her that they were not going to release any Lithuanians, that they would all be deported deeper into Russia. At the time trains, filled with goods confiscated from Germany and elsewhere in the West, were heading into Russia. *(Because the trains were being used to transport plundered goods, the deportations to Siberia were temporarily delayed.)* After interrogations, they began letting a few people return to Lithuania. Mindaugas asked Stasė, if they were to let her go, to go and visit Mama at Aleksotas and tell her where he is. Stasė was allowed to go home. After she came home and had a good night's sleep, she went to see your mother in Aleksotas. Your mother left for Gardin immediately. Stasė helped Mama trade some of her belongings for vodka and cigarettes. She got off the train in Vilnius and went to pray at the Gates of Dawn. *(A holy shrine were Catholics believed Holy Mary had made an appearance)* She promised the Virgin Mary that if only they would release Mindaugas, she'd give him up for the priesthood.

Now I'll tell you what Mama told me when we met at the Vitkus's home:

When she arrived in Gardin, Mama went to speak to the commander, but he denied that Mindaugas was there in prison. Disappointed, Mama paced outside of the prison, until one soldier asked her, "Hey, Matushka, what are you doing walking around here?" She told him that she knew that her son was here, but that the commander denied it. The soldier said, "My shift will end soon. When my replacement comes, I'll go and see if your son is here." After some time he returned and said, "There really is someone here who looks just like you." Then Mama gave him everything she'd brought—the vodka, and cigarettes, and so on. And she got on the train to return to Kaunas. On the train there were a few Jewish men who were traveling to Kaunas to look for Jewish children who'd been rescued. Talking among themselves they mentioned Mama's name. She told them who she was and told them the story of how she'd just been to Gardin to try to get Mindaugas released, and that Mindaugas was the one who'd rescued Jewish children from the ghetto because he'd had a German uniform and was in the guard. The men told her that there was a very important NKVD official onboard the same train and that he was a Jew and that they'd talk to him and see what he could do.

A short time after Mama returned to Kaunas, they released Mindaugas. He was suffering from exhaustion because they'd made them run on foot from Germany to Gardin. They had starved the prisoners and so the prisoners had eaten only what they could find in the garbage. His heart and his stomach were severely affected.

Stasė told me that after Mindaugas returned to Kaunas that he'd come to visit her. She said that since Mama had offered him up to the Virgin Mary, she felt he should go into the priesthood. Only Mindaugas did not have the calling. Then she met him one more time on the street. He complained about his poor health and said, "Stasė, I am dying..."

Now when I think about it, by saving Jewish children the gates of the Gardin prison opened up for Mindaugas, and also made it possible for your mother to finally travel to the United States to be with her children.

Yours, Aldona

Kaunas, August 10, 1947

My dearest Motiejus,

After I received your letter, I wrote you four more letters. This one is the fifth. The other four I wrote each Sunday. This letter comes after a longer break. During that time nothing has changed here for me, only I'm overcome with longing. I'd like to see you and Nijolė, and her brother Algimantas—the sooner the better. I'd like to hold you all close to my heart. How much longer will your residency last? Has Veronika finished her studies? What class would she be in now? What class is her brother in?

General Vitkauskas's family lives very well. I meet them often. They are very good to me. Laima is already in her third year at medical school. Juozas has finished his studies. He is well known for his work with youth.

My life would not be so bad if only I had my strength. Lately my health has gone downhill. My legs are especially bad. I also need to earn bread for myself and for Mindaugas, as well as clothing, but that's nothing—life would not be interesting without work.

My mottled cow gives me about twenty liters of milk. I sell it and make a nice profit. For now, remain in good health. I'll be waiting for your letter.

Yours, K. Braženienė

Kaunas, September 7, 1947

Dear Motiejus,

This is, I believe, my sixth letter to you. Only I don't know how many of my letters you've received. I've received only one letter from you. I'd really like to receive more letters from you. I'm very curious how your residency is going and if you're fiancée's sister is still studying, and if so, what year of medical school is she in.

My life is as it's always been. Autumn is near, and I am saddened; although, the weather is still good even though the nights have grown longer. Oh, and I don't like those long dark nights. I don't want to sleep longer, although, it wouldn't be such a bad thing. If only there were a way that I could close my eyes for a long time and forget my longing...

August 26 has passed. That day was very dear to me. Although twenty-four years have gone by, I can still remember so clearly that day when two little beings came into existence *(the twins Nijolė and Vida)* and how happy I was, how much I loved them, and how much they loved me. I thought that those two little beings would hold my gray and worry-worn head and be the comfort of my old age. But, alas, that horrible war tore them away from me and they have disappeared without a trace.

For you young people it is a wonderful thing to travel around the world. But I can only fly in my thoughts; my feet won't carry me any more. Enough for now. I will wait for your letters.

Yours, K. Bražėnienė

In 1950 while Nijolė was in a sanatorium convalescing from pulmonary tuberculosis, she began receiving letters from Eva Birkman. Eva was the wife of a wounded German who had been left behind in Lithuania. Eva and her husband lived on the brink of starvation, and so Mama felt sorry for her. Mama fed and clothed Eva and her husband and at one time took her in to live with her. When Mama was exiled to Siberia in 1949 Eva wrote to Nijole and hinted that she knew where Mama was but could not tell her. For two years Eva wrote constantly to Nijole, asking her to send packages, which were intended for Mama. However, Eva kept the contents of the packages for herself and hid the fact that Mama was in Siberia, at a time when Mama was in great need of financial support in order to remain alive. Eventually Eva stopped writing to Nijole and only in 1956 in Canada when Nijolė unexpectedly ran into the Valatkas family's daughter Eugenija did she learn that Mama had been deported to Siberia. Eugenija was writing to her own parents through Poland. Eugenija's parents helped find Mama in 1956 in Siberia.

In 1956 Nijolė was working in a New York hospital as a pathology resident. One day in June Nijolė returned home from work and found the first of Mama's letters written from Siberia. It had been mailed in January and had taken almost six months to reach her.

1956

Excerpts from Mama's letters, written from Siberia to Vida in Australia and to Algimantas and Nijolė in America, addressed to an alias: Barbara N. Zareckis, 105 West 72nd Street, New York 23, N.Y.

During the first Soviet occupation in 1941 Soviet authorities began deporting Lithuanians, Latvians, Estonians, and Finns to Siberia. This wave of deportation ended with the Nazi occupation of Lithuania, but was resumed in 1944 when the Soviets occupied Lithuania a second time. Approximately 275,697 were deported at that time, although different sources list different numbers. This is because the deportations were kept secret from the rest of the world and the NKVD did not keep accurate records. Between forced deportations, repressions of partisan activities, and Lithuanians on the deportation lists fleeing to the West, roughly a third of the nation disappeared between 1941 and 1953, when Stalin died. Mama was deported to Siberia in 1949 because her two brothers were priests, because her brother-in-law was a member of the Christian Democrat Party and former Minister of Finance, because her husband had been a member of independent Lithuania's first freely elected parliament, and because three of her children were in the West. The deportations were ordered by Stalin to rid Lithuania of its intellectual class and of anyone who demonstrated the slightest inclination towards self-motivation.

When Mama was deported to Siberia she and thousands of other deportees were placed in an over crowded cattle wagon; among those in her wagon were thirteen Catholic priests and seminarians. Upon arrival in Irkustk the exiles were regrouped into brigades and assigned to forced labor. Mama was assigned to a brigade of some twenty fishermen who fished Lake Baikal on double twelve hour shifts with no break to sleep, both in the winter and in the summer, no matter what the weather was. Mama, in her late fifties and early sixties already, was assigned the task of keeping house for all twenty men in the brigade. Her many daily du-

ties included cooking, cleaning, laundry, chopping wood, and dragging home water from Lake Baikal. The group lived in the most primitive of conditions without running water or heat.

After Stalin's death in 1953 exiles were allowed to write letters to their relatives. After a while some of the exiles were allowed to return home.

Irkuskaya region, Olchonsky region, pas. Chuzhyr, January 30, 1956

I greet you my daughter Nijolė! And also my daughter Vida and my son Algimantas!

I've dreamed of you many times, conjured you up in my thoughts, and begged for in my prayers. I don't know how large a sheet of paper it would take for me to write down all the words that I'd like to greet you with.

I had to leave Lithuania March 25, 1949 and for almost seven years I am living in the same place, and that is on the island of Olchon on Lake Baikal. It is very beautiful here. The little town of Chuzhyr is right next to the Baikal. On the other side of the Baikal there are tall mountains, grown over with trees in some places, and on the other side of the town there are forests and then more forests. There are about 300 Lithuanian families here. You can say that life isn't so bad. Everyone has built themselves a little cabin and keeps a cow and a few other animals. The poorest of the Lithuanians here is me, but only because I'm going on 64. It's been two years already that the doctors have assigned me as a class III invalid. *(Under the Soviet system there was a classification system in place according to an individual's ability to work. A class three invalid was no longer capable of work.)* My disease, which is called high blood pressure, is assigned to this group. It's the second winter already that I cannot leave my room. It's better for me in the summer. That's why life is hard for me here, because I cannot earn a living for myself. I get some aid from my relatives in Lithuania in the form of two to three packages a year. One of my good friends here helped me out with 2000 rubles when I was building my little house for myself. His name is Father Vincas Pranckietis. Next time I write, I'll send you his address because he does not live here anymore. You'll be able to write to him. Now I am sharing my house with a young Lithuanian woman and her husband, who live here together with me. She asks that you look for her brother, Juozas Ulevičius's son, Feliksas, who left for America before the war and is living in Waterbury. Her name is Stepanija Filipavičienė-Ulevičiūtė. She has also helped me during difficult times.

You probably already know that Mindaugas died in 1948 on August 13th and is buried in Kaunas, in the Aleksotas cemetery, besides his two grandmothers. Later I'll write more about him. Now I'd like to ask why Vida isn't living together with you, Nijolė, and why is she in Rome alone? What kind of a job does she have? I know that she was gravely ill and had two operations. How is her health now? What is my dearest Algimantas doing? Did he complete his degree at the university? How did you and Vida complete your studies? What degrees did you receive? Three years ago I happened to hear that Aunt *(Veronika)* died. Where is Uncle *(Karvelis)* and Ugnė now? I remain concerned with your studies. I'd also like to recommend that you study Russian because it is a very beautiful language and the literature is rich. After all, your father was fluent in it. I have learned to speak and to read in Russian fluently.

I believe that you have remained my same three darling children, just as I have remained your same mother, and I believe that the tides of life did not wash away from you those high ideals, and I believe that you have not brought shame onto my gray head, just as I have not brought shame onto you... May God protect you.

I want to end this letter, so that it doesn't become too long. Ending, I am turning to you with a request. We really feel the lack of clothing and shoes. I didn't bring much with me from Lithuania because I was robbed there. And here I could no longer buy anything. I'd like to ask for shoes in size 39 or 40 (my feet are often quite swollen), clothing, underwear, and some blouses that are not of a light color. The blouses should not be tailored because I am old and no longer thin; it would be hard for you to get the size right.

They're saying that they'll let us elderly return home, so maybe by June or July I'll be in Lithuania again.

I'll be waiting for your letters.

Yours, Mama

The Soviet Union suffered from severe food shortages, shortages of medicine, of clothing, and other goods. The people who returned from Siberia did not have the right to register as permanent citizens and thus could not work and also could not receive packages or letters in their own names. They were dependent on others to receive their packages and letters for them. Mama, and thousands of exiles like her, were completely dependent on packages sent from relatives in the West. They would sell the contents of the packages on the black market in order to obtain cash. Often the cash was used for bribes to be admitted to the hospital, to see a doctor, to obtain medicine, basically to do anything that one would have to do in the course of one's daily life. One of the problems was that often the packages did not reach their recipients, because the contents were stolen or the packages were received replaced with items of lesser quality.

Chuzhyr, April 26, 1956

My Dear Ones,

I'm writing you my fourth letter already. But really, you could say it is just the continuation of that one and the same letter. This letter will be my last before the ice breaks up, because maybe this is the last mail that will be able to get out over the ice. In my other letters I didn't tell you not to send food. There is food here, only you need money to buy it. I heard that packages with food in them cost a lot.

Don't send money either. The best thing is to send fabric that I can sell easily or trade for food. Don't send me too much, because I think that it probably isn't so easy for you to earn a living. After all, you need to eat, clothe yourselves, and study. Take care of your health, that's most important. Don't think that I'm starving. We have a garden; I plant potatoes; I have a few chickens that lay. I get along well with my boarders. They leave for work; I prepare their food; feed the pig and the chickens. That is worth a bite of bread. Besides that I knit patterned mittens, sweaters, and I earn a few rubles that way. Now that I've received a letter from you my mood is much better, and so maybe my health will improve too. Of course, my heart doesn't work right and that is why my legs are swollen, but what can you do? Somehow you have to do battle with life. In the future, when you send a package, could you maybe put a comfortable corset, a medical one, more to hold in my insides because they're stretched. Maybe it's from the hard labor or maybe from old age. Stay where you are. Don't go anywhere. I'd really like to have a photograph of all of you. Later I'll send you mine. In my other letters I asked you to look for Juozas Ulevičius and the others. Be good, look for him maybe through the newspapers, and ask that he'd write to the address I gave you. Though I'm writing that they should write directly to me and am asking you to give out your address, you should do what you think is right.

Spring is beginning here. The nights are still cold, but during the day the sun is warm. The nature here is incredibly beautiful. The air is dry. Good for the lungs. It's very important here to have your own, separate house, which, thank God, I do. That is, I have half a house.

You, Nijolė, are the center of our family. Be a good sister to your brother Algimantas. He, the poor thing, is lonely. I feel very sorry for him. I don't think it's so easy for you either. I feel that you've lived through many troubles. Poor Vida has suffered so much with her disease. It hurts me so much that she couldn't complete her studies. I'm happy that my Algimantas will complete his studies and have a profession. Often I dream of you all, exhausted, tattered, but especially Algimantas. I suffered much over those dreams. Now that I've received news from you, my mood is much better. Thank God that you are all alive, healthy, and that you are taking care of yourselves. The future will be brighter. All of this is because of those terrible wars; they've exhausted everyone. I am happy that you maintain contact with each other, and that you stay together like a family and take care of each other. May the Lord grant that you continue to maintain a brotherly love for each other. You are all equally dear to me, I love you all the same, and I pray for you.
I'd like very much to hear something about Aunt. I suffered much over her. I'm waiting for her final photographs. I kiss you all passionately and I'll wait for letters from you. Greetings to Uncle and Ugnė.

Yours, Mama

Chuzhyr, July 8, 1956

My dearest daughter Vida,

I received your letter written June 14, 1956. I was waiting for it eagerly. I received three letters from Nijolė already. Although she wrote to me about all three of you, I like to receive letters from each of you written in your own hand. Your letters and photographs give me untold pleasure—they are incredibly beautiful. How happy I am, my daughter, that you, on your holiest of days, wore your Lithuanian national costume *(Vida's wedding day)*. In your costume you looked like a true daughter of Lithuania. I am incredibly happy that you have not forgotten your beloved homeland and that for a husband you have chosen a Lithuanian. I'd like it if your husband, Algirdas, could write to me in his own hand. Somehow I'd like that. I am very grateful for your prayers, especially for Rasa, that little angel. I believe that God truly listens to her prayers. During the hardest days of my exile I felt a special care from God, maybe as a result of all your prayers. Over seven years I've lived in exile with a very small income and little help. Many people are surprised that being old and alone I managed to build myself a little house, not any worse than anyone else's. As soon as they released me, I sold the house, and now I have 2000 rubles for my trip and for the beginning of my new life. I believe that I'll be leaving here August 15th. I expect to be in Lithuania ten days later. At first I'll stay with the Vitkus family, and then later the Žiulys family. I've lost all my rights to the house on 26 Darius-Girėnas Street.

In Lithuania I expect to meet up with all sorts, but I've grown accustomed to everything and I'm not worried. There's a Lithuanian proverb: "If God will help you, the pig can't get you." I've written you, I believe, seven or more letters. There I wrote about Mindaugas's death. It would be too bad if you didn't receive them. I wrote them after I returned home from the hospital after pneumonia. I wasn't that strong yet. I wrote those letters one after the other without any special order. But, I believe you'll understand. August 13th is the anniversary of Mindaugas's death. If you can, pray for him. When I pray for him, I feel him close, it seems as though I can even feel him breathing. I pray for him, I pray for you, I pray to the Virgin Mary at the Gates of Dawn that she take care of all Lithuanians who are so far away from their homeland. I pray to Saint Theresa that she teach you how to love Jesus in the way that she loved him. That she would show you the bright path to heaven that she followed. I'm glad that you are teaching Rasa how to pray. Six years old is the age to learn prayer. You can't let the moment slip by, not having used it for something good.

I am glad that you remember and value what I have taught you, even though at the time it may have seemed useless and annoying. But it's necessary in life. I let you go out into the world at a very young age.

There has not been a day, not an hour, that I have not thought of you. I prayed to the Virgin Mary that she would protect you from the types of mistakes the world seems so full of. I will end with this letter on this thought. Leaving Chuzyr I will write again and give you my address in Lithuania.

Yours, Mama.

Chuzhyr, July 9, 1956

My dearest Nijolė and Algimantas,

My most important goal in this letter is to thank you for your package, which I received on July 5th. It took three and a half months to get here. Everything was intact. I treated the postal workers to the chocolate because they made sure that I received my package. I thank you especially for the dark blue wool fabric. I've been dreaming a long time about being able to sew myself a new coat since the one I brought from Lithuania is badly torn. Here I could get around 1,500 rubles for that fabric, and already people have made me offers. With that much money I could live modestly for six months, but I don't want to sell the very first gift that I've received from you.

I learned already to live for the day. I don't worry too much about tomorrow. Somehow I believe in the Lord and the Lord has not failed me yet. In the beginning, when I first arrived here from Lithuania, I had almost nothing and I couldn't earn anything, and I suffered over that. Then there was no hope of ever going home. Two times I wrote petitions to the Soviet Lithuanian government, asking permission to return home, but both times they were rejected. My health declined dramatically. The doctors diagnosed me as being in the third stage of high blood pressure and assigned me to a home for the disabled. I was in no rush to go because I had a room here and here I could take care of myself. My blood pressure was 235, my legs and my feet had swelled to the size of pillows. I didn't pay much attention to all that, though I was annoyed that not only I couldn't run, but I couldn't walk briskly. Shuffling around as I was, my situation changed for the better. There was talk about releasing elderly invalids. Then I decided not to go to the home for the disabled and then on January 24th a declaration came out stating that the elderly who did not have anyone to support them could be released. And then on January 28th I received a letter from the Valatkases in Kaunas about you and directly afterwards I sent you my first letter through them. From that time on my mood has changed, and at the same time I grew stronger. Now I have only one thing left to worry about and that is the trip ahead of me. I'm a little bit afraid of it. I'll be traveling for ten days. Clumsy as I am now, it will be difficult. Don't send any more packages to this address. I don't expect to stay here longer than August 15th. By winter I plan to go and live with the Vitkus family in Utena and visit the place where I was born. After that the Žiulys family has invited me to stay in Panevėžys. They all send their greetings to you, but especially Mildutė, who sends her greetings to her godmother Vida. When I return I'll tell them all about you, and then they can write to you themselves. Because of several unpleasant incidents our ties had broken off for about three years. Now we're back in touch.

I am here with an Ukrainian girl, who helped me a lot when I was sick and I couldn't bring back any water, or chop my firewood, or do any other heavy work *(her assigned work load)*. Her name is Ania Koval. She'd worn Vida's national costume, which I'd had with me. Now I sent the national costume to Lithuania to one of our relatives on your father's side who'd sent me some packages. She is very devout and often prays for you.

Before leaving I'll write again. I'll be waiting for letters from Algimantas and I thank him for his package. If you didn't receive the letters in which I wrote to you about Mindaugas, I'll write again. There is this writer here, Greičiūnas. He writes "with an ax in his hand." He sends all Lithuanians his greetings. There's also a woman here called Veronika Kuzmickienė. Her eighteen-year-old son was killed. Her husband also. She does not have any relatives left in Lithuania or here. There's only one, in America, in Chicago, her brother's son, Vytautas Aniulis. She wants very much to correspond with him. Be good, find him, and send him her address. Do it as soon as you can.

Yours, Mama

Chuzhyr, July 15, 1956

My dearest Nijolė and Algimantas,

In this letter I'd like to ask you to send a package to my dear friend Father Vincas Pranckietis. I arrived here in the same cattle wagon with him. *(Lithuanians were deported to Siberia crammed into cattle wagons).* He helped me build my house. Whenever I was sick or had any problems, he'd come immediately and visit with me, comfort me, and support me in any way he could. He held mass many times for Mindaugas, may he rest in peace, and also for you. When I heard that Aunt had died, he immediately held mass for her soul. Now he has moved to another location. He was just here visiting. He visited me. I'd like to pay him back for all he has done for me. He is around your age. For five years he fished in the Lake Baikal—both in the winter and in the summer. In the winter he fished during blizzards and in the summer during storms and changing weather. It would be hard for me to list here all the suffering this man has endured. Lately things have been going a little easier for him. I'd like it very much if you could send him a package that would be worthy of his stature. He would need some very good quality dark fabric with a lining and all the trimmings necessary to sew a good suit, including buttons. His mother can sew it for him. He also needs a pair of good shoes, size 44, and a few pairs of socks, some shirts, and some handkerchiefs. I ask you to do this as soon as you can. Write him a letter and inform him of the date when you mailed his package. Packages take up to four months to arrive here. In the letter you write to him, you must tell him that I wrote to you that he was my greatest friend and ally in exile. All three of you must thank him for that in the nicest way you possibly can. Because Vida does not live with you, the two of you should thank him on Vida's behalf. He is a humanist and a sensitive soul. He has a camera and will be able to mail you photographs that show how we Lithuanians live in Siberia. *(Father Pranckietis's photographs of the exiles lives in Siberia were published in 1989 with his memoir* The Fishermen of Baikal.) I'll write again soon. I kiss you all warmly.

Yours, Mama.

First letter from Siberia in 1956

Chuzhyr, August 6, 1956

Dear Nijolė,

In my first letters to you I wrote about Mindaugas's death. In those letters I wrote to you about his wife and his daughter (Eva was wrong when she told you he'd had a son). His daughter is six years old now and is already going to school. Her name is Dovilė, but we call her Dovilytė. Mindaugas's wife is Genė Puidaitė. She lives with Dovilytė in the Kaunas suburb of Marvelė. Send them a package. Dovilė needs white fabric for a first communion dress, white shoes, and white socks, and a holy medallion to wear around her neck.

I am very happy and I praise God that I found you all alive and healthy and that you're living your lives the right way. Often I think that I'm not worthy of such blessings. All of a sudden I have it all: news from you, and I am free and may return home. After all those tears and all that suffering all of a sudden there is so much joy and happiness. Now all that is left is to see you again. As I write those words, my heart trembles. To see you, just not here, in Siberia...

My health is much better now. Everyone is saying that I look younger. When my countrymen found out that I'm receiving letters from you, and that I received a package, they all began visiting me and asking that I show them your photographs, the things you've sent me, and that I read them your letters. Before, when things were very hard for me, few people saw me and rarely did anyone visit me. I keep writing to you about suffering, but that's because I've experienced so much hardship. But all I have to do is just take a look at other people's lives and I see that everyone has their own hardships, especially during these difficult times, everyone, you could say, but especially those of us who've been separated from our homeland.

I've already begun preparing for my trip home. I've decided that I'll be leaving at the end of August. When I leave, I'll write you a letter. I could write much more, but then the letter will be heavy and it might not reach you, so I'll leave what I have to say for next time.

Yours, Mama

Chuzhyr, August 20, 1956

My dearest Nijolė and Algimantas,

I received your letter written on July 3rd. I'd written to you May 28th, but the letter was returned to me from New York. Our postal system requires that on the envelope you write first the name of the country, then the name of the city, then the address, and in the last place the person's last name, then first name. You wrote first the name, then the address, then the city, and in the last place the country. We're required to write the address the way the post office requires it, and when you write it the other way around, things get mixed up. That's why I think my letter was returned to me.

I am now a free woman and at the end of August or in the early days of September I'll be returning to Lithuania. The trip will be exhausting, until I can leave Olchon. From there onwards I will travel by train to Lithuania. Maybe I will stay with the Žiulys family in Panevėžys. No one knows me there... At first the Žiulys family was afraid to write to me, as were many other people. We *(exiles)* were tossed out of our society as dangerous and were damned for all times. Now a lot has changed. On paper we are free and many of us are returning to Lithuania. I have no right to my house on Darius and Girėnas Street. My life changed when I started receiving your letters. Even if I had to spend the remainder of my life in Siberia, it would no longer be that hard. Now I am happy, I know that you are taking care of me, that you love me. I have nothing to give you to repay you for all your care, longing, and love. I am very grateful for your gifts, which you and

Algimantas sent me. (I already received two packages.) Everything suits me perfectly. Many people come to me and want to buy things from me, but I won't sell anything from these first gifts, not unless I was desperate for food.

August 26 is Nijolė and Vida's birthday. Every year I'd remember you and send you my prayers. This year I can wish you a happy birthday by mail. What else can I wish you besides strength to battle life's troubles and good health. My dearest wish would be for you to return to your homeland, but as I write these words my heart trembles... I am very happy that the Lord has granted me such good children. My greatest joy is that in all the storms of life you've not let go of your faith in God. You suffered many hardships, as I did. I'd thought that everything was lost, though there was a faint glimmer of hope in my heart. And that hope did not disappoint me. Now I have a stronger hope—that you will return home to Lithuania... I kiss you all heartily.

Yours, Mama

Mama's letters written from Lithuania after she returned from Siberia

Utena, September 14, 1956

My dearest Nijolė, Vida, and Algimantas,

I greet you from our homeland. I arrived in Vilnius September 10th at 10:00 at night. I spent the night in Vilnius and then at 7:00 in the morning went to the Gates of Dawn to thank the Virgin Mary for her care and guidance, which I felt all throughout my exile. Mary's portrait was shining by the light of hundreds of candles and was surrounded with white lilies. The chapel and the stairs leading up to the chapel were crowded with worshippers. A priest was holding mass, the people were chanting the liturgy and other hymns in Lithuanian. It was so moving. Tears were streaming down my face. I thanked Mary that you cared for me through all my troubles and that I was able to return home. I prayed for all of you, for Uncle, and Ugnė, and for all Lithuanians, that Mary of the Gates of Dawn would protect them all and help them all return to their homeland. I stayed and listened to three masses. I didn't have the strength to do more. My legs hurt me terribly. While bidding Mary farewell, I thanked her one more time for helping me return to my homeland, and I left my prayers of thanks at her feet. I asked her for her guidance in my future life.

The trip to my homeland was not as difficult as I thought it would be. I left on August 31st and I was in Vilnius already on September 10th. The trip cost me 500 rubles. There were some other expenses associated with my trip, so in all I spend 800 rubles. I'm living with the Vitkus family, three miles from Utena *(in the village of Šilinė)*. They have taken me in, they feed me, and they have invited me to stay. While in Siberia I suffered from loneliness and I was afraid to return to Lithuania without a home to return to. I thought I would be homeless. When I got here I found that everything was different. All my old friends remained as they always were, pleasant and friendly. Utena reminds me of my childhood. Everything is so familiar and dear to me.

I will be waiting eagerly for your letters. They say that letters to Lithuania take eight to ten days to arrive. I've written many letters to you, but I don't have any word if all of them have reached you. I ask you this; when you receive this letter, write back to me right away. I've received all your letters and photographs. I'll send you my photographs later. I want very much to know how Algimantas is living.

Right now in Lithuania there is a lot of rain, the days are foggy, and I haven't seen the sun yet. It rains all the time. Now that I've returned to Lithuania I feel stronger. My legs don't swell as much. I guess the climate of my homeland is good for me. I am wearing the shoes you sent me, which means I no longer have to wear shoes with rubber soles. Now, thank God, I want for nothing. I'm living in my homeland, I receive news from you, what else do I need? Just to live and thank God for living. I want to take on some sort of work. I'm not used to all this free time. Nothing good comes of it. I imagined that life in Lithuania would be cruel, but I haven't experienced anything awful yet, although I haven't been here a full week. I live well here in the Vitkus household. Their cabin is big, there's plenty of room. The people here are educated and sincere.

I'll be waiting for your letters, maybe even from Vida. Rasa will be writing to me. I thank her for her prayers. Bobutė *(Grandmother)* also prayed for her to Mary of the Gates of Dawn. She prayed that she would grow up healthy and that she'd come back to Lithuania to her grand-mother. I send my greetings to Uncle and Ugnė. I kiss you all many times.

Yours, Mama

Utena, October 5, 1956

My dearest Nijolė and Algimantas,

First of all I'd like to thank you for your package, which I received September 21st here in Lithuania from the Utena post office. The post office in Chuzyr forwarded it to me. I thank you for every littlest thing that I found in that package. I'm living with the Vitkus family on their farm in Šilinė. Mrs. Vitkus is my cousin—we are the daughters of broth-ers. She alone helped me during all my long years of exile by mailing me packages, all the time living desperately herself. Her family is big, and during the war they lost a lot of people and wealth, but they managed to get back up on their feet and now they have a bite to eat. Knowing my situation, she gathered up whatever she had and sent it to me, and then when she found out that I'd been freed, and that I might be able to return to my homeland, she immediately invited me to come and live with her. There are four sons and two daughters in the Vitkus family. Their cabin is large and there is plenty of room for me here. I hardly ever meet my other relatives. My other relatives, after I was exiled, hardly ever re-member me. They complain that they've suffered too much hardship, but who didn't at the time? There is a difference between suffering hardship at home and being exiled to Siberia.

The local doctors have examined me and have given me a diagno-sis of hypertension. My blood pressure is 205/110. Besides that they found a chronic infection in my left leg. I believe that the best medicine is a good mood and good living conditions, although both are not the very best right now. The Vitkus family is very good. They all love me and we all eat at one table. Three of their sons are my god sons. We joke that I will be their matchmaker when the times comes for them to marry, and for that I'll barter for a good burial when I die.

What else do I do? They say the heart beats, the eyes laugh, and the tongue gossips. That's how I've learned how to make my hardship easier. To other people, I look very cheerful. And now, thank God, everything is going well for me. I know about you and I am happy that you have remained the way that I let you go out into the world. And if it is the will of God that we one day meet, then we will meet, I haven't given up that hope.

I read your letters everyday. I've even learned them by heart and could recite them out loud. I also gaze at your photographs often. I'm not in a hurry to send you my photograph just yet. I had a photograph of myself made in Chuzyr, but they weren't ready by the time I left. They promised to send them to me, but I haven't received them yet. Recently I dreamed of Aunt (for the first time) and of Mindaugas, and both of them were very happy. All Souls Day is near. I've ordered mass for them.

Around the 15th of this month I will be traveling to Panevėžys. Mrs. Žiulys has promised to come and get me. There I plan to have my eyes checked and to get glasses. There are some good seamstresses there too, so I plan to have some clothing made from the fabrics you sent me. From Panevėžys I plan to travel to Kaunas to visit Mindaugas and our two grandmothers' graves. Then I'll visit Mindaugas's daughter Dovilė and his wife Genė.

I am tormented by uneasy thoughts when I don't receive a letter from you for a long time. I think a lot about Vida and I worry that the tuberculosis doesn't come back. I've written her a few letters already. She should not be knitting me a sweater. Instead, she should be resting, lying down. I can knit a sweater myself, besides, you've sent me three already and that's quite enough. If only I could live with you, I'd be able to help you around the house. If you have any free time at all, study the Russian language. It is very helpful these days to know Russian...

When you decide to put together a package, please include buttons for underclothing, blouses, and different size needles and thread. I'd like very much a medallion for my neck on a chain and Father Yla's prayer book *Lithuanian Prayers and Hymns.* If you can, a few different types of rosaries. I'd like very much to have a wristwatch, a simple one that works well and clearly shows the time. Forgive me for being such a nag and constantly asking you for things. By the time you dress me, it'll cost you a fortune. For now, I kiss you and I'll be waiting for your letters.

Mama

Utena, October 17, 1956

Dear Nijolė and Algimantas,

...I am getting ready to dress myself up with all the beautiful fabric you have sent me, only it's too bad that you forgot to include a fashion magazine in your package. To make the transition from a wartime overcoat and a summer coat that isn't much different without a fashion magazine to look at is not that easy. But our tailors do a better job sewing clothing than over there in America. And our beauticians can do better perms than the one you have, Nijolė.

Living on Lake Baikal I learned survival humor. Our countrymen there are very funny people. When you run into one of them they can make you laugh so hard that you double over. You don't even need "Dick and Doff."

Enough joking around. Now I'll move on to a more serious topic. Because you did not receive the letters in which I wrote about Mindaugas, I will try now, as much as I am able, to explain. Those letters were written in April. At that time it is too difficult to transfer the mail. Sometimes it stays in one place for a week or more, until they can move it, and sometimes a letter can get lost...

As you already know, during the war Mindaugas was on the front lines. When the war ended, having suffered through great hardship, but not wounded, he returned home. *(Mindaugas's return is described in the letter from Aldona Marcinkutė).* As you know, since childhood he had serious problems with an inborn abnormality in the heart valve. The hardship of war weakened his heart even more. Also, his marriage affected his health negatively. The doctors believed that he should live for about five years quietly under his mother's care, avoiding heavy work or worry, eating the right foods and resting well. Then he could have built up his strength and lived. But, unfortunately, he did none of that. After he'd rested a little bit, he decided to enroll in a newly established pharmacology school, where he studied for two years. At the time, he did not have the right to enroll in the university... *(Men who had served in the German army did not have the right to study under the Soviet system. This was one of the ironies of this generation—while these men had been conscripted into the German army against their will, they had to answer for it by being deprived of their rights under the Soviet system.)* While he was studying at the pharmacology school, I noticed that he'd begun dating Genė. I was worried that he'd do something he'd regret, so I started trying to talk him out of making an insane mistake. First of all, he was too young then. He was barely twenty-one. Secondly, he was in poor health, didn't have a profession, and was not at all ready to take on the challenge of family life. He was in the midst of living a child's life, immature, unstable, and traumatized by the war. He was very unstable and there wasn't anyone at the time who had any influence over him. Being alone, and in difficult circumstances, I could not hold him back from unwise decisions. Genė was older than him and she was practical. At the time he needed the influence of good friends, or his family, his brother and sisters. Then he really would have been saved from the tragedy that followed. Whenever the two of us spoke about you, especially about you, Nijolė, his eyes would fill with joy. He grew up to be a good-looking, pleasant, gentle young man, but at the same time he was weak. If there had been anyone from his family around to spend time with him he would have matured into a serious young man and would have known how to plan his future wisely. I saw it all coming and my heart sensed that this marriage would send him to his grave. That's why I fought with him to stop it. But he was stubborn and wanted to have it his way. He married, completed his studies, passed his exams, went swimming in the Nemunas River on a hot day, lay outdoors in the sun, and the next day his temperature rose to 40 degrees centigrade. His face swelled, and his abdomen, and his legs, which used to swell up before all the time. The doctors diagnosed him with a kidney infection. Because his heart valves gave him so much trouble, his overall health declined quickly. At the time it was difficult to find a doctor. Most of the better doctors were away on vacation. I took him to see what few doctors I could find, but they stated their opinion point blank, that his condition was hopeless because his heart valves prevented his blood from circulating. And so, after a month-long illness, he died on August 13, 1948.

At first my relationship with Genė was bitter. For a long time after I was deported I did not write to her, but when they started talking about amnesty for invalids and granting permission for us to return home, I wrote to her. She wrote back to me right away, sent my Dovilė's photographs, a package, and did what she could for me. Everything that was must remain in the past. I simply must forgive her and forget it. After all, Genė remains close to us. I wrote about Mindaugas in the only way that is possible at the moment. If we ever meet, I'll tell you more... Do you remember Kotrynėlė? *(Sarah Shilingovsky, the Jewish girl Mama rescued when she was five).* Her mother and her aunt Baronienė helped me very much with Mindaugas's affairs...

That's how I'll end this letter for now. I'm enclosing the photographs you asked for, and one from Mindaugas's funeral. You'll recognize me standing not far from the coffin. Later I'll send you more. Send my best wishes to Uncle and Ugnė. In my next letter I'll write more. I kiss you all.

Mama

Utena, October 24, 1956

Dear Nijolė and Algimantas,

...I pretty much described Mindaugas's death to you. When we meet I'll tell you much more. His wake was in my living room, where he was photographed with me. The evening before his funeral we carried his body over to the Church. And the next day, after mass, we carried him to the cemetery. I've buried many dear people from my family. It was difficult to part with each of them, but walking beside their coffins I'd never had the thought to walk and walk and to never part. I walked behind Mindaugas's coffin lost in thought, not seeing anything in front of me besides his dear coffin, not one tear fell from my eyes, it was that good and that easy to walk, it seems, I'd go and go a hundred thousand kilometers, just so that I would not have to part with him. And I didn't see when the coffin stopped beside his grave and when it was lowered and when it was covered with dirt...

I was left an orphan. I didn't know anything about your whereabouts. At night I'd sway beside the window, with my eyes pointed towards the cemetery, waiting for him to come home. Sometimes, it seemed, I could hear his footsteps drawing closer, and it seemed as though he were coming, that he was close... Exhausted, one night I dreamt that he came with a small package in his hands. He'd brought me his laundry to wash. I think he was serving in the army. I was worried. He said, "Don't worry, Mama, I can buy my way out." I asked, "How much do you need?" He said, "About 1000 rubles," and he disappeared. After that, I donated as much money as I could to the church just to ease his burden.

In 1949 I had to leave my home. Mindaugas was supposed to be exiled together with me, but because he was already in the cemetery, I had to go alone. That is about all I am able to write at the moment about Mindaugas. There is much much more that I need to tell you when you come to Lithuania... For the moment, let's turn the page on the past, not the distant past, but an extremely painful past. When I think about it, I come to the conclusion, that everything is designed and led by God's plan. Mindaugas, had he lived, would have been forced into exile with me. And so God called him right in the bloom of youth. May His will be done.

Here follows a description of Mama's deportation to Siberia, based on the story she told Nijolė when she came to America:

On March 25, 1949, very early in the morning, the KGB, pounded loudly on the front door and woke Mama. They checked her documents and began searching for Mindaugas, so that they could exile him to Siberia. But he'd died August 13, 1948 and was buried in the Aleksotas cemetery, which was visible through the front windows of the house. Our two grandmothers were buried there as well. Mama showed the intruders the view of the cemetery through the window and said, "Go and dig up my son, Mindaugas, I'd very much enjoy his company on the trip."

Utena, November 21, 1956

Dear Vida,

In your letter I found a few words written by your husband, Algirdas. For those words I am grateful. However, I am most grateful for Rasa's gift—that dear handkerchief—it is a very dear keepsake for me. Last week was a very happy one for me because I received a letter from each of you almost at the same time. I'm finishing up answering each of your letters. At least through paper I can reach those who are dearest to me in the entire world. The letter from Algimantas came first, and that's why it made the deepest impression on me. It's been a week since I received it, but I still can't dry my tears… It would seem, what do I lack? He is alive and healthy, but it is so painful that he had to suffer so much in his youth. I know that it was hard for you and Nijolė, but somehow I believe that it was hardest for him. Thank God that all that hardship is over now, though we still don't know about the future… I think that when he becomes a professional, his life will get easier and be much better. If only his health has not been ruined! I am so afraid of losing him, the way I lost Mindaugas, may he rest in peace.

Although you write to me that I should not be afraid of telling you everything I need, all I can say is, you can't pull your wealth out of a pond. You write that you would even dig me up to take care of me if you had to. Digging is hard work. I know that too well. You promise me that I'll never need to work if I come to live with you. I've worked my entire life and I couldn't sit still for a minute without working. Here at the Vitkus house I've knit socks and gloves for all my godsons. Oh, and I must have written at least sixty letters to my countrymen left behind on Lake Baikal.

You offered to buy me some yarn. I could weave some scarves from it. The women here weave beautifully, only yard is hard to come by. It would be something for me to do, and helpful for me and for others. The yarn should be of good quality, spun, and thin, strong, and in many interesting colors. If you come across black or dark blue fabric for a summer dress, something suitable for my age, please send it to me. I leave it up to your opinion. I believe that you know my taste. I have one everyday dress, and one hanging out to dry—winter or summer. Nijolė writes that there are two packages on the way, one from Uncle. Sometimes I wonder if he doesn't send things that belonged to Aunt, may she rest in peace, or am I mistaken?

I probably won't be going to Kaunas until the spring because this year winter came early unexpectedly. I don't have warm clothing, so I can't travel far. I'd like to end this letter by wishing your happy family a Merry Christmas, and in the hope that we will celebrate the next Christmas all together. I thank Rasytė for her prayers. I am sending her and you my photograph the way I am, although I don't look that great. My age and what I've been through has left its mark. I kiss you all.

Yours, Mama

Utena, November 23, 1956

Dear Nijolė,

...That Eva is shameless for deceiving you and me, for lying, and for using you. She ended up in my home after the war when many people were left homeless and starving. She would come to me asking for a place to stay and for food to eat. I helped her and others as much as I possibly could, thinking the entire time about you, and about how you were all left in a foreign country, homeless, and maybe starving too. In the meantime, one day, carrying my milk can to Kaunas to sell the milk, I slipped and fell and sprained my left hand. So I asked Eva to stay with me and help out until my hand healed. She agreed to it readily, but she wasn't much help. Somehow I managed to milk the cow with only my right hand. She carried the milk. After a week there was no milk left and no one left to buy the milk—that's how she took care of things. Then I had to find another woman to carry the milk, but I was still left with Eva, who I had to clothe and feed. She just went to parties day and night with her friends. She lived that way with me for about six months. After that she returned to her own country, to Germany, and I never heard from her again. I could write much more about her, but I'll leave that for later... My hand healed, but it was never properly set. I had to stay in the hospital for a while, but I couldn't leave my house to Eva, I didn't trust her with good reason. Send my greetings to Uncle and Ugnė. Love and kisses,

Mama

1957

In 1957 Algimantas, Nijolė, and Vida started making arrangements for Mama to join them in the United States. The way the process worked was that first Algimantas, who was an American citizen, made an official request to the American Consulate in Moscow inviting his mother to come and live with him in the United States and promising to support her financially. Once the American Consulate approved the request and notified Mama that she had the right to apply for a visa to the United States as the mother of an American citizen, she needed to gather her family birth certificates and other documents together and request that the Soviet government grant her an exit visa in order to leave the Soviet Union and issue her a passport. The entire process typically took from six months to a year. If the request was denied, the applicant could re-apply after one year. Algimantas invited Mama to the United States twice; Vida invited her to Australia twice; and Nijolė invited her to the United States once. In each instance Mama was given permission to travel to the United States or Australia, but the Soviet exit visa would be denied without any explanation. Nijolė made extraordinary attempts through high-level American officials to pressure the Soviet authorities to release Mama, but all of these attempts failed. In the end it took a $1,000 bribe hand-delivered by the well known Lithuanian-American journalist Salomėja Narkeliūnaitė to get the Soviet authorities to release Mama.

Utena, January 10, 1957

Dear Vida,

Your last letter is especially precious to me because I received it while celebrating Christmas for the first time in my homeland after exile and after our long years of separation. Although we have not yet been able to sit down together for Christmas Eve supper, we can communicate with each other through our thoughts, knowing where we all are.

I thank you very much, dear Vida, for such a special gift—the prayer book of Mary of Lourdes. It is doubly special to me because it is a gift from Aunt and from you. I don't even know how to thank my dearest Rasa for such a special drawing and for her dear words. I'm wondering what I can send you and Rasa to remind you of your home-land and of her grandmother.

I spent Christmas together with the Vitkus family in Šilinė. All their relatives had gathered at their parents' house, only Kazys was missing, but we received our first letter from him for the holidays with photographs. We all read it with joy, and that made our holiday all the more pleasurable. The entire Vitkus family sends you their Christmas greetings, hoping that next year you will sit at their Christmas Eve table together with them here in Šilinė.

My health is much better. I'm using the medicine that Nijolė sent me. You, Vida, always worry over my health, but you never write about your own. I'm sure that after such a difficult illness, you are not com-pletely well yourself. Besides, keeping house and taking care of a family, not to mention Juozas's birth, must exhaust you. He is so plump that it must be difficult to carry him around. I compared his photograph to one of you when you were that age and you both appeared equally plump to me. Now I see clearly that you could really have used my help at this time in your life. But how to cross the ocean? Should I use the boat that Rasa drew for me? When I received your letter, I dreamt of your house. In my dream I bedded you down and then took Juozukas and his crib into another room and put him to sleep. I told Rasa to be very very quiet, so that she wouldn't wake her mother. Algirdas was working in the garden with a shovel. I saw the potatoes and beets growing. I couldn't see the orchard at all, although it was fascinating to see an or-ange tree growing in the yard. Maybe next time Rasa can draw me a picture of that orange tree with the oranges on it?

The Karsokas family sent me fish and flour for Christmas. They've invited me to stay the summer. They've even promised to pay all my travel expenses. If I can, I will definitely visit them. They are very nice people. I kiss you all.

Mama

Utena, March 3, 1957

Dear Vida,

I am writing this letter to you while in a very good mood. On the first of this month I received a notification from the American Consulate that I should go see the local government and request a visa to travel to the United States. Today I went to our local police department and handed over that notification. They promised to inform me of what other documentation I will need. They scheduled an appointment for me to return to see them at 6:00 pm. Until I get everything settled, there will be many trips back and forth and many documents will need to be hunted down. As long as it all ends well.

When I received the notification from the consulate I grew sad. I could not stop my tears from flowing while at church. It can't be that God is that merciful and that he will allow me to die in your arms? I don't know what kind of medication I should take to be able to sleep at night. The slightest worry or thought drives sleep away. Then my head hurts terribly and my ears ring. I have a hard time lifting my left leg and I start to limp.

I have not yet received your packages, but there are three on the way. If they arrive safely, I'll sell the contents and get some money to take care of the documents. Vida, I'll ask you to send me one more thing, a scapular on a strong chain that doesn't rust. Aunt's, which you sent, was taken by Elziutė, in memory of her dear aunt. She kissed it with tears streaming down her face.

In this letter I've written everything together, my joy, my hope, my worries, and my shortcomings. That's how life is. There are people for whom life is much more difficult, people who've lost everything and have suffered much more than me. After all, I still have all of you, my biggest comfort in this world. I kiss you all.

Mama

P.S. I'm enclosing a sample piece of yarn.

Utena, March 4, 1957

Dear Nijolė,

I received your letter, written on February 9th, on February 24th. I've not received Vida's package, which I believe, she mailed back in November. She'd written that she'd sent it by airmail, so that I'd receive it in time for Christmas. Your packages reach me the fastest, Nijolė. The best way is to send it yourself and not through others. I received a letter from my friend *(Father Pranckietis)*. He is thrilled to have received Agimantas's package, which was mailed through Sweden. It would have arrived faster if it had been mailed directly. He thanks you profusely and is overjoyed with the good quality fabric for a new suit. He wrote that the shoes he received were work boots, but he wanted dress shoes. Maybe when you order from a catalogue they don't always send what you've ordered. That happens often with the mail. If that fur coat is in good condition and warm, I'd like you to send it to my friend, but only if it's not too worn. You can't send something used to a person like that. He could really use a coat like that because it gets very cold in Siberia. If you can, put something else in with the fur coat. It would be very good if you could send a pair of dress shoes to go with the suit. His size is 44. When I lived in Chuzhyr, I wore his shoes when it got to be cold. The best thing would be for you, Nijolė, to send the package yourself, as an Easter gift. Though the package would never reach him in time for Easter, do it anyway, and write him a letter, describing what you've put in the package. When you have a letter ahead of time, listing what is in the package, it is easier to deal with the post office.

My left knee hurts me very much. When I walk, my knee rattles like a rusty wheel. The doctor says that it is a chronic infection of the joint. All sorts of problems trouble me now. I'm planning on traveling to Panevėžys. Mrs. Žiulys has come by twice to pick me up. Nijolė, write to them, they are unhappy that I did not chose to go live with them. I couldn't change where I live now. The Vitkus family is happy that I'm living with them. Through me they were able to find their son, Kazys, in England, who they'd thought was dead. He's already sending them not only letters, but packages. You can't even imagine how happy they are about it. The father has grown younger by twenty years. They've given all the gifts to the children. Their difficult lives have gotten so much better because of the packages. They hadn't even caught their breath after the war, when their youngest son, a gifted student, started having trouble with his lungs. They had to make the choice to give up necessities and pay for his treatment. And so, after two years of sanatoriums and other methods, they've managed to save his life. Now he's studying again, although he's not very strong yet. He needed good food and warm clothing. And two more of their sons recently returned from the army. They also needed everything. Now their troubles are over and their future is much brighter. Janė is an able and energetic girl with a good education. All of the family's troubles are on her shoulders, and now the sun is breaking through the clouds.

The greatest joy in my life would be to get to you, children. I am happy in my homeland and my relatives are very good to me, but I still feel lonely. I am tormented by longing for you. My hope is that in the very least I can reach you in my dreams. Sometimes I see you in my dreams, but not ragged and exhausted like before. As long as I'm on my feet, things aren't so bad, but what will happen when I can't hold on any longer? Who knows how much longer it is given to me to live? The Vitkuses are old. The time will come for them to pass the house on to the children and for the children to marry. Then a new spirit will enter the house, more family. The children will have to take care of their own parents then. What will be left for me then? I'm just a lost soul living in their home. That's not a concern just yet, but it will be in the future. Right now everyone here loves me and there's no better place for me to be. It's fortunate that they took me in. Often I can't sleep at night. My thoughts race all over the place and they always stop at the same point. Until now God has taken care of me. Maybe he'll take care of me further. After all, I am old, I am alone, and I am an invalid. In the Soviet Union family members are allowed to join each other, even if they live far apart. It couldn't be that they wouldn't let me join my children, even if they did live in various countries all over the world? I believe that with my whole heart.

Thank you for Aunt's photograph. I'd like a photograph of her from her funeral. I pray for her often.

I'm waiting for Ugnė's photograph. Good luck with your studies, Nijolė. Love and kisses.

Mama

Utena, April 29, 1957

Dear Vida,

I am thrilled to have received your letter after waiting for it for so
long. Reading it, I thought I was going to lose my mind. So many packages and so many things! Why so much? My dear Vida, do treasures fall
from the sky into your lap that you throw them in all directions? Now I
am convinced that your personality and your generosity are similar to
mine. When I was able, I gave all my relatives and friends whatever I
could. I felt sorry for everyone, but life's cruelty and insincerity had
taught me everything.

Of course it is a good thing that you sent gifts to your goddaughter,
but that's enough. Jūratė Bakšytė has aunts who live in the same country
as you. When I lived in Chuzhyr I desperately lacked clothing and
footwear. For six winters I walked around in rubber boots with my feet
wrapped in whatever rags I could manage to find. One winter I wore
Father Pranckietis's shoes and that winter my feet did not freeze. But not
having proper clothing or footwear I froze my joints, especially the ones
in my feet. Every winter I had bronchitis and my final winter there I had
pneumonia. The cold dipped below 40 degrees centigrade, sometimes
even lower. It's hard for me to describe in writing everything I went
through there.

Don't send me any more packages. You've covered me in gifts
from head to toe. May the Lord grant that I manage to wear everything
out. Uncle also sends packages to me, and Algimantas, and Nijolė sends
me so much that I've lost count. Now I have everything, everything I
need. You've probably gone into debt over those packages.

It is spring already and it's beautiful. The birds are singing, the
flowers are blooming, and the frogs are croaking. Soon the butterflies
will arrive. How wonderful it would be for Rasa and Juozas to chase
them, to pick flowers, and to splash around in puddles. I remember when
I was little that was my absolute most favorite thing to do. Now I, like
that insect after winter has passed, have begun crawling outdoors. Now I
can walk from Šilinė to Utena on foot. That is a huge improvement. It is
so wonderful to walk alone through the forest and through the hills.
Everywhere it is green and everything smells wonderful… I like to walk
alone and to daydream. My thoughts revolve only around all you. Every-

thing weaves together—the happy memories and the painful ones. Every once in a while I smile, every once in a while there are tears in my eyes... Writing this letter to you, a tear has fallen onto the paper... *(You can see on the letter where the ink is blotched by the tear)* I want for nothing. I have everything I need, but I am tormented with longing...

Do you remember the little girl Kotrynėlė and the little boy Alexander, whom we hid during the German occupation? I received a letter from Kotrynėlė's mother in Israel, and she has sent me some gifts. Your children are truly beautiful. Juozukas looks like an exact copy of Father Juozas *(Mama's brother Father Juozas Bakšys)*. His features are so much like his. Whoever sees those photographs is shocked. May God bless your family. I kiss you all and I'll be waiting for your letters.

Mama

Utena, May 19, 1957

Dear Nijolė,

You're probably tired of waiting for my letter. I kept waiting until I had something interesting to say. First of all, about our urgent affairs *(Mama's visa to the United States)*. I didn't trust my own opinion, so I had a consultation with a serious lawyer. We are both of the same opinion. I do not need to write a document asking where I should seek assistance. When your documents reach the necessary organizations here, they will contact me. I can upset the balance by appearing too eager. That was my opinion, and the lawyer agreed with me.

From my perspective here, I don't think this will be easy. It's especially difficult for people whose relatives left after 1940. On the other hand, I am all alone here, I'm not a productive member of the work force, and I am an invalid. Although in the Soviet Union the elderly are supposed to be taken care of with either a pension or shelter, I have not received anything of the kind to date. You must do what you can, and fate will take care of the rest... Only Nijolė, I ask that you and the others stop worrying about me. I know very well what suffering is. If I were still living the way I was before, my life would have been over by now. Now my life has changed. Though I am not living in my own home, the

Vitkus family and the Žiulys family takes good care of me. Panevėžys is only ninety kilometers away and accessible easily by public transportation, but still they always come and pick me up with their car.

Up until now my health was very poor, especially in the winter. I'd get dizzy and fall down often. My heart would beat rapidly and I couldn't sleep at night; I'd use a cold compress. My blood pressure was 240. When I returned to Lithuania I received your tablets, the "Serpasil" and I began using them. This spring I noticed that my head no longer hurts and I don't get dizzy spells anymore. My blood pressure came down to 185. I was prescribed "Validol" for my heart and it works very well. Now I sleep well at night. The doctors here tell me that the vitamins you sent, Nijolė, are very good. I'd like to lose weight and bring my weight down to 75 kilograms. Life would be easier then. The doctors have forbidden me to eat meat or fat. They tell me I should eat only dairy products and vegetables, but here in Lithuania they practically don't exist. They say that it would be very good for me to eat lemons and garlic, but they don't exist either. In March I received two packages—one from Sweden and one from Switzerland, from Basil, which really surprised me. Uncle's *(Karvelis)* name was on the return label. I was confused by that...

Why, Nijolė, didn't you write me earlier that your only day off from the hospital is on Saturday? I would never have burdened you with sending me all those packages. Now what I've written is written. From now on do not send me anything else except for medicine. I received a letter from Dovilė. She is angry at her aunts and at Rasa for not writing to her.

They are talking now about the release of all the exiles. I sent out a package with a letter and four neck ties for Algimantas's birthday on May 21st. Vida has written to me that the stork is planning to deliver another little one for them in September. What's it to me if I can't go there and be with her? I feel so sorry for her that she is having such a hard time with small children, and cooking, and housekeeping. If only I could, I'd work day and night to make things easier for her.

I am enclosing a photograph of your father and me from when we were young. That was after the typhus in 1920. I've decided not to frighten you with my most recent photograph. Now you can see for yourselves that I didn't look all that bad when I was young. I kiss you.
Mama

Utena, May 26, 1957

Dear Nijole,

All week I've been trying to finish writing this letter to you, and always something gets in my way. Finally I realized that my intuition was right because yesterday I was summoned to the police station. When I went there, it turned out that it was about my attempts to go and visit you. It turns out that they've received some of the documents from you. The police assigned a few officials to deal with the details of my leaving to visit you. We talked for a few hours. Most importantly, they asked about my family and about all my relatives... There will be many more of those talks to come. I'll need to fill out more forms, and they will be requiring all your addresses, even your photographs... When they finished their questioning, I asked them if there was any hope that I'd be allowed to leave and go to you? The official almost guaranteed that I'd be able to leave, because I am alone here, I am old, and I am an invalid. He thought that it might even be resolved as soon as this autumn. That friendly official, I think, is some way related to Kotrynėlė or Alexander. He said that he liked me because I took care of those children during the Nazi occupation. He even remembered their names and surnames. This is the second time he's dealt with me. You see, while I was in Chuzhyr I'd sent in a statement, requesting that I be allowed to return to Lithuania. In that statement I explained that during the German occupation I saved those children in addition to other Jews. He was surprised that after all that I was exiled. In general, he praised me for how I was handling things and said that it was smart that I didn't go around asking questions and making demands. If they need to, they'll find me themselves or ask me to come see them. He also offered for you to return to Lithuania... He could take care of all the paperwork right here, so that I wouldn't have to travel to Vilnius or Moscow because that would be too hard for me. I don't know how everything will end up, but the beginning hasn't been that bad.

I've received two packages from Vida, one from Kotrynėlė, and one from London. The sender is Bražėnas. I think it's from Algimantas. I've finished your medicine, the "Serpasil." Don't send me anything else, Nijolė, just medicine.

Maybe we will meet after all? Before I had no hope left. But still, it did feel good to help others, the way I helped those children. That Eva, even though she turned out to be a liar, I still pitied her.

June 13th is Ugnė's birthday and her name day. I send her my heartfelt greetings. I'm enclosing a photograph of her on her mother's arms. I have more photos of Ugnelė here. I could send her more. I kiss you. Mama

I hadn't sealed this envelope when the mailman brought me your letter with such a precious gift enclosed—rosary beads. Dear God, how much joy you all bring to me! Not too long ago I received a similar letter from Vida. How beautiful her words are! I read and I get so emotional. It seems to me that I really never did all that much for you, that you'd all shower me with so much love in your words and your deeds. May God repay you for everything.

I'd like to return now to our matters and say just a few words. Like I mentioned before, I'll be called in to talk quite often now. If that gentleman continues to be as sincere as he appeared in our first meeting, then I think everything will go smoothly. Only I worry the most about you. I've noticed that they pay the most attention to you, Nijolė, asking that you return to your homeland... *(Mama did not know that Nijolė had been married to the freedom fighter Juozas Lukša, but she sensed that the NKVD was especially interested in Nijolė's activities in the West. From this letter Nijolė herself understood that the NKVD knew of her ties to Lukša and the freedom fighters in Lithuania.)* I responded, even if it means that they won't let me out, that right now you should not come back. Make your life there. Now they're supposed to release all the deportees from Siberia. We'll see what will come later... You still need to complete your studies, pass your exams. If you came here you'd have to start everything all over again from the beginning. When will you have any time left just to live? Read my letter carefully and do everything you can so that no one can hurt you...

Mama

Panevėžys, June 19, 1957

Dear Algimantas,

Today I received a letter from you and today I am writing to you. I don't know why your letter took so long to reach me. My heart is so happy reading a letter from you. I am indescribably happy, my dear son, that you have not forgotten your mother's homeland, and that you are still living by those ideals that you took from your homeland. I am so overjoyed that you remained an idealist, that you have not become a materialist. Nothing ruins a young person more than money. I believe that you have not closed off your heart from feeling compassion. As I remember you, you were sensitive towards others. At this time the world is drowning in materialism and capitalism. Only God knows how all that will end. Everyone is shouting for peace, but in the souls of nations there is no peace. That horrible war has separated all of us from each other. For twelve years you did not know where I was. And I did not know where you were. Thank God that we now can write to each other. I have hope that we will see each other yet. What fortune it would be if we could meet again in our homeland! I believe that all the efforts you are making on my behalf have reached the proper officials. It seems as though there will be no obstacles here, only that it will take time until everything is organized. I've written more in detail about all that to Nijolė, so I'm sure she'll tell you all about it.

I've received a letter from Kotrynėlė and her mother. They are living in their homeland *(Israel)*. They sent me gifts. I believe you still remember her from when she lived with us. Nijolė wrote that she corresponds with Alexander's parents.

I do not have a stable life. I live in Utena with Stefanija, then in Šilutė with the Vitkus family, then in Panevėžys with the Žiulys family. That's how I'll have to live until everything is settled. I don't know how I will endure such a long journey, but it's still too early to talk about that.

My dear son, do not think that your letters tire me. Quite to the contrary, they bring me much joy. I wish you persistence in all your goals and good health. I believe that we will meet again. Every morning and every evening I pray for you to the Mother of Heaven, that she may protect you and keep you safe from all misfortune. I kiss you many, many, many times. *Yours, Mama*

Panevėžys, June 24, 1957

Dear Nijolė,

Recently I received a letter from Algimantas, dated May 1st. It took about six weeks to reach me. Reading his letter, I remembered vividly when I'd let the three of you, Nijolė, Vida, and Algimantas, out into the wide world in 1943, during the German occupation, to search for learning, because the Germans had closed down the universities. I really cannot remember if Algimantas left with you or one semester later. I think that you and Vida and Algimantas must remember that well... Some times I'm asked to talk about these things here... Now that I've received a letter from Algimantas, and in that letter he remembers his homeland vividly, I've had the desire to share some memories with you... I am pleased as I can possibly be that God gave me such good children. Most importantly, you have not forgotten God, and your homeland, and you love your mother so. My dear children, you should know that I love you as much as you love me. What joy it would be for all of us to meet again here in dear Lithuania. Right now, after you've just expended so much energy on your studies, you need to live a while where you are and rest, and then later, once you've gotten your energy back, you'll be more useful to your homeland... Your homeland, whether she is experiencing hardship or poverty, is always a precious treasure. Right now in our homeland nothing is lacking... There is even too much of everything. Everyone is racing, conniving, just to fill their pockets and to fill their bellies well... People like to drink wine. That's the most important goal these days. Young people go on trips together, party, dance, sing, visit theaters and watch films. Life is boiling, bubbling...

I don't know if you will understand my letters the way they ought to be understood. My thinking has grown old and my writing as well... Finishing this letter, I send my greetings to you and to Ugnė. Pass on my greetings to Uncle.

Mama

Utena, August 20, 1957

Dear Vida,

While I was in Kaunas I wrote you a long letter. I hope you received it. After all my journeys, I've returned to live with the Vitkus family. I am resting now, as I hurt my leg during this trip. I visited Algirdas's parents twice. They welcomed me pleasantly and gave me gifts. They are a very nice older couple. Only, I can't understand why they live according to the old customs and why they are so shy. Maybe my openness made them feel more uncomfortable?
My dear Vida, the 26th of this month is yours and Nijolė's birthdays. Every year I remembered this day with tears of pain in my eyes. Now I remember this day with tears of joy. In my letter to Nijolė I sent birthday greetings to the two of you. I still want to say happy birthday to you, Vida, separately. As that very serious and painful hour giving birth draws near, I want to wish you endurance and patience to bear all the pain. For some reason, I often think that the Lord is sending you twins. If that happens, don't be afraid. Take everything that comes from the hand of God. You and Nijolė are twins and you've grown up so nicely. Vida, I pray the most passionately for you. I kiss you all warmly.

Mama

Utena, August 21, 1957

Dear Nijolė,

When I returned to the Vitkus household from Kaunas and Panevėžys I found your letter and your package with the medicine and eye glasses. My health, over all, is much better. In Kaunas I walked around a lot during the heat of July. I walk slowly. It's difficult for me to walk uphill; I walk a bit and I have to stop and catch my breath. In Kaunas the first thing I did was to visit Mindaugas and your two grandmothers' graves. I found Mindaugas's grave unkempt. The cross I had put up was faded and crooked, and the grave itself was overgrown

with grass. Now with the Žiulys family we've decided to fence it in with
a fence made of Lithuanian oak and to fix everything up and paint it.

While I was in Kaunas I visited Vida's husband's parents. I saw
them twice with Genė and Dovilė. They hosted me wonderfully and
gave me gifts. They are a very pleasant and sympathetic older couple. I
also visited Eugenija Valtakaitė's parents. Her father is paralyzed and is
living in his own home, but when I glanced around, it seemed to me that
they did not lack anything. For me, having lived the way I have, it even
seemed strange that people who live so well could even dare complain
about anything. If I were to compare my own life, especially when I
lived on Lake Baikal, what could I say? They've been corresponding
with Eugenija since 1946 and what I can't understand is why didn't they
tell me about you? After all, they knew what I was going through. They
complain about the hardships they went through. But they've remained
in their own home. Not only did I lose everything, I was exiled without a
bite of bread to eat or clothing to cover myself with. I'm not complaining to anyone. I thank God that I've found you and that I've returned to
my homeland. I've brought back many riches for my soul and my mind.
The war was responsible for everything after all. For some it passed
without much disturbance, but for others, it was bloody.

I also visited Father G. *(Gruodis)* who lives 80 kilometers outside
of Kaunas. Do you remember when he lived in that house *(the Jesuit
Gymnasium in Kaunas)* where Algimantas and Mindaugas studied? Now
his hair is white as an apple blossom and he is very pale. He's living in
an old apartment, where it is unbearably cold in the winter, and is taken
care of by a nurse, not a layman. He is living very humbly without adequate food or clothing. He suffered much and now as an invalid has no
proper surroundings and has no peace. I spent eight hours with him. He
was overjoyed to see me, and asked after you and Uncle. He was very
grateful that I'd visited him. He remembers all of you in his prayers.
When I said good-bye to him I promised that you would support him as
much as you could. Since Vida was bragging that this year has been
good to her, I've written to her telling her what he would need to have
sent to him in the nearest future. It would be a good thing if Uncle could
support him in some way. He is a friend of Uncles from back in Voronez. I think Uncle will remember Stasys... Pass on my greetings to
Mrs. Vincė *(Jonuškaitė-Zaunienė)* and Mr. Domas *(Doctor Jasaitis).* I

think that he remembers when we used to call him "little spirit" back in Voronezh.

I asked Genė to search for my marriage certificate in the archives and if she found it, to mail it to you right away. My marriage to your father happened July 20, 1920 in the Utena church. They've not called me back over our affairs. According to how things work, now I should receive a notice from the consulate in Moscow, telling me what I need to do, because he's sent my documents there.

It would be good if you, Nijolė, could go and stay with Vida to help her. The thought often comes into my head that God might bless her with twins this time. Of course, that is a blessing, but together with that blessing comes a lot of hard work. I am still afraid that her illness might come back and I still cannot imagine that the two of you are living separately and that your lives are different. I still see you as two very young, barely mature, girls, both wearing identical outfits. Although I've lived a lot and have suffered a lot, time flies past quickly with both pleasant and painful memories. I didn't notice when I became an old woman, not fast anymore, ungainly, when my body changed, my hair went gray, my face became lined with wrinkles. You two only look matured to me. People who've known me a long time say that my face hasn't changed, only that I've gained weight.

While I was in Kaunas I filed a notice that my house should be returned to me, because there are other people who want to buy it under the table. I made that impossible. If they're giving it away to others, they can give it to me. I gave Genė my notarized permission to take care of that matter for me. If I left, I'd rather have the house go to Dovilė. It is her inheritance after all. Otherwise strangers will take it.

Send me the books you've bought for me as quickly as possible. If I don't need them, I can pass them on to someone else. Saint Ann Katherine's "Vision of Christ's Suffering" I think I can get in German. How are those packages for my Anna? Finishing this letter, I kiss you and Ugnė heartily.

Mama

P.S. I've finished my letter, but I haven't written what's most important. I can no longer hold onto my own thoughts; they're flying all over the world's countries. On the 26th of this month it is yours and Vida's birthday. For your birthday I wanted to send you both some pretty Lithuanian woven ribbons, so that you could tie them in your hair, the way you used to do when you were still living in Lithuania, only I didn't have enough time to finish weaving them. I will send them to you later, at Christmas, when you'll be reunited with Vida. Every year, when I remembered this date, I'd send the Lord prayers, that you'd remained alive and healthy. Today I have nothing more to wish you, only to thank the good Lord that he listened to my prayers and that you've remained the way I wanted you to be. Most importantly, good people. Today I'd like to wish you, having suffered such terrible hardship, and having recovered from it, not to forget God ultimate goal—do not drown in materialism, don't get involved in splendor and emptiness, to remain loyal daughters to your homeland, to not forget your homeland, and to help her in this difficult time. Those are my most sincere greetings to you on the occasion of your 34th birthday. Loving you both passionately,

Mama

One more little thing—while I was here in Kaunas I had some clothing made by one of my old friends. Her daughter, Danutė Valaitytė, remembers Ugnė from when they were both in their first year at the gymnasium in Kaunas. While I was there, she wrote Ugnė a letter. I believe that Ugnė will be able to answer her letter and put in her photograph. Nothing bad will come of that. It would make Danutė very happy. I thank Alexander for his beautiful photographs. I've received a package from London. I believe that it is from Mr. Gringauz. Thank him. As a keepsake, I'm enclosing a photograph of the four of you in Jasonys. You are on the right, Nijolė.

Mama

Utena, October 6, 1957

Dear Vida,

A week ago I received your letter. Mrs. Vitkus brought it to me from Utena. We were both afraid to open it because we did not know what we would find inside: tears or joy? Thank God that everything has gone well and that you and your little girl are healthy.

In Kaunas I was flooded with old memories: Mindaugas's grave, that little church in Aleksotas... It was the anniversary of his death. I requested mass. The sexton, who was Mindaugas's friend from that place where he studied *(the Jesuit Gymnasium)* decorated the hearse so beautifully and lit so many candles! The people sang "Angle of the Lord"... Everything looked the way it did during his funeral... The church is so cozy, so clean, that you feel as though you could stay there forever...

I went to see our old home a few times. You wouldn't recognize it from the inside; it has been quite neglected and damaged. A Russian man lives in my room and sleeps in my bed. Do you remember that bed? Big, white, beautiful? I told him that that bed belonged to me! Though I can't do anything about it until I get the rights to my house back. I made out a notarized power of attorney for Genė. She'll be going to Vilnius with it, to the Supreme Soviet. If they gave it to others, maybe they'll give it back to me. I don't have anywhere to live or anything to live from. They have to take that into account!

All the packages that you've mailed to me arrived complete, except for one box of coffee and one piece of soap. I think that the scent tempted some one there in the post office, since the flavor is so delicious. I treated a rare guest to some of your coffee. The only problem is that I don't have a proper coffee pot to serve it (do you remember how it was at Aunts?). The candy and chocolate will go to Dovilė because she and Genė are my dearest guests. I will treat Alius Vitkus to the cocoa because he suffered from the same disease as you, Vida. Some times you just have to bake a traditional cake for someone, but it isn't easy because you can't get cane sugar or cooking chocolate.

You asked, Vida, who still needs packages. Many people need them, but how could you possibly earn all the money you'd need to send them all? In the first place, take care of your family. You, Vida, should hire someone to help you, at least with the heavy work. You have a large family, but only one person working to support it. You should put something away for a rainy day. It is beyond me to understand how Algirdas is capable of earning that much money. He must work day and night.

If it's not too difficult for you, the first thing Dovilė needs is clothing for her first communion. Genė needs fabric for a light-weight summer coat, sand colored with notions, and a raincoat. They both need shoes. That would make them both so happy and they'd have something to be proud of. Genė, after all, is a widow, and Dovilė is an orphan. She misses her father terribly. The next package would be for the Vitkus family. Kazys sent them each an article of clothing, but they are a big family, so it is difficult for him to clothe them all by himself. They lack everything. The Žiulys family also needs a package with all sorts of clothing. (Enclosed is a list with each person's age, size, and other instructions).

I don't want anything for myself, Vida. I have everything I need; the only thing I lack is good health. I ask the Lord to give me a little more strength, so that I could walk faster. Through the window I see how an old woman, hunched over with a cane, is moving quickly and I want to cry. I am not hunched over, my back is straight, but I cannot walk. It's been three Sundays already that not only can I not walk to Utena, I can't go in the carriage either. When I returned from Panevėžys I brought back the flu with me, and that developed into a strong case of bronchitis, which almost became pneumonia. I am waiting for medicine from Nijolė to ease my breathing.

Vida, you wrote that with each ship that sails for Sweden you will send me some fabric. Thank you and thank you to Algirdas, only I ask that you don't send it at your own expense. Here people sell fabrics and our Lithuanians like the tasteful kind with a factory symbol.

Finishing this letter, Mrs. Vitkus and I congratulate your entire family with that little bundle of joy. I thank you for giving me my granddaughter and I send her a passionate, passionate kiss. Mrs. Vitkus also sends you all kisses, especially her new little relative.

Yours, Mama

Utena, December 15, 1957

Dear Nijolė, Vida, and Algimantas,

With tears of joy I send my greetings to all of you gathered together for the first time after so many years in Vida's home. I feel as though I can see Nijolė and Algimantas flying in an airplane above the ocean. I follow the plane with my thoughts and then it lands beside Vida's small house. I feel as though I can see the three of you with your arms around each other, reunited again. I am rejoicing with you together. After all, a mother's heart is never separated from her children. When the children are happy, the mother is happy. Be happy, my happiness is dependent on that.

Today is Sunday and I stayed home. It is quite cold now, maybe around 15 degrees below zero centigrade. For two weeks I made the trip to Utena every day. The doctor prescribed a quartz lamp for my ear. I don't know what he is planning next. My ear is still not alright, although I can hear better and it is not ringing as much. I'd like to get my hearing back.

I've been here and there and I've come to the conclusion that the best place for me to live is with the Vitkus family. With them everything is simple and sincere. The winter is cold, but this year I have warm clothing and shoes. The landscape is pretty here, like in Jasonys. Utena is not far and the road is not mucky. I can walk directly to the post office.

Vida, thank you for the warm scarf and the warm fabric for a dress. Now I have something to tie around my neck and keep my ear warm. I wanted a black scarf so badly. And it is so pretty, with white borders. But, unfortunately, it was in Stefanija's package, and she didn't want to give me the black one because she already had a white one, so I took the white one. It is pretty and warm, but it gets dirty quickly. Besides, I've become accustomed to wearing only black. I don't feel comfortable wearing something colored. In general, people here really want scarves and head scarves. I've woven a few small scarves from the colorful yarn you'd sent me. When all my friends and acquaintances saw them, they practically yanked them all off of me. I knit myself a pretty and warm sweater out of the black yarn.

I think, Vida, that I wrote to you earlier about pillow covers. Nijolė sent me fabric for pillow covers and sheets, but along the way they were "shortened." While writing to you, I received a letter from Kaunas from the former Vincė Kvėdaraitė (now Kripaitienė). I visited her when I was in Kaunas. She and her husband returned from Siberia, they'd lived there for fifteen years (since 1941). You and Nijolė probably remember her. She used to carry Ugnė around in her arms. She, the poor thing, is very sick and has no clothing. If you can, put together a package for her, from the three of you. Maybe Ugnė could contribute also? At least write her a letter. I kiss you all.

Yours, Mama

Utena, December 22, 1957

Dear Vida,

Thank you, Vida, for the package you sent to me through Sweden in September. The one that you mentioned in your letter. The raincoat is perfect and it suits me well. The scarves are very pretty, as was everything else in there. Probably Nijolė is there with you, as is Algimantas. Be happy, my dear children. Hours of joy don't last very long. When I think back on my past, even with all the painful memories it contains, I still manage to find moments of joy. For example, the children, Alexander and Kotrynėlė brought me so much joy, even though I had to risk my life for them. My heart soars with joy, even now, when I remember them. A few months ago I received a letter from Baronienė. She described her tiny, but beautiful, homeland, Israel. She wrote about Jerusalem, Nazareth, and other important places. Recently I also received a letter from her daughter, Dina. She described her mother's death to me. I cried when I read her letter. That woman was truly enlightened, and she'd suffered much. She died at the age of 66 of a stroke. Her daughter Dina already had three children. She and her mother were often in our home and happily they were saved from a certain death, they met again in our house, and they were filled with joy. I was filled with joy as well.

When I received that first letter from you I cannot describe how joyful I was. Now I am also filled with joy that I have you, that I receive letters from you, packages. I sometimes drop a tear onto my letters to you. Forgive me, my dears. Sometimes it weighs on my heart that after I've written a letter to you that I might have written about something unpleasant, and that would make your lives more difficult. Sometimes I remember what I've said and I am sorry for it.

If we met, you'd probably never recognize me. I'm fatter, my hair is gray, and my face is wrinkled (though many people say that they are surprised that I still look so young after all that I've been through). The way I look on the outside is not that important. On the inside you'd find me much richer. I've become even more of an idealist, an optimist, I know more people now. My heart, though always sensitive, has become even more sensitive, though I quickly spot people's insincerity. My mind is left clearer than ever. I've become brave; I can answer all sorts of questions that any gentleman may ask… You see how your mother is. At the very least I know how to brag to my children. And so, I've lived a long time, but as long as I am alive, I am still learning.

I'll be waiting for letters from all of you. I haven't gotten any for a long while. I miss them very much. I kiss you all.

Mama

Utena, December 29, 1957

Dear Vida,

It's the first time that I've received your letter and photographs in time for Christmas. Poor Juozas looks as though he's unhappy about something; you can even see the traces of tears on his face. He really does look like Father Juozas. Rasa has gotten so big. I recommend, Vida, that you teach Rasa to help you. Get her used to it. You need to teach them responsibility, so that they could feel for their mother and father and help them. Don't get her used to empty appearances, like many mothers do. I don't like how Dovilė is being raised. The girl is smart and talented (she is a lot like Mindaugas) but she is used to dressing up and going dancing with a full skirt. That's the spirit here, that's how girls are being raised. Children are not being raised to be responsible, to feel empathy for others, to sacrifice for others. When I was seven, my brother Antanas was three, and Veronika (your Aunt) was the same age as your Marytė. My mother did not let me run around and play with the other children. I had to watch Antanas all the time and I had to rock Veronika in her cradle. I am grateful to my mother that she taught me how to work and how to be responsible. It makes me happy to remember now how I was Veronika's little nanny. It was harder for me to control Antanas. He didn't listen to me, he even would hit me, but I watched him so that he wouldn't get himself in trouble or get hurt. That made it much easier for Mama to do her work... Be healthy, my dearest daughter.

Yours, Mama

1958

Utena, January 12, 1958

Dear Vida,

When you receive this letter, Nijolė will most likely no longer be with you. Now I will be waiting for long letters from both of you with descriptions of your reunion, of all the time you spent together.

This Sunday I went to Church. I listened to a beautiful homily for the feast of the Holy Family. It's too bad, Vida, that you weren't here to hear it. It was like a pedagogical lesson. Listening to this homily all my thoughts were about you and your family. When you look now at how children are being raised here, it is painful. Parents are only concerned with the exterior appearances of their children. They do not pay any attention to the inner spiritual life of the child. Maybe you think that your mother was too strict because I did not give into certain request that you had at the time. Now that you are grown ups, I hope that you value the care I put into raising you to be good and noble people. I think that I'm not wrong when I think about you in that way. At least that's how it appears to me. Now, Vida, I can only wish that you raise your children to be respectable and intelligent people for "God and their Homeland." It is not easy to raise children the right way; it takes a lot of sacrifice. Do not let them stray far from home without any good reason or goal. The best thing is to accustom them to their home because home life is everything. He who does not love his home is left to wander his entire life and will be unhappy. You need to teach them to love God and to love their Homeland. If a child is given a strong foundation, no matter what comes later, no matter how hard, that person won't be lost.

I think that I've pretty much written what weighs on my heart. I'll be waiting for your letters and photographs. I kiss you all many times.

Mama

Utena, March 10, 1958

Dear Nijolė,

In this letter I want to brag that I've already received a document from the American Consulate in Moscow, announcing that on their side all the arrangements have been made for me to enter the United States. Now I need to request my government that they give me permission to leave. I went to see the Utena regional government about this matter. They explained everything to me and told me which documents I needed to include with my request. Everything would go smoothly, if only there wasn't a mix-up with my birth certificate. Luckily, I found them in the Utena archives. The problem is that on our marriage certificate your father's name is written as Konstantas, and his father's name as Mykolas. On his death certificate his name is written as Konstantinas, and his father's as Mikalojus. This is the cause of much confusion. Now I will be searching for your father's birth certificate. On the birth certificate I'll most likely find Konstantinas and Mikalojus. If I can find that birth certificate, then everything will be much easier.

There is one more thing that is not clear on the Consulate's document (it's written in Russian). One of the letters is wrong and that changes the surname. I'll need to explain that in English there is no Ž, only Z. I'll attach to my request Algimantas's letter in which my name and his surname appear and in which he invites me to come live with him, and explain that the documents are already in Moscow, in the American Consulate. The government told me that his letter to me should help.

I'm very lucky that I found a lawyer in Utena (he is a Russian) who is an old friend of your father, and who knows our entire family. He's been taking care of all my documents, requests, and forms. Not just anyone is capable of that. Enough about that.

My health wouldn't be half bad if it wasn't for all these worries (they've accompanied me my entire life). When I complete putting together all my documents and hand in my request, then I'll take a rest because all of this is exhausting me. When I received the letter from the Consulate I went to the church and cried the entire time. If anyone had asked me why I was crying, I would not have been able to answer them. I'm just emotional and that's all. Now I have to go to Utena and take care of business, of which there is more than plenty. The sidewalks in Utena are slippery and I'm afraid of falling. Stefanija helps me get around. How is Ugnė doing? I send her my greetings and have enclosed a picture for her from the priest at Utena church. Pass along my greetings to Uncle. I kiss you.

Mama

Utena, April 1, 1958

Dear Vida,

I've received that lost one *(the package),* which took eight months to reach me. I did not find some of the items on your list inside it. All of the fabric is very nice and very fashionable. I am writing you this letter on April Fool's Day. Believe me that I'm not lying to you. Easter is close, and it feels like Christmas. The fields are covered thickly with snow, the nights are cold, the temperature drops to 20 below zero centigrade. Yesterday and today it snowed hard, and the wind carries the snow across the fields. If I were twenty I'd happily be out enjoying the snow. Now I just look through the window and watch the snowflakes as they fall. And what do my leg and arm do? My arm writes you this letter, which is much more legible than before, but in the middle of writing it freezes and tires. Then I immediately pull on a wool mitten, one that Nijolė sent me while I was still living on Lake Baikal. My hand warms up, rests, and then I begin writing again. And my foot, that grand lady, I keep wrapped in two pairs of thick socks and stuffed into my warm shoes. The room is not warm, especially when a strong wind blows. In general the numbness in my fingers and toes is slowly going away. When I just sit down to write you a letter, Mrs. Vitkus comes in and begins to annoy me, "Did you thank Vida for the fabric for the bedding? Did you tell her that I say hello." And Mr. Vitkus calls to me from up on the stove, where he is lying down, "And send Vida and her entire family my greetings." He is lying on the stove without bed coverings and down is flying everywhere. This letter to you is going to be one of my silliest. Even Mrs. Vitkus is arguing with me why I am writing you all of this. She says that Vida will think that they've let everything go. You see, she's raised a lot of children, and they, playing around, tore up all the pillows.

Okay, enough fooling around. All I can do is wish you Happy Easter and wish you well, Alleluia. Maybe dear God will allow us to celebrate next Easter together. I kiss you all and I'd like to ask Rasa to pray for her grandmother's health.

Mama

Utena, April 13, 1958

Dear Vida,

Thank you for the precious gifts that I found in your letter. Oh, Vida, why have you convinced yourself that I'll be coming right away? My affairs have only moved forward from your side, but over here, I haven't started a thing yet. Five weeks have gone by already and I've not filed my request because there are all sorts of errors in the records. To receive a passport, all of your dates and names need to be correct.

There could be no bigger joy than for the entire family to come to-gether into one huge bunch, and I do believe, that fate will allow this to happen. You must pray a lot, because prayer can knock down all sorts of obstacles. I've noticed from your letters that you think of me as behind the times. My dear child, I am not behind the times at all. The opposite is true. Through all that suffering and all that hardship I've moved forward. I understand none of it: not women's obsession with fashion, not older women smoking, not a modern lifestyle, only a life that is in line with God and the laws of the Church, a life that is decent, respectable, and doesn't affect your health, a life that can be held up as an example to your children. You must remember that the goals of our lives do not end in this world. I am happy that my children have not broken off their ties with our highest goal—God our Father. My biggest joy would be for you to be one with God and not let go, not even for a moment.

I do not know how Algimantas is doing, but his letters give off a religiosity. Our life goal should be to follow the Will of God. Christ's words, "Lord, not how I want everything to be, but how you want it to be" makes it easier for us to bear all the suffering and hardship of life. You may dress up in expensive clothing, go to parties, only don't lose yourself, in other words, do not lose hold of your soul. Our body is a vessel that contains our soul, which is constructed according to the image of God, and which has been redeemed from the sin of Adam and Eve by the blood of Christ. That's why you must keep your soul pure from sin, so that the soul can thrive in it.

Well, that's enough, my hand has grown tired. I kiss you all.

Mama

Utena, May 1, 1958

My dear son Algimantas,

My first words are those of congratulations on the occasion of your birthday on May 21st. I have much hope that on your next birthday I will be able to show you my motherly love by clutching you to my loving heart. I've collected all the necessary documents, I completed the applications, and I wrote up my autobiography in detail, in a word, I've done everything that is necessary to request a passport. I've handed everything in to the head of the police in my region. From here it will be sent on to the appropriate office in Vilnius, and then on to Moscow. I wrote a letter to the United States Consulate explaining where and when I submitted my paperwork for the visa. Filling out the application I had to explain accurately when and under what circumstances and for what reason the three of you emigrated to America and Australia. Because I didn't know all of that, I wrote down that you left in 1948. Here, at the regional level in Utena, that much information was enough, but Vilnius and Moscow will most likely demand more detailed information about your emigration to the United States. Therefore, anticipating more questions, I'm asking you to write to me as soon as possible, to explain when you emigrated to the United States, what year and what month, for what reason, and under what conditions. I'll need to know where you work and what you do and your most accurate address (I put down the address I had for you on the application). Can you write in more detail what kind of a job you had upon your arrival in America, what you studied, your profession, etc. That would be very useful. Nijolė and Vida will have to do the same thing.

You left Lithuania in 1943 when the Germans closed down Kaunas University. You went to Austria, to Innsbruck University to continue your studies (that's what I put down on the application). The Ministry of Education requested the Germans that a group of students from the first and second year be granted permission to continue their studies. The three of you ended up in that group. Today I wrote the same thing to Vida and Nijolė. I don't believe that the two of you emigrated at the same time to America or that Vida emigrated to Australia at the same time, that's why each of you must write to me separately.

I received the letter from the Consulate February 28, 1958, and I handed in my passport request April 29th. It took two months for me to gather all the necessary documents and to write my autobiography, and to fill out all the forms, and prepare my request. Because of all those problems and because of all the running around I had to do, I even became ill. Now all that worry and work is over. My health has gotten better, and all I have to do now is to sit quietly and wait for the decision.

Today is May 1st and all over Lithuania and the entire Soviet Union working people are celebrating. The cities have been decorated beautifully. People are also dressed up and in a celebratory mood; they are marching, waving flags, and filling up the squares. My soul is also in a celebratory mood. It is spring in Lithuania; there is no more snow in the fields, though it is still quite cold. This year, because there was so much snow, the water level in the Nemunas had risen quite a bit. Some areas of Kaunas, those under sea level, were flooded. The water reached Genė's house in Marvelė.

And so, I've written you a little. Now I'll be waiting for your letter. Definitely write. If other questions arose, I'd be able to answer them appropriately. Every day I offer up the third part of the rosary for the three of you and pray to Mary that she may watch over you.

I kiss you, my son.

Yours, Mama

P.S. I think that when the war ended the three of you, that is you, Nijolė, and Vida, did not return to your homeland because at that time it was still dangerous to live in Lithuania. Bandits were overrunning the country and Lithuanian citizens were being massively deported to Siberia. I think that that is the only reason that you were forced to travel to a far away land to seek out a living, suffering great hardship, poverty, and worked long hours in factories or other heavy industries, just so that you could continue your interrupted studies. Now life is peaceful in Lithuania and life is good. It is especially easy for young people to obtain an education because the government gives students stipends, dorms to live in, and other necessities. I am convinced that that is the only thing that stopped you from returning to your homeland. I am convinced that you love your homeland, that you miss it, and that you are suffering living so far away from it. I am also ready to leave my homeland with pain in my heart because I am completely alone here and I can no longer earn my own living here.

And so, my dear son, I think that I correctly solved your fate. That horrible war did it all. It tore families apart, and sent people all over the world to suffer and live in poverty. Nowhere is it better to live than in your own homeland. May the Lord grant that those horrible wars never happen again, that everyone may return to their homeland, to their families. I believe that in the long run everything will be resolved and all nations will learn how to solve their problems in a productive way, so that we will be able to live in peace. That's all for now.

Your loving Mama

Utena, May 22, 1958

Dear Algimantas,

I received your letter written on May 5th. My application for a passport along with all the necessary documents has been sent on from Utena to Vilnius, and from there it will go to Moscow. That very same day I wrote a letter to the Consulate of the United States in Moscow telling him when and where I applied. Now that I've completed all this worrisome work, I am resting and waiting for the results. I think that this entire affair will take a long time and that there will still be some uncertainties to deal with.

I'd like to ask you one more thing. Write to Vida and ask her if she needs money. She spends a lot of money on all my affairs. I don't need so much for myself, but there are a lot of people who helped us during the war and I felt that I must repay them. For example there was Father Gruodis and others. Vida has sent them all a package, but there are still others whom she promised she'd send packages to. I also help the Vitkus family because I live here with them and because their life is very hard. I want to pay everyone back so that I could die with a clean conscience. Now there is this one relative of your father's who he took care of. I've given her a few things. It is very unpleasant when you give things to one person and another stands there drooling. Soon I'll have taken care of everyone. Of course, when life was hard for me the only people who helped me were the Vitkus family. But that's how life is, when you have nothing, then no one notices you, but as soon as you have something, everyone wants a piece of it.

It is spring already. Everywhere it is green. In the early morning, just as it begins to grow light the nightingale chirps, the coo-coo bird coo-coo-es and all the birds begin to sing in many different voices. I open the window, stick out my head, and listen to the concert of birds. In this way I begin to daydream and I think about you. My heart hurts when I think that you cannot breathe the air of your homeland and listen to the birds singing. I believe that one day you will return to your homeland. Good-bye my dear son. I kiss you a thousand times.

Yours, Mama

Utena, June 2, 1958

Dear Nijolė,

...I'm sure that I've written to you that on April 28th I handed over my application with a mound of documents to the Utena regional government. They told me that May 5th they will send them on to Vilnius and from there to Moscow. I put all my documents together in an orderly manner, according to all the requirements, and sent them on very nicely to the government. They approved them and accepted them. There can be questions from Vilnius or Moscow, if something isn't clear to them. My application, autobiography, and request were written by Mr. Aleksiejev, a well-known lawyer and judge, and your late father's dear friend. Although he is Russian, he knows Lithuanian well. Both Russian and Lithuanian were very useful as I assembled my documents. He knows our entire family well. His wife, a pediatrician, remembers you and Vida very well from when you were little. In a word, despite the fact that putting together this request exhausted me, it went well. I wrote a letter to the American Consulate in Moscow explaining where and when I submitted my paperwork. (They'd written in their letter that I needed to do that). Now I am peaceful and am waiting for the results. I think that it will take a long time.

I wrote to Vida about the down blanket. Here in Lithuanian the climate is cold. Even in the summer you sometimes need something warm to cover yourself with, especially out in the country the homes are cold. Heat is expensive and there is a shortage of it. That's why I'd like to have a warm blanket. This year the Vitkus family is planning a renovation because their masonry stoves won't get them through another winter (they barely kept us warm last winter). I pay the Vitkus family 200 rubles a month for my room and board, over two years that amounts to 5000 rubles. I will sell the fabrics from Vida's package, get the entire 5000, and give it to them all at once, so that they can use it for the renovation. At the time of the renovation they will build me a new room. I have many expenses because I was left practically naked, having lost my house and all its contents. I'm not buying any furniture. I've now managed to dress myself. Even if I eat very little, it still is expensive. My doctor's visits are expensive, my medicine, and where am I to get the money from? And that money does not come easily. You have any sort of business with anyone, and immediately they want you to pay, especially when they know that you receive packages. I try not to see people unless there is an urgent need, and I've begun to avoid my relatives. Vida sends so much that it is just horrible. I've received all her packages, only one was held up along the way for eight months.

I've received two letters in a row from Algimantas. I'm still waiting for a letter from Vida. Then I'll have all the information I need from all of you, in case something is missing. I'm beginning to acclimatize to life in Lithuania. At first I felt uncomfortable, I felt as though every one I met was ready to swallow me whole... No one has made life unpleasant for me... Genė is fighting it out with the authorities over our house. If she can get the house back, I will sign it over to her and Dovilė. Stay healthy. So much for now. I kiss you. Pass on my greetings to Ugnė, Edvardas, and Mrs. Vincė.

Mama

Utena, June 19, 1958

Dear Vida,

I've not received a reply to my request for a passport yet. I had to furnish additional information on how you left Lithuania and how you've lived to date. I also had to go and talk about our past family situation and about the present. They mentioned Aunt, Uncle, and Ugnė. I gave them accurate information about our family's past. I could not say much about the present because since you've left Lithuania I do not know very much about how you live and I do not want to know. They were surprised by my answer. I had an answer for that too... Don't mention anything about them in your letters (write to Nijolė and Algimantas and tell them the same). I don't know anything about Uncle and it is best for me not to know anything; I don't want to hear any news about Ugnė either. *(Mama did not want Nijole, Vida, and Algimantas to write about the family because they were politically undesirable as known anti-communists, and knowing too much about them could lead to further interrogation for Mama.)*
It's enough for me to correspond with you. I am not interested in corresponding with anyone else. I am tormented by memories of those who've died, Mindaugas, your father. That's why I'd rather not be put into the position of opening up old wounds... Please ask Rasa to pray for my health, because I am not well. I push aside all unnecessary thoughts that exhaust me. I'd like to write much more to you, but I'll put that off for later...
On Sunday Stefanija and I went to Linkmenys, 40 kilometers away. There's a family there who've just returned from Siberia. I'd lived with them. It was wonderful to see them. When I go to Kaunas again I'll visit Algirdas's parents and I will write to you about it. For now, stay healthy.
Mama

Utena, August 3, 1958

Dear Vida,

Today it's been raining since early morning, and so I did not make the trip to church. I'm praying at home for all Lithuanians who are far away... I'm asking God to keep them all alive, safe, and to help them return to their homeland. Today is Rasa's birthday. I wish her a happy birthday and hope that she grows into a beautiful and intelligent daughter of Lithuania, and that once she's completed her education that she returns to her homeland and works for its gain.

Yours and Nijolė's birthdays are coming soon. I, your poor mother, cannot send either of you a gift. I'd like to send you both a Lithuanian national costume, but it's not so easy to get beautiful ones. Maybe I'll weave a set myself. So for now I will wish you good health and God's blessing.

It's been a month since I've returned from Kaunas. My health is back, but that "spasm" still gives me a hard time. I'm still hoping that I'll get stronger, to lose weight, maybe God might still grant me the opportunity to travel to you. When I think over my entire situation, I cannot find any reason why I would be denied permission to go to my children; it would be cruel not to let me go. I haven't ever committed a crime; I've never hurt anyone. If my relatives are dangerous to anyone, why should I be blamed for it? Besides you, I have no other blood relatives. My sister is dead, and I don't know anything about the others... I have no material wealth, I live from the packages my children send me, I am old, and I am sick.

In my application I wrote in great detail about my situation, my own life, and my relatives and parents' lives. I repeated it all during the interrogations. I've thought everything over, and my conscience is clear because I cannot think of anything that could prevent me from going to you. I have nothing to hide. I think that the government will take a positive view of my situation. It would be too painful to have children who wanted to take their mother to live with them, but instead to have to end your life in a nursing home. I'd like to write more, but...

In a few weeks I will have guests from Kaunas—Genė, Dovilė, and Dovidaitis and his wife. They like the Aukštaitija region, where the landscape is so beautiful. I kiss you all. *Mama*

Utena, September 7, 1958

Dear Vida,

It is September and the weather here is clear and dry—the last few days of summer. It is so sad. The birds aren't singing anymore, the storks are congregating and getting ready to leave their homeland to spend the winter in warmer climates.

In Kaunas and Vilnius it is virtually impossible to get an apartment. Many of the exiled are returning from Siberia. Their situation is very difficult because they don't have any place to live and it's difficult for them to get registered. It's almost impossible in Kaunas and Vilnius because there are many foreigners there. *(After the war Russians were relocated into Lithuania in large numbers to live in the homes and apartments formerly occupied by Lithuanians who'd been exiled, killed, or fled. In this way the Soviet government achieved ethnic cleansing and colonized the Baltics).* I'd like to write you much much more, but... Whether I want to or not, it's time to finish this letter because I don't have anything interesting to tell you...

Marytė is probably already running around; she's almost two already. I kiss you all and will be waiting for your letters with photographs.

Mama

Panevėžys, October 12, 1958

Dear Nijolė,

I know that you are expecting a letter from me, as I am expecting one from you. Unfortunately, in this letter I have to complain to you that Moscow denied my request that I be issued a passport to travel to the United States to live with you. In their answer they wrote that my request to leave the Soviet Union has been rejected. And so, all our efforts and all my hopes that I will be able to reach you have died. About three individuals applied with the same request at the same time, and all three have received the same answer. It is very painful that in my old age I don't have a corner that I can call my own, or someone to care for me, an invalid, after all. Hope had made me stronger, had given me energy, now everything is dead... I won't be able to say anything better than that in this letter because my tears are covering the paper. I wonder who I've hurt, what I've done that's so terrible, that they don't even allow me to go to my children? I am old, after all, an invalid; why not give me the last few moments of my life to be happy? In my life I've known little joy; rarely did the tears dry on my cheeks. I've always waited for a better day, but it has never come... I came to Panevėžys to have a suit sewn for my trip and at the same time I received the answer.

Nijolė, if you can, send me some beautiful pictures by famous artists like Rafaelo or Murillo. I like them so much. When I was exiled, all my art disappeared. Now I will have my own room, so I will decorate the walls with them. Pass on my greetings to Mrs. Vincė, Edvardas, and my other friends. I wanted to see them all so badly! I kiss you.

Mama

Panevėžys, November 1, 1958

Dear Nijolė,

I am writing you this letter from my hospital bed. On October 21st I was able to get myself a place in the hospital. I was lucky, because there is a long line of very sick people who are waiting in line to get a place in the hospital. I was surprised when they placed me at the front of the line. Lately my health has been very poor. They x-rayed my heart, but they did not tell me what the results were. *(At the time in the Soviet Union the patient did not have the right to know his or her own diagnosis).* Only I overheard them talking among themselves about what a terrible state my heart was in, that it isn't working well, and then I overheard one of them say, "If you want to save her, you have to do it now." After ten days in the hospital I'm feeling better. I slept for three nights and one day—I haven't slept like that in a very long time. The buzzing in my head has quieted and I almost don't have headaches. I don't remember feeling this good in a long time. Now I've learned what I need to do and what kind of a diet I should follow, although obtaining this knowledge almost cost me my life. The Lord knows what he is doing. If I'd gotten the permission to leave and go to you, I probably would not have survived the trip. Now I have hope that I will grow stronger. And my lawyer is going to file my request again, and then, if they give me permission, I'll have hope that I'll get to you. Now I will not need to run around offices collecting documents because I have all the originals and their copies. Besides that, my lawyer has been restored to his former position (he'd been demoted before) and he'll be able to take care of everything without involving me. All he will need to get from me is my signature. When I check out of the hospital, I will ask the doctor to write up an account of my health, so that I cannot be called in for questioning whenever they feel like it. I've left all your letters (and Vida's student pass with a stamp from 1943 – 1944) with them as proof of when you left Lithuania and for what reason.

All my life I've never paid much attention to how I walk; I always walked faster and faster, I was used to it. But now when it is necessary for me to walk slowly and to rest a lot, I often forget about that, especially when I've got work to take care of and problems that need to be solved. So, now my health has taken a turn for the better and I'm determined to take good care of it. I understand how much you worry about me, and that pains me. For now, Nijolė, don't worry about my affairs, you've got plenty of your own. I'll only ask you to send me medicine. I know that they are expensive. I'm enclosing a few prescriptions in this letter. Not all of them are for me. Send them by airmail and quickly. The ampoules are for Uncle Žiulys, to strengthen him. We will pay the tax on the medicine here. It won't be that expensive here. When you send the medicine, could you enclose a pen?

Now I will wait calmly for whatever God doles out to me. I will accept everything from His hands, life or death. His plans are not our plans.

I don't know how much longer I will need to stay in the hospital. Now it is winter, so it is a good time to lie around. In the spring I'll return to Šilinė. Now I have a lovely, big, and sunny room. All it needs is to be painted. Genė was able to find two of my pictures, but the beautiful Madonnas have disappeared. Spring brings everyone back to life. The care is good here in the hospital and the doctor is contentious. In Lithuania we still have talented doctors from the older generation. I'd become so weak that I no longer could pray the rosary. The spasms had affected not only my foot and hand, but my speech as well. It has not come back altogether yet. The doctor says that my heart will grow stronger, but that without medicine I will not be able to live. What ever happens, I'd like at least to be able to take care of myself.

While writing to you I've mixed up my sheets of paper and I'm flitting from one thought to another. There are some very noisy ladies here in my room, so it's hard to find some peace and quiet. I'll finish now. Pass on my greetings to Ugnė, Mrs. Vincė, Lionė, and if you see him, Mr. Gringauz and Alexander (do they live far from you?) If you meet up with Domukas, give him my greetings. I kiss you, dear Nijolė.

Mama

Utena, November 7, 1958

Dear Nijolė,

Oh! What a terrible thing I've done wearing you out like this. Such emptiness, those pictures. I was thinking about pictures without frames. I can have the frames made here. You can roll up the pictures into a cardboard roll and send them through the mail like that. But leave it for now. You are faced with exams. Don't even write to me often, you don't have time for that. When I ask you for medicine, send it, because that is a necessity. I am waiting for the comforter, because winter is drawing near. Nijolė, there is no need to spoil me. I am completely taken care of, although my money situation is difficult, I often need quite a bit of it. That's why I have to sell certain things. Medicine is free here, but it is expensive. There's a proverb: "If you don't grease the wheels, you won't go anywhere." I feel like traveling, to visit the churches, and my old friends. Now the doctor has forbade my traveling without a companion. It takes thirty minutes to get to Utena, so there's no time to freeze. It was cold in the Vitkus house, but now after the renovations and the new stove and the warm comforter it won't be cold anymore.

All my life I never had the time nor the inclination to take care of myself. Now too, until this trouble started, I did not worry too much.

Now I appreciate my health and am concerned over it and am resolved to take care of it.

I took the negative reply calmly, but my nerves were shot. The doctor's diagnosis is as follows: "Morbus hypertonicus, typus cardio-cerebralis, lento pregrendiens. Atherosclerosis, cardiosclerosis, atherosclerotica stenocardia, insuff. Cardiovascularis II. Status post microinsultus cerebri." I think you'll understand my disease from that. Now I've learned what I need to protect myself from. The most important things are food, sleep, good air, and not exhausting myself working, thinking, talking, or worrying. I need to maintain a good mood.

Therefore, Nijolė, leave those pictures alone. Genė promised to bring me a couple from our old house. Somehow she managed to get them. Take care of studying for your exams and completing your studies.

My lawyer is a good man. He knows our entire family. Already he has made inquiries on how to open up my case again. To receive a passport you need all sorts of documents and to take a lot of care. That's why the high blood pressure became a spasm. If I'd been warned that something like that could happen, then I would not have rushed around. I believe that God will allow me to grow stronger. I've lost weight and that is very important. Now my lawyer can take care of everything without me because he has all the copies of my documents. All he needs is my signature. I think that I'll be able to go home for Christmas much stronger. I'll never give up hope. I had to live through a lot in Siberia, all alone, but I thank God for that. I experienced a lot, I learned a lot, and my conscience is clear. Nowhere is it better to live than in your own homeland and in your own home. Genė will probably not be able to get our house back. I probably could get it back on my own, because it belongs to me, and because no one takes a daughter-in-law seriously. Having good lawyers on your side, and with a lot of expense, it still isn't clear if it would work out. My health does not allow me to take this on, especially with all the traveling it would take. Genė and Dovilė are planning to come visit me soon.

And so, my dearest Nijolė, don't worry about me, it's not so bad, and finally, it is all God's will. Pass on my greetings to Mrs. Vincė, Mr. Gringauz and Alexander, Lionė, Ugnė, and Mr. Edvardas. Do you remember Matas K.? *(Uncle Karvelis's nephew)* He died in Siberia May 7, 1947. I kiss you, Nijolė, many, many times.

Mama

1959

Panevėžys, January 14, 1959

Dear Son,

Thank you for such a pleasant letter. Don't worry about me so much. I have left the hospital. My health is much better. Even now I am under my doctor's care. I am very concerned that you pass your exams and that you are able to finally take a good rest.

My lawyer has told me that if we want to repeat our request for me to leave the Soviet Union and go live with you, you must write a letter to the American Consulate in Moscow and inform them again that you would like to take your mother, that you would be responsible for supporting me, and that the Consulate must send me another official letter, just like last time. Then I will make a second request to my government, requesting a passport and permission to travel to you. I've heard that sometimes it takes three requests before they finally let you out. My lawyer says that we need to repeat everything, everything. If you need a copy of my marriage license, write to me, I have copies. Sacrifice a minute of your time and write a few words to your aunt and uncle, Žiulys. I've been here for a longer time now, and they are taking care of me.

In the beginning of March I plan to return to the Vitkus home. Spring and summer are near. Nature will help restore my strength. The doctor tells me that in addition to medicine, I must have a good mood, good surroundings, and friends. But where will I find all that if not together with you? If I could travel, I'd visit my old friends and I'd feel better. Stay healthy, my dear son. Believe in God. I kiss you.

Yours, Mama

Panevėžys, February 8, 1959

Dear Nijolė,

I'm very happy that you are feeling more at ease over my health. This illness began while I was in Siberia in the winter of 1953 (maybe even earlier, but in a milder form) at a time that was very hard for me. That was the first time I went to see a doctor, and the doctor found that my blood pressure had risen to 240. I myself had no understanding what that blood pressure reading meant, and the doctor, who was very busy seeing a massive number of patients, didn't bother to explain it. The only medicine available was some iodine tablets. It was not possible at the time for me to have a restricted diet and besides I didn't know much about diet. I had to do hard labor and I suffered much. Then there was the trip to Lithuania. Notwithstanding that the trip was successful; I had a lot of hardship and trouble because I had to take care of all the details myself. Whenever I climbed out of the train, I'd have to cling to the closest person and walk with them because my head was spinning. When I returned to Lithuania I began checking my health with an internist. Up until this year I was under a doctor's care and my blood pressure dropped to 180 and my health was alright. A year ago when I started organizing the paperwork to come to live with you I over-exerted myself putting together the documents and then lived through a shock. Again, I didn't know that I was not supposed to exert myself or worry myself. The result was that my right foot and the fingers on my right hand went numb to the wrist, and despite that my heart was working well and again I began to experience dizziness. The doctor recognized it as a vascular spasm. I was very upset; I thought I would no longer have a hand and a foot. At the time the best thing would have been for me to admit myself to the hospital. Although health care is free here, it is very complicated to get admitted into the hospital (just like all of life is very complicated here.) That's why I tried to cure myself by resting at home, but my health was already so poor. The entire time my blood pressure remained around 200. Last October, when I received the notification telling me that my request for a passport had been denied, my health grew worse than it was before. My friends advised me to try to get myself admitted to the hospital in Panevėžys because it had certification and was better supplied with medical personnel and medicines. I understand my condition pretty well and I am convinced that it is no longer possible to cure me of the hypertension because I am too old. This February 10th I will be sixty-eight. I overheard the doctors talking among themselves when they checked me out of the hospital, and they said that my condition was stable. They did not succeed in lowering my blood pressure below 180 in the five weeks I was in the hospital. I think that it might be reduced by about ten more. When I receive your letter and the medicine you sent me, I will check it again. After that, in March, I will return to the Vitkus family. I'm bored of being here because I have no work and because the weather is so bad that I can't get out—it's slippery everywhere. When the doctors released me from the hospital, they impressed upon me that I had to live without any excitement or worry. It is very important for me to maintain a good mood. It would seem that life has taught me every-thing, but how will I pass this exam?

Now many of our countrymen are returning from Siberia. Even my good friend Pranckietis is in Lithuania. I don't know if Algimantas sent him a package. If he did send it, then we have to take care of things with the mail because if they can't find the addressee, they will send it back. I've written to him, but I haven't received a reply yet.

My friends from Siberia have promised to come visit me, and in-vited me to go visit them. Now I have a large and nice room in the Vitkus house, so I have a place where to invite guests. It's cozy in the Vitkus house, I feel free there, and I don't have to worry about food. They take very good care of me. Now their lives have become much better and they live without want.

For the second time already my doctor has prescribed "Collojod." He says that they are essential for me. If you can't find it, you might find something similar.

So, I've written a lot. Now I will give you a break from all my ill-nesses. I've been praying to the Lord with different prayers to help you in your most difficult hour. I kiss you.

Mama

Utena, March 19, 1959

Dear Vida,

I'm already late wishing you and your family a happy Easter. I had promised my doctor and myself that I wouldn't worry about anything or think about anything. But is it possible to sit by calmly and wait for a huge holiday? Everybody yearns to spend the holidays among family. You expected it; I expected it. Although, knowing these conditions, I doubted too. That's why that bad news astounded me. After my illness I became lazy, doubtful. Before I couldn't stand to be idle for even an hour, and now I wander from corner to corner, not feeling myself. Maybe you've spoiled me. You've given me everything I need, and so I've become lazy... I wish you all joy over these Easter holidays and I kiss you all warmly.

Mama

Utena, April 19, 1959

Dear Nijolė,

You cannot imagine my joy when I received your letter. I worried over not knowing your exam results. Before I received your letter I dreamt of you exhausted, even sick. When I woke up my eyes were full of tears. I was afraid that you'd become sick after all that studying, then, after all those years of study, you wouldn't be able to earn a living. Here it is much easier to get an education and take exams, although doctors work long and hard hours. Health care is free, but there are large numbers of people in the hospitals.

I think that you know well what it means to have your homeland and what it means to be in a foreign land. It is better to starve in your own country than to be wealthy in a foreign land. What about those hundreds of thousands of talented young people who dreamed of a bright future in their homeland, and instead spent many years of their lives in exile, in jail, and in concentration camps, enduring hardship and poverty. All their hope for a bright future died. It's true, many of them have come back, and maybe many more will soon be able to join them. But their lives here are pitiful. Most of them have nowhere to live. Our countrymen are insincere, few people empathize with them. There are people here who live well, only they dress up and party all the time. We could talk a lot on this subject. As far as that gossip, which we hear often, all I have to say is that we're used to it and don't take it to heart. There has always been gossip, everywhere.

Day and night I pray for all of you, but especially for you, Nijolė. I feel very sorry for you. Are these the last of your exams? When you hear your results, write to me right away. I'm eagerly waiting for your package with the medicine, and especially the cardio phone for the doctor. I won't need medicine soon. I've exhausted you with my requests, and it is all very expensive. Our doctors prescribe a lot of medicines; that's how things are done here.

Now I have nice clothing, I have a lovely room; I've gotten a bed, a sofa, and three chairs. The down blanket you sent me is light, airy, and does a good job warming my rheumatic joints. A few years ago Alexander's father sent me some good quality fabric for a man's suit as a gift. I sold it and got 1300 rubles for it. Probably a thousand rubles is a lot of money to you. True, for us it is not such a small amount either, but it doesn't go that far because prices are high and everything is expensive. Now I will have all the necessary clothing I need for the rest of my life with the exception of small things here and there. Last year Vida sent me a lot of fabric because I had to contribute to the renovation; otherwise life would have been impossible. Now the Vitkus family will not collect anything from me over the next few years for room and board because they have deducted it from my contributions to the renovations. They provide me my meals, wash my clothes for me, and do it all sincerely. They are the only relatives who took me in when I was completely destitute at a time when their lives were just as difficult. The entire family is very sincere. The parents are old, but they are still lively. Janė is a wonderful girl, only during these last two years she's had to work very hard. This year she has a job in an office that is much easier.

I will try to find out the last names of those women who also handed in a request for a passport. They were about my age. Vida wrote that 1000 people from our country were permitted to enter Australia. Not even waiting for anything, she handed in her request for me. Maybe I might be lucky.

Finishing this letter, Nijolė, I will ask that you watch your health. I keep you in my prayers as much as I possibly can. Thank Muska's Mama *(Mrs. Šodienė)* for remembering me and pass on my greetings. I kiss you many many times.

Mama

Utena, April 30, 1959

Dear Nijolė,

Again I'm writing to you. Last Sunday I went to see my lawyer to find out the last names of the two women who were trying to get passports the same time as me. They are Emilija Kviklienė, born in 1893 and Babkaitienė, who is somewhere between 40 – 50 years old. The first wanted to go and live with her children, who were born in America. She came to Lithuania before the war and stayed here. The second wanted to join her husband. I did not find out the last name of the third one, though she lives somewhere not far from Utena. She wanted to go live with her son in Canada, but here she has another son and two daughters. They did not let her leave because she has people who can support her here. The first two received a negative answer around the same time I did and with no explanation why. The lawyer said that after one year has passed since the first request, you are allowed to repeat your request. You have to do everything you'd done on your side all over again. I ask you all, especially you, not to worry too much over this—whatever happens happens. I am very concerned that you finally pass all your exams and take a break. My conscience is bothering me that I've created so many problems for you with all my affairs and requests. Now, when I receive the medicine you sent me, I will no longer ask you for anything, just an occasional letter now and then telling me about yourself. Algimantas is probably tormented over having to write.

Mama

Utena, June 17, 1959

Dear Nijolė,

Janė just brought home a package from the post office that is so large I never could have expected. Don't rush to send me these packages so often, at least not until you are able to earn more money. I have everything I need; it's only people around me who need more.

Not too long ago I met my friend *(Father Pranckietis)* and I told him that you'd be sending him some gifts. He is very grateful. His life, and the lives of others like him *(the exiles who returned from Siberia)* is very difficult. Most of them get pushed around like dogs and have mud slung at them. Not too long ago an article appeared about Uncle *(Karvelis)*, which was too horrible to read. It made it seem as though there could be no worse person on earth... I kiss you many many times and I pray every day to Mary that she would watch over you and help you in all your life's work.

Mama

Utena, June 29, 1959

Dear Vida,

Not too long ago Aldona wrote and bragged that you'd written her a very long letter. Of course, she wrote her impressions of her visit with me here. I know that she wrote about my life as though through rose colored glasses. It's true, on the surface that's how it seems. Added to that is my appearance, which looks much better than I feel. It's not likely that any one could see how I feel inside. Well, it's good that someone else writes because my letters probably just ruin your good mood. There are happy moments, but they are rare. If I were more active, I could get out more and distract myself. It's true, that are good roads for the cars and that public transportation is good, but for that you need to be healthy. I am often dizzy and because my leg hurts me, I cannot climb into a train or a bus. I'd be happy if I could get to Utena on foot. That would be a good walk for me and a good distraction. It's also too hard to go by horse, because they do not belong to us, and because they're afraid of cars.

In general, my health is poor notwithstanding that my blood pressure has gone down. The medicine just keeps me going. But I lack the most important medicine of all, positive feelings. This generation is very different. They have not lived through what we have lived through and they cannot understand us. It's hard for us to adjust to them. Sometimes it's even difficult to breath in this atmosphere... It's hard to live without your homeland, but it's even harder in your homeland... If we were all together, life would be altogether different.

Not too long ago I read an article directed at Uncle. I shivered when I read it. They touch upon Aunt's funeral, and even your marriage, but they lie. They make it seem as though there couldn't be a worse person in this world. *(That article probably mentions Nijolė's, and not Vida's, wedding. Nijolė was married to the well-known partisan Juozas Lukša-Daumantas, who was killed by the Russians in the autumn of 1951. That article was meant to slander Uncle. Mama did not know about Nijolė's marriage at the time.)*

I no longer have any hope of reaching you, even though it is better to have hope, even if it is a false hope. Of course, probably the best thing would be for me to live in Kaunas. But they won't give my house back, and besides, it has been practically destroyed. If I did get my house back, I'd invite the Kripaitis's to come live with me because they have a bad apartment and because I'd enjoy living with them. I would not feel so lonely living with them.

Uncle complains of loneliness, but he is still able to work and that fills up his life. What is there to say about things that are not impossible... We must suffer; maybe we've brought it upon ourselves.

Not too long ago I met with Father Pranckietis. His situation is unpleasant. It's not clear, but he might have to go back... *(Exiles who returned without permission were forced to go back.)* He was thrilled when I told him that you were preparing a package for him. We must pay attention to those who after almost two decades have returned to their homeland, having suffered through hardship, and do not have a place to stay.

I'd like very much to be closer to Mindaugas's grave. This autumn I will exhume our two grandmothers' remains and bring them here. He will stay there alone...

I don't know what's happened to grandfather *(Father Gruodis).* He hasn't answered my letters in a very long time. Maybe he's been touched by some unpleasantness? I don't know what to do about Algimantas? If only he'd answer at least one of my letters.

There is a great demand for nylon stockings. People pay 50 rubles for a pair. *(Almost a week's wage.)* If you could send me a large quantity, that would be good economic security for me. I don't know what's more convenient and cheap for you.

It's probably the middle of winter for you now. And here the heat has just begun. When it cools down, I will go to Kaunas. I'm in such a bad mood; maybe the trip would do me some good. So, I've written a lot. I'll only ruin your mood. I kiss you and I'll be waiting for your letter.

Mama

Utena, July 30, 1959

Dear Nijolė,

You letter really upset me. God's ways are not easy to understand. One spiritual leader said to me when Mindaugas died: "Don't suffer over it, God knows what he is doing." What today seems very painful in a few years might seem unavoidable. And it's true. When I look back on the past, starting with your father's death, then I find truth in that spiritual man's words. If father, may God rest his soul, had lived, we would have continued living in Jasonys, and there is no question that living there our entire family would have been deported to Siberia. Your entire youth and all your education would have been lost. Now, although it is hard to live without your homeland, you've acquired an education and are living good lives. If Mindaugas had lived, they would have exiled the both of us (because it was him who they were looking for). Then everything would have been lost. They released me because of my old age, but if he'd been with me they'd never have let him or me go. He would have been completely ruined, an invalid of the soul and of the body (his health was very bad). Now when I think on those children *(the Jewish children Mama saved)* I realize that it was a huge risk. Many people told me that I was a stupid idealist; even Uncle warned me that I am unthinkingly heading for danger. It's true that it was dangerous and once I lived through that danger. I went to see Kotrynėlė's mother at her work place. The Gestapo detained me. I was trembling all over. Only by pretending that I was completely stupid was I able to get away. Now it is so good that those children survived and if I understood your letter correctly, the Jewish community is trying to help me. Now I've renewed hope that God's road will take me to you. When my request to go to you was rejected I was so upset that I lay down practically in my grave. It was even dangerous for me to sit up in bed because I was having a high blood pressure crisis. I overheard a group of doctors talking about how I could have a heart attack. When I went to see my doctor he said, "Now you can travel, but if you'd tried to travel before you wouldn't have made it." It's the same thing again. Everything happens because of God's will. When a person is beaten blow by blow, she loses balance, and she herself no longer knows what to think, or what to do.

As you can see in the photograph, I am fat, although I've managed to lose some weight. How good it would be to lose more. It would make life much easier. I look healthy and so others are jealous of me, but I am jealous of their health. I eat as little as I can, without any fat, but my weight remains the same. This photograph was taken by Father Pranskietis. I was visiting them not too far from Panevėžys—by their house on the fence.

Last week was the Vitkus son's wedding. Genė and Dovilė came and so did Dovydaitis with his wife. We went to see the lawyer to see if somehow we could get my falling-down house back. In September we will have to go see Juozas Vitkauskas. Maybe he'll help us be able to buy it back. I kiss you.

Mama

Utena, July 31, 1959

Dear Vida,

Yesterday I received a letter from Nijolė. I am surprised to what ends and with what kinds of people the question of my going to live with you has been tied. *(Nijolė's efforts to have Mama released, starting with the highest officials of the government of the* United *States, is described in the appendix.)* It can't be?

Dovilė is bright. Unfortunately, she is not getting a good intellectual or Catholic upbringing either at home or at school. I advised Genė to transfer her to the former "Aušra" Gymnasium for girls. There are still some teachers there from the older generation and the education is better, but Dovilė didn't want to transfer, and Genė agreed with her... I kiss you all.

Mama

Utena, August 22, 1959

Dear Vida,

...I think that you know me well enough to know that I never had any patience for emptiness. My soul was always filled with more noble works, and that's why it's always been hard for me. I'm still battling so that I wouldn't fall apart completely, but the disappointment of not being able to see you has stunned me. Although I've recovered and my energy has almost returned, I'm not sure where to go with it? All the time I have to shuffle around because inquiries are constantly being made... All my peace I experience in church, but lately the church has been under attack; priests are cruelly and indecently attacked and slandered; just like all the saints and the holy trinity is slandered, even Mary, Mother of God. Now there is a new method—to create communism by destroying religion, especially the Catholic faith, because religion is considered superstition that darkens the people's minds. These are painful, but at the same time interesting, times.

My mood would be much better if I were able to reach you. The Vitkuses are good people, but they don't fill up my life. I think about you all the time and that gives me strength. It's too bad, Vida, that you cannot complete your studies. My greatest desire was to see you all with professions. The world is still not in order. We are all screaming for peace. God only knows what kind of peace that will be or if it will ever come at all. It is good to have a profession. God knows how and where you will have to live. Write soon. I kiss you all.

Mama

Panevėžys, August 26, 1959

Dear Nijolė,

...Tomorrow I return to Utena. The trip has cheered me up. It is a three-hour comfortable ride by train. It's the second day that it's been cooler and my blood pressure has dropped from 180 to 160. The doctor told me I needed to have ten ampoules of "Padutin" and ten ampoules of "Endoton," and to lie down for a week, so that my heart would be strengthened, because I told him about your plans for me. He praised you for your good idea. Everyone's opinion is positive, but for some reason I don't have much faith that it will work. When I returned to my homeland at first I had much more enthusiasm, optimism, and hope. Lately, that's all slipped away. To recover I need positive things to happen and positive surroundings that would fill my soul. Unfortunately, here everything is negative, everything is slipping downwards, and there are some very hard moments. You feel as though you won't last much longer. We *(the exiles)* are the rubbish of this age and often even our own people don't understand us. If you happen to meet other people who've had the same fate, then your heart recovers. You and we are the extreme, you left in time, and the others of us have been thrown out. The center is filled with an entirely new type of person, people of a new spirit or without any spirit at all—colorful on the surface, but empty inside. A nation mostly expresses itself through color... Pass on my most sincere greetings to Mr. Edvardas, Mrs. Vincė, Alexander's father, and Kotrynėlė. Thank them for all their efforts on my behalf. I kiss you.

Mama

Utena, September 7, 1959

Dear Nijolė,

I keep writing one letter after another. Now I'd like to share something important with you. One Lithuanian traveled to your country in 1944. His wife and son remained in Lithuania. He, like you, is doing everything he can to get her to be able to leave and go to him, but all his efforts were disregarded, as in my case. Not too long ago a high official from our country was visiting in your country. That Lithuanian, rumor has it, some how was able to get close to this official and ask him to release his wife and teenage son. Right now that same woman is writing letters to Lithuania from your country. Your aunt in Panevėžys told me about it yesterday. She claims she knows this story for a fact. We read in the newspaper (maybe you read it too) that about the middle of this month a high official from our country will travel to your country and will spend a longer time there. Maybe you some how could talk to that high official about me. People here are of the opinion that important officials like that can help in these instances. The exhibit from your country will be leaving soon; it's closed now. I kiss you and I wait for news.

Mama

The story of this family is the following:

The father and daughter were separated while fleeing from the approaching Soviet army in 1944 from his wife and young son. The father and daughter succeeded to escape and emigrate to the United States a few years later. The mother and son could not escape and were deported to Siberia. They were released 12 years later after the death of Stalin. The father finally found his wife and son in Lithuania and put all his efforts to get them out of Soviet occupied Lithuania and join him and daughter in the United States. However, all the efforts were in vain and their request to leave were several times rejected. When Khrushchev visited United States, during a banquet in his honor in Philadelphia, the daughter, with the help of an official openly approached Khrushchev and burst in tears, asking his help to obtain an exit permit for her mother and brother so that they could join her and her father in the United States. Khrushchev faced with this situation promised her to release her mother and brother.

Nijolė, when she heard this story, also wanted to approach Khrushchev and ask him to release her mother. She went to Washington and with the help of protocol chief Wiley Buchanan submitted a letter requesting Khrushchev to release her mother from the Soviet occupied Lithuania. She also intended to watch his motorcade and try to advance herself toward it, however she could not do it, went back to her hotel and spent the night crying reproaching herself of her failure to make a public dramatic show for her mother's release.

Panevėžys, October 25, 1959

...After Khrushchev's visit to the United States there has been talk that both nations have made an agreement to exchange citizens with the goal of reuniting families. Supposedly, our country promised to release elderly and lonely parents, allowing them to join their children. If that's the truth, then I'll be seeing you soon. If only I could get better faster! I kiss you all.

Mama

Panevėžys, October 26, 1959

Dear Nijolė,

...I've hardened myself to all sorts of experiences and shocks, and it seems that all of them, whether good or bad, I'll be able to cope with impassively. I am very surprised that in your country such high and honorable individuals, from our perspective, give such promises and with such concern, and that they actually contact you and inform you of what they've done. In our country officials only do that sort of thing for a select few. May God repay them for their good hearts. Now my greatest concern is to get better soon and to wait for that greatest joy, if only I am worthy of it.

It's good that you will do what you are planning to do, if only you met with Algimantas more often. It is much harder for lonely men than for lonely women (here it is almost impossible to manage to get by if you are all alone). You write that he has much more free time than you or Vida. I've judged from his letters (although he does not write often) that he does not have much time and that his work is hard. He mentions his homeland with great longing. You know, Nijolė, a sister's heart cannot feel what a mother's heart can feel. Because I am far from him, you must show him a sister's love. Couldn't he live somewhere closer to you? He wrote to me in his last letter that he still hasn't passed all of his final exams.... You uncles send you their greetings. They've sent you a gift. I kiss you.

Mama

In this letter Mama mentions "your country's high officials." Most likely, at the time Nijolė had written to her, telling her about the steps she was taking to obtain permission for Mama to receive a passport to travel to the United States.

Already in July, 1956, Congressman Charles J. Kersten had written a letter to the Vice-President of the United States at the time, Richard Nixon, asking his help in requesting that the American Ambassador in Moscow contact the Soviet leadership to discuss the question of Mama's release to the United States. Nijolė had known Charles J. Kersten very well since 1953 when he came to Europe to collect statements from refugees in order to analyze for congress how the Baltic nations were incorporated into the Soviet Union.

In the appendix of this book are Kersten's letters and letters from other US officials who were trying to help obtain Mama's release. Among the letters is one from Doctor Samuel Gringauz, whose son Alexander was saved by Mama during the Nazi occupation, in addition to letters from other important individuals in the government at the time, as well as two letters from Richard Nixon. In addition to all these letters, a letter was passed on to Khrushchev from the chief of protocol Wiley Bu-

chanan. Unfortunately, all of these efforts did not help secure Mama's release...

Panevėžys, November 21, 1959

Dear Vida,

I wrote my last letter to you on the tenth of this month. *(Many of Mama's letters did not reach their recipients.)* Your letters take ten days to reach me. I don't know how long it takes my letters to reach you? I've received all your letters and photographs. This letter I am writing to you already able to sit up at a table. I walk and move very little. I don't feel so bad, only I am worried about those two packages that I haven't received until now. They are treasures. By selling their contents, I could save up enough money to pay for what is most essential right now, namely my medical expenses. I will remain in Panevėžys until March. The Vitkuses are worried that I've left and that I've not returned for such a long time.

While I was writing this letter Father Pranckietis was passing through and stopped by to visit me. The poor man has lived through some huge unpleasantness. *(Most likely he returned to Lithuania without being officially released.)* It's only been a year since he's returned from Siberia and now it looks like they'll be sending him back. They don't want to register him; the same thing has happened to many people from Siberia. People like him are beaten off like dogs. It was very painful that I did not have any gifts for him because the packages you promised me have not arrived yet. He is dressed very poorly, and like always, without my even noticing it, he tucked 100 rubles under my pillow. He really needs a winter coat. I wrote to Algimantas long ago, but like always, silence. You probably don't even have the kind of fabric that would be suitable for a winter coat there in Australia. I'll have to ask Nijolė. I kiss you all.

Mama

From the left: Father Pranas, Konstancija and Jurgis Bakšys, and Father Juozas. Standing: Konstancija (our mother) and Veronika. Around 1916

*The Bražėnas family in 1931. Konstancija and Konstantinas ,
the twins, Nijolė and Vida, Algimantas and Mindaugas.*

Konstancija Bražėnienė

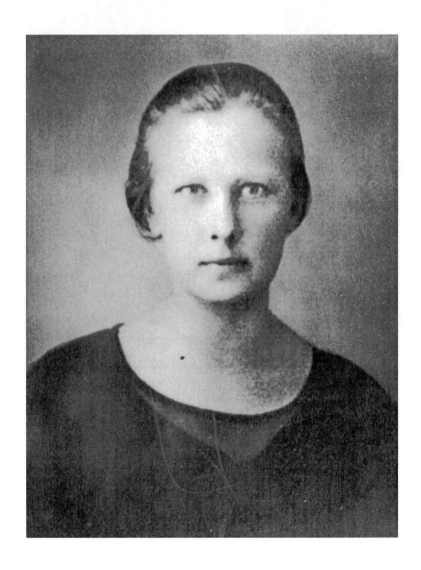

Mindaugas Bražėnas, 1944. Eighteen years old.

This map shows the journey exiles took from Lithuania to Siberia. The arrow indicates the island on Lake Baikal. USSR

Konstancija Bražėnienė celebrating Christmas Eve with a group of priests and clerics in Siberia, 1950.

A handwritten list of priests from the Kaunas seminary who'd been deported at the same time as Konstancija Bražėnienė. This list was mailed together with her first letter from Siberia in 1956.

Kauno kunigų Seminarijos auklėtiniai su kuriais kartu viename bagone važiavome į Sibirą ir kartu Baikalo Jaloje gyvenome.

1) Pranckietis Vincas
2) Konstantinas Eernis
3) Abromavičius Vladas
4) Butkus Izidorius
5) Butvimikas Antanas
6) Augustinavičius Jonas

    ką tik išventinti kunigai

1) Anieliauskas Vitautas
2) Minkevičius Albinas
3) Raugas Stasis
4) Vaškevičius Valerijus
5) Gidutas Leonas
6) Mitritas Antanas
7) Itašaitis Jonas

    klerikai 4 kurso

Konstancija Bražėnienė in 1956 when she returned to Lithuania from Siberia.

Fiorenzo Paronetto, Nijolè's husband

The Vaitiekūnas family in Australia: Rasa, Algirdas, Andrius, Vida, Algirdas, Maryte, Juozas

These photos of Konstancija Bražėnienė were taken by the journalist Salomėja Narkeliūnaitė.

These photos of Konstancija Bražėnienė were taken by the journalist Salomėja Narkeliūnaitė.

Konstancija Bražėnienė with her granddaughters Lucia and Laura in New York, 1967

Konstancija Bražėnienė with Laura in New York, 1967

Konstancija Bražėnienė's grave in the Rockland Cemetery, New York.

Nijolė Bražėnaitė-Parronetto and Fiorenzo Parronetto

1960

Panevėžys, January 1, 1960

Dear Vida,

This time it took me a little longer to write you a letter. Mrs. Valaitis came to see me to sew my clothes. She is a very good seamstress and she's doing me a huge favor because I would not be able to travel to go see her. I want to go to you wearing clothing that suits my figure and my age.

The Kripaitises are eternally grateful to you for your gifts. Now they can dress themselves and hold their heads up. They've suffered so much, and life continues to be hard for them. They have big worries over their apartment and it is hard for them to fight for it because they don't have any money. Until now they've lived like everyone else—as though in a hole in the ground. Mrs. Kripaitis wrote to me in her letter that you've supported her not just materially, but morally as well. When you are destitute it always makes you feel better when someone shows you pity. If she had a better apartment, I could stay there for a longer while. They've been allocated an apartment on the fourth floor, so that wouldn't work for me. So, what can you do? You must be satisfied with what you have and thank God that you have somewhere to go. I kiss you all.

Mama

Panevėžys, January 19, 1960

Dear Vida,

Since Christmas my health has improved. I can already spend the better half of the day out of bed. The most important thing is to have suitable food, a good mood, and good surroundings, but here all of that is almost impossible to achieve. And so, I must suffer. What can you do? Things are the way they are. I am determined to return to Utena either in early or late March. Spring will start then and spring tempts me there.

I'm still preparing to go to you. I'm thinking, that if I'm able to go, I will take a few small suitcases with me. Here I have my clothing made by a very good seamstress who accommodates my figure and my age. I don't think that you'll be ashamed over how I'm dressed. You've sent me so much nice fabric that it would be embarrassing to go to you dressed poorly. In one of her letters, Nijolė mentioned that she could send me another down blanket. When I cover myself with a down blanket I am not cold at all, even in a cold room, but I ought to have a spare blanket for when I go to Utena to go to church. Often I must stay overnight there, and so it would be good to have an extra blanket and a blanket cover. If you sent me a blanket cover, I could pour down inside it and sew a separate blanket for Mrs. Vitkus. She is old and has rheumatism. She needs something warm to cover herself with.

I wrote to my lawyer, Mr. Aleksieyav, and asked him to take care of my documents. He promised. I kiss you for now.

Mama

Panevėžys, February 22, 1960

Dear Nijolė,

A few days ago I received your letter. You wrote that you sent me an official invitation to come and live with you. I think that the best thing would be to send it through the American Consulate in Moscow, just like you did the first time. You shouldn't expect that I will be released; you don't know what I know. Uncle *(Karvelis)* is often mentioned in the press, and others, all connected with me. I've completely given myself up to the Lord's will. If he allows me to see you again, then he will grant me the health to do it. My health would improve, if I had the right living conditions. I've come to stay here just because of the access to better medicine. Because I've been admitted in the past to the hospital in Panevėžys, that's where my medical history is. Many of the doctors there know me, but especially the head internist, and the heart and hypertension specialist. He pays attention to my hypertension and atherosclerosis, and administers serious treatment. And this time, as soon as I arrived here, they admitted me right away and took good care of me.

Aunt received the notice that your package has arrived, but she's been in Kaunas for two days already, so the notice is here waiting for her. I kiss you.

Mama

Panevėžys, March 26, 1960

Dear Nijolė,

I was released from the hospital a few days ago. The doctor had recommended that I be admitted right away because my blood pressure was going up very often and my heart beat was irregular. I was in the hospital for three weeks, the pounding subsided, and my heart started functioning normally again. I lay in bed the entire time and I'm out of the habit of walking, so until I get used to walking again it will be difficult. Even my hand shakes as I write to you. I'd like very much to have a device at home, so that I could check my own blood pressure. Not all the doctors here have one, but it would be easier to check it at home. My doctor in Utena has been sentenced to a year in jail. Sometimes here the doctors get that kind of a vacation...

Oh! If only I could tell you everything! Well, maybe some day... It is impossible for you to imagine how we live...

I don't understand what Edvardas *(Turauskas)* finds in my letters that is so interesting? I've received a letter from my government informing me that my name has been written into the list of names of those who want to leave for the United States, and that I should receive a letter of invitation, inviting me to go to you. I'll finish for now. I kiss you.

Mama

Mama's name was included in the list of people desiring to join their relatives in the West thanks to the efforts of Vice-president Richard Nixon when he met with Khrushchev in Moscow and had their so-called "kitchen talk."

Utena, April 12, 1960

Dear Nijolė,

Though I've just written to you, *(the letter never arrived)* I'm writing again because so many thoughts have gathered in my head. Again there's a lot of talk here about people being allowed to leave, but as soon as you want to find at least one fact you can't get anything. From what I can gather, a few families were able to leave with permission from Khrushchev himself, when he was there visiting you. I've not yet heard that someone was able to leave through the method that you are using. I went to see my lawyer and we had a long conversation about this. It turns out that the notice I'd received had been sent by the American Consulate. It states there that I have to receive a document from you, like the one you are preparing for me now, and then write a request to my government and explain. I think about it and I'm afraid of that journey. Would my health hold up?

Although the Vitkus family is very good to me and I have my own large sunny room, I am missing something. I need the love of those closest to me. Are you convinced that they will let me out? After all, my release will depend upon our government. Was your important guest, who was in Moscow, *(vice-president Richard Nixon)* able to do anything? These questions torment me. Some times I think to myself that you will most likely return to Lithuania. Maybe the big heads will solve some problems this summer and things will go back to normal. It would be the greatest joy if all of us could meet again in Lithuania. I don't know by what means I could improve my mood or get my energy back, but I really need something. Write to your Aunt Žiulys and thank her for taking care of me. The Vitkuses greet you. I kiss you.

Mama

Utena, April 23, 1960

Dear Vida,

Today I received your package, which took four months and eleven days to reach me. Thank you. On the second day of Easter I received a lovely letter from Algimantas. It seems that, after all, he has matured into a serious and religious man. He is taking care of my affairs in a serious manner. Only God knows if they'll let me out. Right before Easter Father Prunskis's mother, who is 72, flew to America to be with her son. Father Prunskis is a journalist and was active with that group that was in Washington when Khrushchev visited. He approached Khrushchev and asked him to release his mother and got his word. After seven months she left.

God knows how it will be with me. I received a letter from the Consulate in Moscow telling me that my name has been entered into the list of names of people who want to go live with relatives in the United States. Now I just need to receive a letter of invitation from Algimantas. I keep thinking that they'll find a reason not to let me out. *(They did. Nijolė's marriage to Juozas Lukša)* Or maybe that's just my fear talking? That's all I'll write for now. I kiss you all.

Mama

Utena, April 30, 1960

Dear Nijolė,

Don't be surprised that I'm writing to you with a shaky hand. My right hand and leg have been affected by a "micro stroke" and that's why they're not altogether normal. *(The handwriting is barely legible)* You can surround yourself with hundreds of the best doctors, but if you don't have peaceful living conditions you cannot be healed from hypertension. This disease demands rest, quiet, a good mood, and other gentle conditions. I didn't have that in Uncle's home, not to mention sleep. For days at a time I did not have peace and quiet and stopped sleeping altogether. Your pills did not help, nor any other sleep medication. I left Panevėžys with my blood pressure at 190. With my head spinning I returned to Šilinė. It's been a month now that I am here. Right from the beginning I was able to take a few steps. Little by little I've been growing stronger and am able to walk not too badly.

Often I think about the trip to you and sometimes I even get the shivers when I think that I might not be able to last the trip. We heard that Father Prunskis's mother, who is 72, was able to make the trip and that she is doing well. But, she probably doesn't have hypertension and is strong. They say that her flight took fourteen hours. I'm curious whether your government consulted with our government when they put together that list. Well, for now, stay healthy. I kiss you.

Mama

Utena, June 7, 1960

Dear Nijolė,

I'm writing to you first because I've received the medicine you sent me and the device. From Algimantas I've received the documents for my travel to the United States. The address is correct on the envelope, but it is written with mistakes on the document. I'll bring it to my lawyer right away. He's taken all my documents and has taken upon himself the task of writing the request; I won't have to do a thing. In his opinion, we'll be able to correct the address by writing a letter of explanation. Now all the requests to leave are handled right here in Lithuania, and, if they allow you to leave, you can get your passport right here in the region you live. At the end of the week I'll know if the address has been corrected, and if everything is alright, we'll write the request right away and I'll notify you.

I have a very sincere doctor who is advising me to go to my children as soon as I possibly can. Nijolė, send a larger quantity of that same medication for grandfather *(Father Gruodis)*.

Mama

Utena, July 2, 1960

Dear Nijolė,

I've handed in my request on June 26th. Although I have little hope that I'll receive a positive reply, at least my conscience will be clear because I will have done everything that it is possible to do. If they don't let me out, don't worry over it, God knows what He is doing. My health is poor, I might not be able to make it. While preparing the documents my health took a turn for the worse, and I had to spend a few weeks in the hospital. Otherwise, I really miss my family. They are building a road right beside the Vitkus house. It's not clear whether their house will end up being in the way. If it is, then I'll no longer be able to stay with them. Genė has made many requests for me to go live with her. But, that is still in the future. Maybe the time will come when we will all be able to go wherever we want. I kiss you.

Yours, Mama

Utena, October 2, 1960

Dear Nijolė,

I've been released from the hospital, but I still am not well. If I were to receive permission to leave, I could not go right now, but maybe later. My blood pressure does not even allow me to make sudden movements. I can't get around my room very well because I sway to the side. Now I no longer have any hope of seeing you again. I still can't write to you myself. Often I am overcome with pessimism and hopelessness. Don't suffer over it if something happens to me. My blood pressure can kill me or paralyze me. The trip to see you is a difficult one. You need to spend ten days in Moscow. But God's Eye sees it all. This unfortunate illness has eaten up a lot of my money and is putting a strain on the people around me. The Vitkus family is having a hard time because of me. Remember them. Write. I am waiting. If you can, write more about your life. *Yours, Mama*

Utena, Šilinė, October 24, 1960
(Written by Janė Vitkus)

Dear Nijolė,

All time I wrote letters for Mama, but this time I'd like to write a few words of my own. Today the Žiulys family took Mama to Panevėžys for the winter. Life is not too bad for her here with us, but the medical care, especially in the winter, is better in Panevėžys. The roads get bad and cars can't get through. It is better to spend the winter in town. There the doctors are better and the medical care is much better, and she needs medical care practically every day. Up until now, Nijolė, when Mama would dictate her letters to me, she did not want to tell you everything about her health. This year she is much weaker than she was last year. She spent almost the entire year in bed. She walks a little occasionally, but then she must lie down again. Because of her nerves her blood pressure is very high. It got higher when she started making preparations to go and live with you. She has an indescribable longing to see you, but she is not well. One day she'll walk around a bit, and the next day her blood pressure is high. A doctor here in Utena took care of her, but she couldn't do much. Maybe it'll be better in Panevėžys. Nijolė, I don't want you to think that there isn't anyone here who can take care of her. She has everything she needs here and we will continue to take care of her as though she were our own mother. We will be going to Panevėžys to visit her. Now we will keep her in our prayers and ask God to grant her health so that she may go to you. And so, Nijolė, I wish you well from everyone in our home and may you succeed in life.

Jane

Panevėžys, November 8, 1960
(The next few letters were written by Aunt Žiulys)

Dear Nijolė,

It will soon be a month that I am living with Uncles Žiulys. Out of the goodness of their hearts they invited me to spend the winter with them, since the medical care in Utena is minimal. Although the doctors cannot help me very much, it's still better to be under their care. I've grown weak, I can barely walk, and I lie down most of the time. I am eager to receive your package. I've sewn myself a few nicer outfits because I was expecting to go to you, but I don't have every day clothes, not even night clothes.

My situation is difficult because neither with the Vitkuses nor with uncle are there people who are home during the day to take care of me, and I'm tired of spending my time in hospitals. It is expensive to pay for the medical care. Write to your uncles and find out what they need, so that you could repay them for caring for me. Write openly, tell me how your life is going. I am very concerned about how you are feeling and your situation.

Maybe the new government will be able to agree and we will be able to travel freely over the borders. I don't know how much longer I will have to suffer like this, because I am not young. Maybe I am a great sinner that God has punished me to this degree.

I am just happy that despite all that hardship you've been able to put your lives in order, but I will not know that happiness. Pass on my greetings to Vida and her family, and chastise Algimantas for forgetting his poor mother and not writing even one letter. Next time I will try to write myself.

Mama

Nijolė, if you send something to Mama, could you please include a size eight warm hat for Ridutė. She'll be starting school and we can't get her a warm hat here.

Your Aunt

Panevėžys, November 20, 1960
(Aunt Žiulys's letter)

Dear Nijolė,

I am very hurt that you have offered to pay me a salary for taking in your mother. I would never have taken on this kind of responsibility and worry for any kind of pay. If I had the health and the time, then I'd earn my pay. We keep your mother here simply because we feel sorry for her, and she has no one else besides the Vitkuses and us. We do as much as conditions allow and as we are able. We completely understand how difficult her circumstances are, although she does not understand us.

Nijolė, I don't think I need to explain to you what it means to take care of someone who is gravely ill, and especially a person like your mother, when she plunges into utter hopelessness. Although even before the war she was extremely sensitive and nervous. Now she worries over every slightest detail, and especially when she doesn't receive a letter from you in a long time. When she receives a letter from you she feels much better and her health improves. Right now she couldn't travel anywhere.

Therefore, my dear Nijolė, don't worry about us. For the time being, thank God, we have enough food, although we must work very hard to get it, especially Justinas. I would only like that you, who've known us from before, would understand us, and that would be the very best payment for all our trouble and worry. I do not want to receive any kind of pay from you, and when the bills accumulate, then we work it out. I kiss you.

Your Aunt

1961

Panevėžys, February 11, 1961

Dear Nijole,

A letter came from the Consulate that I should not worry about taking care of the documents since it takes so long. It looks as though I will receive permission to travel, but I'm not so sure I will be able. Pray for your poor mother, because when I look back on my life I can see that I am really pitiful and I don't know how God will be able to help me. Although my health has improved, I will still be spending a lot of time running around seeing doctors and taking care of things. Besides that, the trip is a long, and I'm not quite prepared for it. In a word, it's difficult to say what will happen right now. I am with your uncles, but the documents will be mailed to Utena, and again, I must travel in the cold weather. Write to uncle and aunt and thank them for me. Despite everything, they are very patient and good to me. I've caused them much unpleasantness with my disease and my nerves. In their home there is light, warmth, and water. I don't have that in the country. Things are now worse at the Vitkus house.

If I am able to travel to you, you will be shocked to find that your mother looks altogether different—exhausted from illness; I've even lost my hair. It's not clear what will happen with me. My life is over and in my old age I will need to suffer a lot and live in want.

Right now it is difficult to sell fabric because there is a lot of it around and the price is coming down. It's better in the big cities, but I'll probably have to go to the Vitkuses soon and there won't be anyone around who could handle the selling for me. Algimantas has not written since Christmas. The same with Vida. I kiss you many times.

Mama

Šilinė, February 17, 1961
(Janė Vitkus's letter)

Dear Algimantas,

When you begin reading this letter you probably won't be able to figure out who is writing to you. I think that you must know about the Vitkus family, but you might not know all of us, even me. This letter is written to you by Janė. Your mother is now living in Panevėžys. Her health has improved considerably lately. She has begun to walk and can even do a little work around the house. Each day she is making plans to go live with you.

A week ago I received a notice from Moscow announcing that Mama's request has been denied. Right now I don't know what to do. I cannot tell her, because if I do, it will upset her terribly and that will affect her health and she might become bedridden again. We are all of the opinion that you should start organizing the documents to invite her to go live with you once again. A woman here left not too long ago. They say that it took four tries before they let her go. When you begin organizing her paperwork she will not know that this request has been denied. Algimantas, don't write to her and tell her that her request was denied, but write to her and tell her that you are taking care of paperwork to speed up the affair. Her only goal in life is to reach you all and to see you again.

Finishing this letter, I'd like to send you my best wishes and wish you good luck in your life.

Jane

Utena, February 24, 1961

Dear Nijolė,

I am now in Šilinė with the Vitkuses. I am unhappy because I will no longer be able to correspond with you. I am very upset and my nerves are ruined. The Vitkuses wrote to you both and to Algimantas and asked you to repeat your request for me to come and live with you. I think that you should not bother. I am too sick to travel. I've found myself in a very unpleasant situation. Now I will really be left without a home, without food, and without everything that is dear to my heart... I am a big sinner; I've done wrong, and I've angered God himself and Mary, Mother of God. I go from one sin to the next. Don't think that I'm trying to frighten you; I am only writing the truth. I will never see you again. Stay healthy, send my greetings to Vida and her family, and to Algimantas. I kiss you.

Mama

Kaunas, February 26, 1961
(Written by Genė Bražėniene)

Dear Vida,

I believe that you will be able to understand me because you are a mother and you know yourself what children mean to a mother. I went to visit your mother and I was very disappointed with her life and with her health. Don't be alarmed, it might not be all that bad, but she is very depressed by the loneliness of old age and by how much she misses all of you.

In general, I don't stick my nose into how she lives. She takes care of herself the best way she knows how. But now I am forced to write to you and to ask your advice. Living in Utena she raised the money to renovate the house, built herself a nice room in that house, but now she can no longer live in it because there is no one there who can take care of her. The same thing happened in Panevėžys. Up until now I thought that the best thing for her would be to live with her own relatives. But now I saw that having done so much good for everyone else, she is left homeless and with no one to care for her. That is why I am asking you to forget about the relatives and friends. Only don't forget about her and comfort her. When I went to see her I found her absolutely obsessed with worrying over tomorrow and without any perspective for the future. As soon as I can I will bring her back to Kaunas with me. Maybe new surroundings, different people, and a quieter lifestyle will improve her health.

You'd written to me earlier and told me that you thought she ought to live with me and Dovilė, but I thought at the time that she was better off living with those people whom she was trying so hard to please. After she lives with us for a while she will be able to decide on her own where it will be better for her.

Pass on my greetings to all your little ones, and especially to Algirdas. I'll be waiting for your letter.

Genė

Utena, March 10, 1961

Dear Nijolė,

Happy Easter! I wish you health, joy, and success in life. My request to go and live with you has been rejected. I must begin everything all over again from the beginning, and I'm not sure if that will work. Maybe in time the borders will open and we will be able to travel freely. I've heard that a Lithuanian Choir from your country will be performing here in Lithuania and that Lione Juodytė is in that choir (*Mama took care of the orphan Lionė in Jasonys*). I might be able to meet with her if I can make it to the concert. Don't worry my dear Nijolė, this is my fate. Who knows where I must live, although for the time being I am living here in this house with the Vitkuses.

Although Uncle and Aunt Žiulys wrote you a very nice letter about me, I am no longer welcome in their home. If I go to stay with Gene, it will only be for a short while. The Vitkus family is changing, so I won't be able to live with them any more. Don't worry, my dear Nijolė, I'll survive.

Your loving Mama

Utena, March 19, 1961

Dear Nijolė,

I've just received your letter. We can try repeating the process once again. Algimantas needs to invite me one more time. Now it seems as though the relationship between our countries is improving, and so maybe in time we will be able to travel back and forth.

Now I don't know where I will stay because there are huge reforms going on at the collective farms and the Vitkus family is being split up. No one is to blame, neither Genė, nor the Žiulyses, nor the Vitkuses that I can no longer stay with any of them. I am very sad. Some how everything has fallen apart. When I think about it, I've grown away from God. For now I'm still living with the Vitkuses. My nerves are in bad shape. I am not registered with the Vitkuses, and I can't stay with Stefanija. *(Under the Soviet system citizens had to register the address where they lived with the regional place.)* I don't know why I am not able to get along with people where I live. You must do everything for yourself, and that is hard for me. Although every one is writing to you that I am welcome to live with them, in reality that is not so. Of course, they're not chasing me out, but everywhere I must pay for my food and all sorts of other things. Be well. I kiss you a thousand times.

Mama

Kaunas, March 20, 1961

Dear Nijolė,

I've received your letter. I'm very sad that my misfortunes have upset you all. Don't worry about it and don't take it to heart. It is hard for me to orient myself. I am not registered with the Vitkuses. Stefanija might have stopped my registration, and so I float between two places. Only God alone knows where things will end. I am guilty for everything that has happened to me in life. Everyone writes pleasant letters to you and everyone wishes me well, only I can't fit in anywhere. I am guilty of so many things that I no longer know what I'm guilty of.

Do not send any packages to the Žiulyses or to anyone else, because they are very expensive and cause a lot of trouble for you. It's better to put some "greens" in an envelope for Easter. Maybe Vida is having a hard time getting by? Don't worry and don't fret. I feel sorry for all of you.

I do not have a stable address right now. My rights were not recognized, that is I was not rehabilitated, and that is why they would not register me. I made a mistake when I returned from Siberia that I did not settle down in Kaunas near my home. Now I've made a mess of things.

I worry over all of this, although I still have a bite of bread to eat. If they don't let me out, I'll just have to accommodate myself to these conditions and live. I feel sorry for you and worry over your health. You are very thin. I know that you are all alone and that you suffer a lot. I pray for you. Be happy. I kiss you a thousand times.

Mama

Kaunas, March 24, 1961

Dear Nijolė,

I've received your letter. You shouldn't worry about me. Now I am living with Genė. I don't know how long I can stay here. It's best to send the package to Genė's address, although that's not certain. This is my situation, wherever I go, I get in the way. I don't know how to adjust to the situation. I feel sorry for you for suffering over me like this. I received Vida's letter with the photographs. She does not look good. I'm so bad at living; I just ruin people's lives and torment them. You, Nijole, must have a hard life and must not get enough to eat. I eat well, although my life is not pleasant. What can you do, things will happen as they are meant to happen; you can't jump in the ground while you're still breathing. I am guilty myself for being denied permission to leave. I wasn't careful and didn't take care of things. I don't know what to do. I don't know how to get out of it. Be good, and don't worry. I feel sorry over all your suffering.

How things are going here is hard to say. For some things are going well, for others they aren't. In general, the situation is not so bad. Everybody has work, but I have none. I kiss you many times.

Mama

Kaunas, March 28, 1961
(Genė Bražėnienė's letter)

Dear Vida,

I've received your letter, and Mama is here already. You worry very much over her. You shouldn't worry so much; there is no other way. Even if she were granted permission to leave, would she ever make it? She has changed completely now and looks completely different. In sum, she worries that life is hard for you, that you are experiencing hardship, and that you are thin. Write to her and calm her down. Write to her and tell her that your finances are in order because she worries over that.

As far as the packages go, there is no need to send them as often as you did earlier. She doesn't need that much for herself. Don't worry about me and Dovilė, we'll take care of ourselves some how.

I wish you well for the spring holiday that's coming soon and I wish you joy and success. Greetings to everyone. We kiss you.

Genė and Dovilė

Kaunas, April 7, 1961
(The letter is barely legible)

Dear Nijolė,

I haven't written to you in a long time, but I have nothing new to tell you. Right now I am living with Genė, but life is difficult because they lack an extra room. My state of mind is poor because there is nothing that I can do about applying for a passport. I imagine you and Vida in a very difficult situation because you must do everything for yourselves. My affairs are at a standstill. Maybe if I'd stayed in Utena, I'd been able to take care of things, but that was no longer possible. I don't know how everything will end. Now even God has abandoned me and I cannot pray anymore. I am falling apart. I hear that many people are able to leave, only I alone seem incapable of taking care of things. My relatives don't love me anymore and don't want me around anymore, and I am not well.

I see you worried, and Vida too. I'm afraid that there wouldn't be a catastrophe in her family. A man is good as long as everything is fine at home, but when there are shortages, then he loses interest. I kiss you all many times.

Mama

Kaunas, April 13, 1961
(The letter is barely legible)

Dear Nijole,

I haven't received a letter from you in a very long time. I imagine you very worried and exhausted, and without anyone to comfort you. My affairs are at a standstill. I must begin everything all over again from the beginning, and that takes a very long time. I can't do it alone. My future is abhorrent; I'm hanging on a thread. I'm not registered anywhere and I am in a terrible mental state; I have no energy and no strength. Everything is unclear. Everyone curses me. If I don't leave and go to my children, I will have no life here. I kiss you.

Mama

Kaunas, May 16, 1961

Dear Vida,

I've received your letter, but those photographs are too big. I need passport size photos. And I can't make them and besides, nothing will come of it anyway. I have no citizen's rights; I was not rehabilitated when I returned from Siberia. Everyone is writing you pleasant letters, but, unfortunately, no one will have me in their home. It's hard to sell off the fabric, especially since I can't do it myself. I feel for you and all of you. It hurts that I cannot help you in any way, that I can only hurt you. Don't worry about me. I am very sinful, and that is why God is punishing me now. Don't pay attention to what I've written. It's just my nerves and the bad situation I'm in. Write. I'll be waiting. I kiss you all.

Mama

Kaunas, July 12, 1961
(Genė's letter)

Dear Vida,

Thank you for your letter to me and Dovilė and for your gifts. Forgive me for not answering your letter for so long. I work too many hours and so I never seem able to find the time. Mama's health is poor. There is a weight on her heart and she sleeps poorly at night. Besides that, her legs are terribly swollen. Vida, don't go through the trouble and the expense of organizing her trip to Australia. She'll never make it. Although it is painful, you must accept her fate. I will take good care of her, so don't worry about that. I haven't become a materialist yet, and for Mindaugas's sake, I will take care of her. Tomorrow is August 13th--thirteen years since his death.
Pass on my best wishes to your entire family. Good luck.

Genė and Dovilė

Kaunas, August 29, 1961

Dearest Nijolė,

What has happened that you don't write to me any more? Vida wrote that you've been married. Don't tell me that this gets in the way of your writing me at least a few words? My health has deteriorated. My feet and my calves have swollen all the way up to my knees and at night I find it difficult to breath. I cannot sleep at night. Although the doctor has prescribed some medicine for me, it doesn't seem to help much. I have a rash on my right leg and a watery discharge oozes out through it. When I weigh it all, it seems to me that I don't have much longer to live. If only I could see you again! The international situation promises nothing good. Just arguments and more arguments.

Write to me my darling. It's very difficult not receiving any letters from you. I don't leave the house because I can't move very much, and so I'm short of breath. I suffer and regret having let you go out into the world on your own. Of course, if you hadn't gone to the West, you would have ended up in the East. Who knows where it would have been harder? Things worked out best for the people who were able to remain in the same place, only not in our situation. How is Uncle doing? I receive letters occasionally from Vida and Algimantas, only not from you. Write to me, Nijolė, and tell me who your husband is. First of all, is he Lithuanian? And what is his profession? I am waiting desperately for a letter from you. I kiss you.

Mama

Kaunas, August 29, 1961

Dear Vida,

Dear Lord, where has Nijolė disappeared to? You write that she has married. It can't be that that has separated us?

You cannot even imagine how much I suffer living in these surroundings. I need to digest Uncle's situation and our situation. I could tolerate it all if I were in good health. My heart is weak, my legs are swollen to my knees, and there is a rash on my right leg, which is emitting a watery discharge. I cannot sleep because as soon as I lie down I am short of breath, and so I spend the entire night sitting up, or swaying and panting for breath. My doctor has prescribed some medicine, but it doesn't help. I predict that I won't live much longer because not only is my physical health weak, but so is my moral health. I can't believe that Nijolė, who always took such good care of me, would forget me so easily? I've been thinking that it might be that Nijolė is no longer among the living, because I don't believe that she would not have told me about her own marriage? And who is that husband of hers? Is he Lithuanian? Does he have a profession? *(It was difficult for Nijolė to admit to her mother that she had married a foreigner, an Italian, a wonderful man, a scientist, whom she met while a resident in pathology, and after many years had passed since her first husband, the partisan Juozas Lukša-Daumantas's was killed by the Russians in Lithuania. She was afraid that Mama would disown her, but in reality Mama loved Renzo very much.)*

Get your children accustomed to physical work. Here everyone must work, and those who are not used to work, suffer. I long for letters from you because that is my only comfort. The international situation predicts nothing good—just talk and arguments. I kiss you all.

Mama

Kaunas, September 27, 1961
(Genė's letter)

Dear Vida,

Although Mama received your letter, she hasn't answered it. Her health has grown seriously worse. There are open wounds on her right leg and she cannot walk. The doctors tell us that it is because of atherosclerosis, and that's why the wounds won't heal. Right now she is home, but I'm doing everything I can to get her in the hospital. Here it is not so easy to get a bed in the hospital, even with a serious illness like this one. I'll be waiting for your letter. All three of us send you kisses.

Genė

Kaunas, October (?) 1961
(Genė's letter)

Dear Vida,

I've not received your letter. We received your package a few days ago. I was able to get Mama admitted into the Kaunas Clinical Hospital. Her leg is not healing, but they cleaned out the wounds. They were very deep. It will take a long time for them to heal. The doctors believe that they will heal eventually. Her blood pressure is normal for the moment.

Dear Vida, write to her often. I cannot describe how she looks forward to your letters. She could not write the last few letters because she was very weak and because the wounds on her legs hurt her very much. Now she will write to you herself from the hospital.

Vida, when you send your next package, put only good quality things in there, even if it means that you must send less: good quality sweaters, wool fabrics for dresses, nylons, blouses, stockings with black ankles... Don't be angry that I'm writing this, but it's easier to sell those things, and Mama needs money right now. Dovilė has enclosed her photograph for Rasa. I kiss you.

Genė

Kaunas, November 16, 1961

Dear Nijolė,

I've received your letter with the photographs. I saw Algimantas in your wedding photographs. You, that is, you and Vida, worry about me. I think Algimantas does too. He wrote me once that if only he could, he'd become a bird and fly back to his homeland and live there all the time. My heart goes out to him. I love you all very much and miss you very much, but I no longer have any hope of seeing you ever again. Write and tell me about Vida and Algimantas. I don't think they tell me the real truth about themselves. You, Nijolė, have grown very thin. God willing, may your life be easier and your husband be sensitive towards you. I wonder if he understands our situation. We are moving with quick steps towards communism and we expect that the rest of the world will follow.

They've done the operation on my leg already, only they haven't taken off the bandages yet. I don't know how it will turn out. In general, I don't feel well. The anesthesia made me sick. The whole time my heart was weak. Maybe in time it will improve.

Write more about your husband and about you. I wish you happiness. There was a time when I dreamed of visiting your husband's homeland, but it wasn't my fate. I loved my homeland and my people very much. My homeland has remained the same, but its face is very different.

My life has not been pleasant. The only thing that has kept me going is my faith. Maybe that moment when I must travel to eternity will come. Your letters are like a breath of fresh air. I wait and wait for them... Write and tell me if Vida is doing better financially. Her large family exhausts her. Does she have anyone to help her or does she do it all alone? Is her husband good to her and does he understand her? For now I kiss you and your husband and I wish you joy and good fortune. I could not decipher your husband's name.

Mama

Kaunas, November 17, 1961

Dear Vida,

I've received your letter and your package. It hurts me that you apologize for not writing enough and for something else that I didn't understand. I love you all incredibly and I miss you. I could not leave with Nijolė then because I could not leave your two grandmothers without anyone to take care of them. They would have died of starvation. Besides, Algimantas and Mindaugas were still at home. They were all dependent on me. My conscience would not allow me to leave them behind. *(In the summer of 1944, when the Russians were already close to Kaunas, Nijolė returned from Giessen to Lithuania with the aim of bringing Mama back to Germany with her. Vida was very sick, but Nijolė left her behind on the impulse to return to Lithuania. She received*

*special permission to make the trip, but the department that issued her
papers told her that she must be insane to take such a dangerous trip.
Kaunas was completely empty, but the trains were still running. On the
Lithuanian border she met many refugees trying to escape the Soviet offensive. When Mama saw Nijolė she was very upset and told her to go
back right away. Nijolė tried to convince her to come with her, but
Mama refused adamantly, saying that she could not leave their two
grandmothers behind without anyone to care for them. Father's mother,
Veronika Braženienė, was partially paralyzed at the time. Mama told
Nijolė that she could not leave Vida behind in Marburg because she was
very sick and insisted that she return to Vida right away. If Nijolė hadn't
returned immediately, Vida would have died. That was the last time Nijolė saw Mama...)*

I am tormented by how the entire world is at unrest. That "joy" that
has reached us, might reach you.

I know that you have a lot of work and that you have a big family
to take care of and that you've helped me so much. I think only of you
and I know that you are thinking of me. I'm afraid that the same thing
doesn't happen to your children.

They've already operated on my leg. They took skin from my thigh
and put it on my calf. They haven't taken the bandages off yet. Whether
it will get better or not, God only knows. Vida, my dear, don't worry
about me. Don't ruin your health. I think that it would be better if the
Lord took me. It would be easier for me and for you. I press you all to
my heart. I love you all very very much.

Mama

Kaunas, November 26, 1961

Dear Nijole,

I've received a letter from Algimantas in which he writes a little bit
about you. God willing, that you may be happy. He wrote that the
Lithuanian community opposed your marrying a foreigner, but that now
they've calmed down. Write about yourself. Tell me about how you live
and how you are feeling. What is your work like? Have you been able to

rest after all that hard work? You haven't written me anything about Uncle and Ugnė. I believe that you meet with them. Does your husband even know a little about our homeland? When you have a child, raise him in a Lithuanian spirit, so that he would know about our poor homeland. I never would have believed that Algimantas would become such a patriot. May the Lord grant that he may return to the homeland and that all of you return. Right now it would no longer be pleasant for you to live here. What language do you speak with your husband? Do you have any ties with Lithuanians? Do you earn a lot of money and do you earn enough to live? I miss you all terribly.

Vida has accused me of not leaving with you when you came back at the end of the war to get me. At the time I could not leave our two grandmothers alone to die of starvation and Mindaugas and Algimantas were still at home. My conscience would not allow me to leave them behind because they were all dependent on me. I clothed them and I fed them. It weighed on my heart to let you two girls go, but there was no other alternative. Now my situation is much worse. If only I could, I'd fly like a bird to join you.

My leg has been operated on and is healing, but there is still the question of how strong it will be once the wound has healed? The wound can come back. My heart is weak and that's what leads to these other problems. I don't have good living conditions. I think only about you and about the future. I can see the end of my life before me, but I'd so like to see you once more... Definitely write to me about Vida's life. Is her husband faithful to her and is he sensitive to her needs? Do Uncle and Ugnė write to you? Is Ugnė planning on marrying? Does you husband like our family, although he doesn't know us very well. I kiss you both many many times. Write me your husband's name.

Mama

Kaunas, December (?), 1961
(Genė's letter)

Dear Nijolė,

Thank you for your letter and for your greetings on this holiday occasion. Dovilė and I congratulate you and your husband belatedly, and we wish you both much joy and good luck. Dovilė and I are both healthy and we spend our days in school and at work. I'm so busy all the time, I don't even notice how quickly the years run by. Dovilė will soon be thirteen. She is growing fast.

Mama is home again. Her leg is almost healed. She can walk around the room, only her health is not all that great. Sometimes she is short of breath and has chest pain. Though, in general she does not complain much.

There is no reason to thank me for taking care of Mama. I believe that anyone would do the same if they saw another person suffering.

This is all that I can tell you in answer to your questions: I will hand in the request for rehabilitation again and when I receive an answer I will write to you. Until she is rehabilitated you cannot even think of doing anything. Besides that, they look very closely at each individual's past, at their relatives, and in general, at everything.

You asked if Mama receives enough packages. Truthfully, she worries that you send her too much and that you are making your own lives difficult by doing so. For the moment she has enough money and seems satisfied. She never complains. I do not know whether she is happy here with us, but we do everything we can to make her comfortable. We care for her, we wash her clothes. She does not need to worry about those things. We all eat together, but most of all she misses you.

I kiss you and I'll be waiting for your letter.

Genė and Dovilė

Kaunas, December 31, 1961

Dear Nijolė,

I received your Christmas greeting. The envelope was full and for that I thank you. You've asked me to choose a name for the baby you are expecting. I will write it in my next letter. Now I'd like to give you some very serious advice as an expectant mother: Offer up your infant now to Mary, so that she would watch over him and so that she would keep him as a servant of Christ, or that she would prepare him for the priesthood, or for a worldly life as an honest and respectable man. In a word, pray to Mary that from the very beginning of his life to the end of his life that he would be in Her care and that She would direct him to Jesus Christ. That is how religious women offer up their infants. *I* might not have been able to express myself well, but I think that you will understand my thought. I can't say much about how to raise him while he still hasn't been born. Often my heart is wracked with pain when I think about how you will probably no longer be able to work for the good of your homeland.

Now I am living with Genė. They've operated on my large wound, but there are still small wounds and some tiny wounds that I am nursing here at home. I was in the hospital for two and a half months; they did not keep me any longer than that because the hospital was over crowded. At first I could barely stand up. Now I can walk very well. You wrote that my handwriting is more legible and that I seem happier. Before I worried a lot over not being able to leave and go to you. Now I still suffer. But, as they say, you can get used to anything. My situation is not pleasant, but I must suffer through it. God only knows if anything better is ahead of me. On February 10th I will be 70. I will be entering the seventh decade of my life. My health is only getting worse. Now I can only walk across the room. My leg was in horrible condition; it was infected and was bleeding pus. Luckily, I was able to get admitted to the best hospital in Lithuania with the best surgeons. Otherwise, they probably would have had to amputate or worse. These clinics were built and supplied during "our times." *(The time of independence)*. It pains me to think about all that. The people who rebuilt everything, who created it all, cannot even live in their own country. Poor Uncle, think of how hard he worked, and look how he was repaid. *(Petras Karvelis was active in rebuilding the Lithuanian state during its independence between 1918-*

1940. After the Soviet occupation of Lithuania he was slandered in the press constantly). How I feel sorry for my countrymen who are sick with longing for their country living in a foreign land. Here they are teaching young people to no longer care about their homeland and about religion... People drink a lot and are adulterous. Those are just a few impressions out of thousands that I could write to you.

I forgot to tell you that I am short of breath whenever I move around a little more than usual. You asked whether I still had any hope of ever reaching you. It's hard to say. They still have not returned my right to citizenship and that makes everything much more complicated. I will try to write a request to the highest government office, maybe that will help. We hear all about the troubles in the world. I don't know what's really true?

Finishing this letter, I have a huge request. Although Vida sends me packages, mostly people here are interested in summer weight fabric, for example, white nylon with a flower print, like what you sent Milda Žiulys, or with other bright colors. Besides that, there is a market for fabric for wedding dresses, elastic nylon stockings, bolts of cotton, slips. Dovilė tells me that black scarves with ornaments are in style now. When the ladies go to the theater they toss them over their shoulders. I am enclosing a square of fabric as a sample. Everyone is impressed with this fabric. If you can, include one more pretty nylon blouse and light weight sweaters. I don't know if all that will be too much for you. The package would arrive in the spring, just before summer, and that would make it easier to sell. The public here in Kaunas likes to dress up and will do anything to get their hands on anything that sparkles. There are many foreigners living here from our faraway homeland... (*Russians were relocated to Lithuania to take the place of the Lithuanians deported to Siberia in order to colonize the Baltic States).* They all live in the cities and many of them don't care what they do with their money... And so if it wouldn't be too difficult for you, I'd like you to do this for me. People like to show off and sometimes they don't even know what they want. I don't think it is a good thing to live a life just of parties and dances. I don't think people earn very much money, but they know how to get it by other means, and when they do, they do it in style.

When you write to Uncle, Ugnė, and Edvardas, pass on my greetings. Is Uncle very old and what does he live from? I think that he must miss his homeland very much. Does he have any hope of coming home?

Have you been able to visit Aunt V.'s grave? Poor Ugnė probably barely remembers her homeland… Why aren't there any Lithuanians were she is living? Why can't she live where Uncle lives? If only she doesn't forget how to speak her own language!

Finishing this letter, I congratulate you both, and I kiss you both! I try to push these thoughts aside. When I think about all of you, I get the feeling that you'll never return home to your homeland. Although my life is ending, I'd like to see you all in your dear homeland. Be well.

Genė and Dovilė

1962

Kaunas, January 25, 1962

Dear Vida,

I've received you package. Thank you very much. Everybody liked what you sent, and that's why the entire package has been distributed already. My leg is not entirely healed, but I can walk better now. My good leg is often swollen and at night when I wash it, it gets irritated. I'm suffering from a cough.

Nijolė's time to give birth is drawing near, and somehow I am uneasy. If only everything ends well. He wrote to me that she is searching for a trustworthy nanny because she does not want to give up working altogether. She went through a lot of trouble to become a doctor. I cannot read what Nijolė's husband's last name is and I've never heard of his first name. I could not find it on the Catholic calendar.

The Cult of Mary is defiled here. Most young people don't even know about Her. Two priests are on trial right now. Quite a few priests and bishops have been dragged into the case. Otherwise, young people here enjoy themselves quite a bit. They go to the movies and so on. And so we are moving rapidly towards communism. They say that then life will be very good. I kiss you all many many times.

Mama

Kaunas, February 18, 1962

Dear Nijolė,

I worry that I haven't received a letter from you in a very long time. I've written you, I believe, two or three letters. I've picked out a few names. Did you pick any of them? March and after that April is drawing near. I think about you all the time. If only God gives you a happy and easy delivery. Every day I pray for you to Mary, that she may look after you and your baby. Maybe it was wrong of me to write to you about the package. These are difficult days for you and your health might not be so good. Vida is very good about sending me packages, but sometimes she doesn't send things that are sellable here. There are people here who don't even know themselves what it is that they want. Over the radio and in the newspapers they talk and write a lot about marching towards communism. They think that communism will take hold all over the world. They think that all the colonies will want to get rid of foreign domination and join up with us... I wonder how Ugnė is doing in Paris? There is unrest there. We hear in the news that there is unrest all over the Western world, and that only here there is peace. Whatever they announce, we've heard it all already. I'd like to know more about your country, but the radio buzzes all the time. *(In the Soviet Union it was nearly impossible to hear foreign news. Programs like Voice of America were blocked with static).* Enough of that.

My health is not good. It is difficult for me to breath, especially when I first move in the morning. The wound on my leg still has not healed. Both my legs swell, especially my good leg. I'm losing weight and my appetite has decreased, but that's not important. I am anxious to receive a letter from you. I am so worried. I keep thinking that something bad will happen to you. I kiss you both many many times.

Your loving Mama

Kaunas, March 17, 1962

Dear Vida,

I've just received your letter with the painful news about Nijolė. Dear God, how badly I waited a letter from her. My heart was uneasy over her. And what could have hurt her? Maybe her body was exhausted and that's why it could not support the pregnancy, especially twins. Why didn't God take me instead of those two little children? I am old, after all, and useless, just a burden on everyone. My life is not very pleasant, but what is that compared to the tragedy that has happened to Nijolė? Vida, I beg of you, please write to me and tell me everything that happened with Nijolė, not hiding anything from me, because I will not rest until I know everything in great detail. I kiss you all many many times and I'll be waiting for a letter from you.

Mama

Kaunas, March 18, 1962

Dear Algimantas,

Yesterday I received the painful news about Nijolė. Vida wrote that she gave birth to twins and that both were stillborn. God only knows what it was that hurt her. I think that the news of her tragedy must have reached you. Vida wrote that she was very upset. When you receive this letter of mine write to me right away and tell me everything about Nijolė. I worried over her terribly.

Write about your life and how things are going for you. Why don't you get married? You'll get old and no one will want to marry you anymore. When you were at Nijolė's wedding, you were able to see her well. She looks very thin on her photograph. Does her husband love and respect her? Was she and is she happy? Vida writes that she is spiritually very strong.

My life without you is very very sad. My health is also poor. If my life were good, my health would be better. Here they talk a lot about your country. They say that there are many unemployed people and that there is all sort of crime. Here they keep talking about communism. God only knows what that 18th conference will decide, most likely nothing good. Today are the elections to the Supreme Soviet. Well, that's enough for now. I will be waiting for your letter. I kiss you many many times.

Mama

Kaunas, April 8, 1962

Dear Nijolė,

I've just received your letter, which I was pining for. Vida and Al-
gimantas wrote me a little about your loss. I am troubled over it because
often physical and moral shock can affect your health. What can you do?
I know that it is difficult to accept, but you must take everything that
God hands out to you with patience. Maybe He knows what He is doing?
I believe that God will give you at least one child. I suffer over your loss.
I worry that you won't be overwhelmed by this. Judging by your letter, it
does not seem as though you were weakened by this if you're already
back to work. Eat well and rest. Summer is close, so maybe the two of
you can take a vacation and go to a resort. Maybe vacations are paid
where you are and maybe you get maternity leave too. You might have
less work now, but you no longer need to prepare for exams. Take care
of your health. You've used up so much of your strength and your mind.
Sometimes I wonder whether your exhaustion did not hurt those babies.
There are some who are of the opinion that women who are under a lot
of stress and work too hard can become infertile. In your case, I don't
think you could apply that because you were fertile, only the children
were stillborn. *(The twins had an in-born blood vessel disorder that
caused their death in utero)*.

These days they say that medicine helps everything. Especially
here, our country brags and believes that their medicine is the most advanced in the entire world. It's true, but granted that they've made a lot
of progress in that area, somehow many people are sick. Very often
people suffer from cancer here. We often have shortages of medicine because we are very compassionate and we send our medicines away to
countries that have managed to free themselves from capitalism, like
Cuba, and others... When I think about it I don't think that medicine is
almighty. Most diseases get diagnosed too late and therefore cannot be
prevented. Therefore, medicine is not able to save lives, but scientists
dream of creating lives. Here they reject the idea that God created everything, and they say that life appeared without God. Right now scientists
are trying to create man, but of course, from organic matter. We'll see
how that works out.

Now the young people are growing up not knowing God and everybody is being turned against God and against the "legendary Christ." They say that Mary of the Gates of Dawn was really Barbora Radvilaitė *(a sixteenth century noble woman),* because she looks like her. I could tell you a lot. They've closed down the Įgula Church in Kaunas and I've heard that they'll be closing down others as well.

Lately my head has hurt me a lot. One time I got so dizzy that I almost fell out of my chair; I barely made it to bed. When I get dizzy my heart doesn't do so well either. In general, I don't feel well. Mostly my head hurts and I get dizzy.

Easter is drawing near. I'd like to wish you and Renzo a happy Easter and wish that God may bring you a son or daughter, or both, for next Easter. Good bye. I kiss you both many times and I'll be waiting for news from you.

Mama

Kaunas, May 2, 1962

Dear Algimantas,

Soon it will be May 21st. Your 40th birthday my dear son. That is a long time, but it has gone by quickly. Although there has been much hardship and suffering, and it is difficult to remember them all, especially when I lost all of you and had to end my old age alone. I still haven't given up hope of seeing you again, but when and how? Of course, that is only my hope, which most of the time goes unfulfilled...

I believe that all of you believe deeply in God the Father and that is a comfort to you, as good as any in this world. That is our Catholic faith. I believe that on Sundays and on other holy days of obligation you go to Church, listen to Mass, go to communion, and confession. I recommend to you, my son that you go to confession for your entire life with the Ten Commandments in front of you and the five laws of the Church. I think that you have Lithuanian priests there and the catechism. Buy it and analyze it. Maybe you can also get religious books. Maybe you can get Saint Ann Katherine's "Visions of Christ's Suffering." Saint Ann Catherine Emelich had visions from Holy Thursday until Easter morning. Her visions have been written down in German and were translated into Lithuanian by Talmontas. That strengthens your faith and reveals Jesus Christ's suffering to you. Also, it is a historical document. I think you can probably find it there. Write to me if you cannot get it there and I will send you my copy.

Finishing this letter on the occasion of your fortieth birthday I wish you good health and God's blessing and other pleasantries. Stay well, my dear son. I kiss you many many times.

Mama

Kaunas, May 7, 1962

Dear Vida,

...I haven't received a letter from Nijolė for a long time since she was sick. She wrote that she began working again. When I look at her photograph I am gripped with fear that she is so thin and that she looks old. Even her chest bones stick out. He looks healthy. Nijolė will learn Italian, but will Renzo learn Lithuanian? I don't think so. Lithuanians learn foreign languages. We are a talented nation, but we are also a tragic nation, scattered all over the world. Do all your children speak Lithuanian well? The poor things do not know their homeland, and that homeland is beautiful and rich, but for ages has been worn down by enemies, who always present themselves as friends, as do-gooders. On top of everything you're supposed to praise them and thank them... It's hard to even think about it, talk about it, or write about it.

Recently I received a letter from Algimantas. He has become very conscientious about writing. I wished him a happy 40th birthday, the poor lonely man. He wrote that little by little he is climbing up the ladder at work. He often mentions that he misses Lithuania. Once he wrote that if only he could, he'd become a bird and fly home to his country and live there all the time. Reading his letter, written like that, I became sad and start to cry...

I kiss both of you and all your children.

Mama

Esendon, Australia, May 17, 1962
(Vida's letter to Algimantas)

My dearest little Mushroom, *(In our family, that was our nick name for Algimantas)*

First of all, happy 40th birthday!!! Really, can't time just stand still? It's hard to believe even. Also, a huge hip hip-hurray for your pro-motion to the 4th category. I'm guessing that there'll be a big inheritance waiting for my children, unless you decide to do something about your future. I cannot understand how you can grow used to loneliness. Or maybe I'm wrong?

I don't know if I've written to you that I've taken care of all the pa-pers for Mama to come to Australia. I have to reserve a flight for her. Her papers are at the Australian Embassy in Moscow. They'll send her a letter directing her to take care of her paperwork so that she may leave. Of course, it's going to be torment with an uncertain end. However it turns out, at least from our side we will have done everything that we can possibly do. Much older people have come to Australia from Lithuania. Maybe it'll work out for her. It's been six weeks already that I haven't heard any news from her. Have you gotten anything? Yesterday I mailed her an eleven pound package filled with all sorts of light mate-rials. I don't know if she received the two I mailed her in February.

Everyone is well here, thank God. Andrius is a little boy already. He'll probably out-do the others with his cleverness and originality. Juozas is losing his teeth and is spitting through a huge gap in his mouth. Rasa is in the sixth grade. She is already a young lady. She just com-pleted her examination for the second year of piano. And Marytė is in kindergarten and spends her days singing and playing. Next year she will go to Rasa's school.

By the way, did you complete your studies or did you just leave everything that way, hanging on a thread? Although, maybe you don't need your studies anymore since you're doing well at work anyway. We all send you kisses, the young, and the old, Uncle Algimantas, on your fortieth birthday.

Ficka (Vida)

Kaunas, June 29, 1962

Dear Nijolė,

It's been a long time since I've received a letter from you. I keep on thinking about you and worrying over your health. Vida wrote that you feel tired in the evenings. I worry. I don't know how your finances are. I'm curious how much meat and dairy products cost over there. How much does it cost to get by? It seems as though apartments are very expensive over there. Occasionally someone from your country visits here and, naturally, in the newspapers and over the radio, they talk about how expensive medical care and education is in your country. They say you have to hand over half your salary to pay your rent. It would be wonderful if you could write to me about all this. How much does it cost to eat a meal in the cafeteria? Our newspapers report that you have high unemployment and that people are on strike. Over here there cannot be any strikes and there's plenty of work if not right here that in expansive Kazakhstan. For the moment we have food, but you must stand in line to get it. We are angry at your country for testing nuclear weapons and mixing up all of nature… In July in Moscow there will be a world congress for peace, for universal disarmament, and to ban nuclear testing. There will be 2000 participants coming from 100 countries and they will back your government up against a wall. We'll see what will come of it.

I'd really like for you to write more about yourself. My leg is healed, but both of them swell up. My health is very poor. I've grown very thin, my chest has collapsed, and it hurts. I've been affected by hardship, suffering, and disease.

I will be waiting for your letters. Is your work hard? I know that practicing medicine takes up a lot of time. Here doctors work like slaves. Where is Renzo from? Did you visit his home? Maybe you'll travel to Italy again this year? Is it difficult to get someone to help at home where you live? Someone to clean and to cook? I kiss you and Renzo many times.

Mama

Kaunas, July 22, 1962

Dear Vida,

A few days ago I received from Moscow the documents from your country inviting me to travel to your country. Now I will begin trying to get a passport. Of course, if they let me out, and if I am well enough to travel, I will go. I think the process will take about six months. Lately I am short of breath again, I can't make sudden moves, lift my arms, or especially I cannot lift heavier objects. Starting tomorrow I will talk to the doctors about how I can strengthen myself. Often I sweat and I feel dizzy. The wounds on my legs have healed and if I weren't short of breath, I could walk well. You probably imagine that your Mama is jus the way you left her. But no, I've changed a lot. That anguish, that worry, life without your family eats you like a cancer. And so, if I were to travel to you, I'd be a burden. But I want to go, although I'm terrified of the trip. When you receive my letter write back and tell me how long the trip is. There's no one to ask here.

I am enclosing a list of things that Genė's brother-in-law has re-quested. I don't want to burden you with this, but I need to thank them for all the good they've done for me. That's how I'll end this. I kiss you all and I'll be waiting for your letter.

Mama

Kaunas, August 16, 1962

Dear Nijolė,

Although I received a letter from you recently, I still want to write to you and share my thoughts on our affairs. It's been a month since I received the documents from the Australian Consulate in Moscow, but to this day I've not been able to submit my request for a passport because I've needed so many various documents, photographs, and so on. It took me a month to gather them all. Today a lawyer came to my home. I gave her all my documents. She will write the request and give it to the gov-ernment the next day.

Recently I received a letter from an international organization in Paris that has offered to accompany me until the end of my trip. I will need to notify them when I receive the documents from my country. Genė would accompany me to Moscow, and from there it would be agents from the international organization. Vida wrote that she has registered me with the International Red Cross and that she has paid my fees. I feel much better now that I see the trip is becoming a reality. If I were stronger, I wouldn't be afraid of the trip, but being this sick, some times I'm afraid. Some how I'll do it, if only I get the permission. If they rejected my request this time, then I'd have to try again. It seems that it is very rare for someone to get permission to leave on the very first try.

I've enclosed a letter from Milda Žiulys in which she asks you to send her a medical atlas. Write to her. She didn't dare write to you on her own, so she is writing through me. I kiss you and Renzo many many times.

Mama

Kaunas, August 25, 1962

Dear Vida,

In this letter I want to inform you that I've handed in the documents from the Australian Consulate and the documents for my request for a passport to the visa and registration department of the regional police. I wrote to the Australian Ambassador in Moscow and told him when and where those documents were handed in along with a request for a passport and a visa. I think that it would be even better if you were to write to them because they asked you to inform me. I received their documents on July 16th. It takes a long time here to assemble everything you need for your request. And it's also vacation time. A lot of people are on vacation, and so it takes several tries before you can get things done. It's even harder that I can't walk around on my own, and so I have to ask other people to take care of things for me. Genė helps me, although she does not have a lot of time. And Vincė Kripaitienė. The lawyer came to my house, wrote everything down, took it herself and handed it in, and then wrote a letter to the Ambassador telling him when and where the documents were submitted. Now we must wait for their answer. The lawyer believes that the answer will be a positive one, but we'll need to wait a few months to find out.

Two weeks ago I received a letter from the Red Cross in Paris in which they announced that they'd take care of me during the trip and that they'd even help to get me from my home to Moscow and they'll take car of getting me my ticket. They asked me to notify them when I receive my passport and my visa. It would be good if you could write to this organization. Their representative is in Australia. It makes me feel good that there is someone who will be caring for me during the journey. I am very grateful to you and Algimantas for all your troubles. Maybe God will grant that after all this trouble we will attain our goal.

That's enough for this letter. I'll be waiting for your letter. Nijolė doesn't write. Is she on vacation? I kiss you all many times.

Mama

Kaunas, December 14, 1962

Dear Nijole and Renzo,

With this letter I'd like to wish you both a Merry Christmas and a Happy New Year. I'd like to wish you good fortune, happiness, success in your personal lives and in your careers, but especially good health, which is most important. I can no longer count how many holidays have gone by in which our family has been separated and how many more will still pass because this latest request for a passport, which had given me so much hope, has failed. On the 10th of this month I received a letter informing me that my request has been denied. They gave no explanation why. It hurts... Don't suffer over it, there is enough suffering in our lives already. The lawyer advised that my children should write a letter to our chairman of the cabinet ministry Paleckis and ask him why they will not allow me, a seventy-year-old woman, ill as I am, alone, and with no one here to support me, no one to take care of me, and no permanent place to live, to leave and go live with my children. Vida lately had been trying to get me to go and live with her. I wrote to her that she should write to this address: Vilnius, Chairman of the Executive Board, Justas Paleckis. The lawyer said that many people do it. She will write a letter to Moscow and to Vilnius. You need to make some noise, maybe it'll work.

Someone else told me that I should write to the Soviet Union's representative to the United Nations, Gromyko (I don't know if he's there right now). They advised that I should write to his residence, which is near the Soviet Union's Embassy in New York and that I should ask him why they don't let an elderly mother go, and ask him to release me. I don't know if it's possible to get near him. This is something that you, Nijolė, should take care of. But it's only a suggestion. Who knows if those kinds of things help. I'll only be able to repeat my request in a year. I'll need to repeat all the formalities, including receiving an invitation from you.

That's my holiday surprise for me and for you. My health had gotten stronger, but now I don't know what's going to happen next.

I have enough money right now. I pay 25 rubles a month for my upkeep. There are other expenses. I'd like to ask you, Nijolė, to request a mass for Mindaugas's soul. I dream of him some times. Because we have very few priests left, the line for requesting a mass is very long.

I correspond with Father Gruodis. He is living right now in the Anykščiai region (Balnikų paštas) in a dark and destitute province. He will be seventy soon and he is very ill. It's a lucky thing that Sister Elena Šimokaitė lives with him. She is a nurse and so she takes care of him. Vida sent him some food, but when the package came it had been rummaged through. He prays for all of you; holds mass where he is, and recently held mass for Mindaugas, may God rest his soul.

Do you meet up with Mr. Gringauz and Alexander? And Kotrynėlė too? Send them all my greetings. Greet Mrs. Zaunienė from me. Does Edvardas write to you? Greet him from me. I remember him as a noble youth. Send my greetings to Uncle and Ugnė. Give them all a piece of the communion wafer I am enclosing in this letter. It's from the Aleksotas church. I'd like to have Ugnė's photograph. Write me more often, if only a few words. Finishing this letter, I kiss you and Renzo many many times.

Mama

Kaunas, December 24, 1962

Dear Vida,

I'd like to write you a few more words. My lawyer has written a letter to Khrushchev himself, which was delivered to him in Moscow by Kripaitis. We mailed a second letter to the Ministry of Internal Affairs in Vilnius. And you, Vida, write to Paleckis, like I told you to.

Right now priests are under attack. They even attack the Pope himself. You even are forced to hear all sorts of blasphemous things about God himself. I kiss you all many many times.

Mama

1963

Kaunas, January 21, 1963

Dear Nijolė,

It seems to me that I haven't heard from you in a long time and that I myself have not written to you in a very long time. When I receive a letter from any of you, I declare that day a holiday and I spend it reading your letter over and over again. That is my entire life.

A few days ago Karsokienė and Flora and her husband came by to visit me. They were bragging to me that they'd received a letter from you. *(Nijolė is Karsokienė's son's godmother).* She offered to go to Vilnius to see what she could do about my affairs. She says that she has a good friend there. The commission in Vilnius is made up of a few individuals. Of course, the highest ranking people are involved... They carefully analyze the requests of people who want to leave the USSR and join their relatives. They analyze your entire life; they even dig up the dead and check out their life histories. For example, they are interested in Father Juozas *(Bakšys, who died in 1924),* and Uncle, and Aunt *(Veronika who died in 1951)* and you, who are inviting me. And then they come up with their resolution and send it on to Moscow, where they simply check it over and declare their own answer—either negative or positive. Many people write to Moscow and make contacts there, and for some, it works. Right now I also wrote to Moscow. As it turns out, you won't get anywhere unless you make some noise. Obviously, you should do what you can over there going through our country's representatives or even international organizations. I already wrote to Vida about it. After all, reuniting families separated by war is an international matter, especially when dealing with someone as old as I am. After all, I am 71 and I am an invalid. I can't answer for all my relatives. Of course, they also take into account how much wealth my family had, but they don't count how large our family was or how much debt we had. We lived as we could as was dictated by our times. I personally supported Jewish children who were saved from a certain death. Many Jewish people hid

173

in my home. I took the risk and imposed the risk onto my entire family...

Everything is expensive here. The official buying price for one dollar is 90 kopecks. With that you can buy one kilogram of sugar. Therefore, even if you sell the entire contents of a package, it does not cover the expenses of the person sending it. No one sends money here, only things. Besides, how much does a dollar buy over there and how much does a dollar buy over here?

After I learned that my request had been denied again my health took a turn for the worse. My blood pressure was at 220. The doctor prescribed the same medications again. After a month of being ill, this is only the second day that I'm feeling better.

Pass on my love to Ugnė and to Uncle. I kiss you both many many times and I'll be waiting for your letter.

Mama

Kaunas, February 1, 1963

Dear Nijolė,

I received your letter of January 23rd. There's no reason for you to be referring to yourself as a "black sheep." *(Because of censorship Nijolė could not explain to Mama why she referred to herself as a "black sheep." The reason was that Nijolė knew that the commission knew that she was the widow of the well-known partisan leader Juozas Lukša-Daumantas. Mama did not know this).* Our entire family is a family of "black sheeps" who get in the way of permission being granted for me to leave. There's your father, Father Juozas, Aunt, Uncle, and I myself, because in my name I owned quite a bit of wealth. In their opinion, we're all guilty. Every one of us has been carefully analyzed. The worst culprit is Uncle. So don't worry about it. You can't hurt me. They are counting sins made earlier. Moscow also rejected my request. The road is the same for everyone. Everything is in God's hands. There is truth in this world, only not everyone adheres to that truth and that is why so many must suffer.

Since Christmas I've written you either one or two letters—I can't remember. I'm curious whether you've received them. Algimantas wrote to me that you are looking well; that you've gained some weight. Thank God, it was hard for me to see you like that, looking like a skeleton. I'm so happy that God has blessed you. Vida wrote that she has successfully given birth to a son. All of her children look happy on photographs.

My entire life has passed by in worry and hardship. Other people look at me and think that I've had a very good life. You know yourself how hard it was for me all alone to work and to take care of such a large family. If you were to count how many funerals there have been in our family, you'd see how many of them I had to suffer through alone. The greatest tragedy of my life was that I was not able to leave with you. But how could I have left your two grandmothers to starvation and death without anyone there to care for them? Besides, Algimantas and Mindaugas were still at home. What can you do—that is our fate—both mine and yours. So don't worry about it. Neither you, nor I, nor all of us together are at fault here. Someone has to be the one to be sacrificed... As they say: "If you're not with us, then you're against us." What can you do when we don't think alike or move in the same direction? If I could write down all the injustices here, it would take up pages and pages. The only thing left to say is: Whoever has the power is the one in charge. And so I repeat, do not worry over it, and write to me as often as you can. I will write as well. When I read your letters and when I write to you I feel as if we are really talking with each other. I'd like to finish this letter by sending you and Renzo both a kiss.

Mama

Kaunas, February 3, 1963

Dear Vida,

I received the letter from you that I'd been worrying over and waiting for. Thank God that everything went well. The entire time I prayed to Mary to watch over you during your most difficult hour. Now Rasa can no longer help you because she's back in school. You'll have to do all the work on your own taking care of Algirdukas. You haven't

written to me whether you received my package with the national costume and whether you liked it. At the time I couldn't find anything
prettier. Over here these days all sorts of amateur performers wear the
national costume and it's popular at dances. And those dances are
endless—they dance and dance. You wrote that you'll be mailing me
another package next month. Put in some wool for knitting. I cannot sit
still without something to do. I especially need to move my right hand,
which has been affected by paralysis, so that it wouldn't get stiff. I don't
know if they wear wool mittens where you live. Kripaitienė and I are
planning to knit some pretty mittens for you and Rasa.

All of my requests have been denied. It's like tossing peas at a wall.
Now I'll only have the right to submit another request in a year. I'll have
to do everything all over again. Vida, you should do everything you can
over there to get some attention. They say that there's some sort of an
international organization in Italy. If some sort of an agreement has been
made, why then aren't they letting people out? I think that mine is an
international case and that everywhere else in the world people may
travel wherever they please. I cannot understand why our government
divides people up into children and stepchildren. After all, I have not
committed any crime under their existing laws. And before that I never
did anything to oppose them. Whatever system of governance was in
place, I lived according to its laws. Is it fair to punish someone over the
past?

I've received a letter from Nijolė. She is very upset that my request
has been denied again. I've not given up hope and I've become accustomed to these hard knocks, even though it unnerves me and breaks my
heart that being as old as I am, I do not have the right to join my
children. Oh well, whoever has the power makes the decisions.

I'm going to finish now because there's something like an insect
buzzing inside my head, I'm getting dizzy, and my heart is palpitating.
That heart of mine is never still. I kiss you all from the smallest to the
biggest and wish you all good luck, joy, and God's blessing.

Mama

Kaunas, March 3, 1963

Dear Vida,

A month has passed since I received letters from you and Nijolė. It doesn't seem like a long time, but it's long for me. Only your letters can revive my poor heart; they work better than medicine. I read your letters over and over many times and each time I find something new in them. That period of waiting with the hope of seeing you again has ended. Now the only thing left is for you to go and rattle the doors on the international scene. Here, they still respect international opinion. The way I see it, reuniting families is an international affair. No where is it stated that only citizens of a certain ideology, material wealth, or from a specific socio-economic background may be reunited with their children, especially in the case of the elderly who don't have anyone to support them or care for them. It is cruel. Here, they look closely at your family. Every grown-up takes care of themselves. How can a mother be responsible for the actions of her grown children? Or for her relatives? That's how it was during Stalin's era, and now it's supposed to be different... On the radio and on television they keep singing that same tune... Uncle was mentioned in today's paper. Our countrymen really know how to slander their own...

Each time I write to you I forget to remind you of a few details. Here you cannot buy zippers for long skirts or for dresses. You also can't get thimbles. For some reason Algimantas rarely writes to me. I kiss you all and I'll be waiting for your letters. Have you christened Algirdukas already?

Mama

Kaunas, March 8, 1963

Dear Nijolė,

Today they are celebrating "International Woman's Day" here in our country. All night long I lay awake and thought about my predicament. I've come to the conclusion that we should appeal to an

international woman's organization (there are several different ones in
various countries). We should ask them for help with my affairs. It
seems to me that one international organization or another should have
some sort of influence. You ought to explain my situation—that I am old
and that I am alone and I am very ill. The years are flying by quickly and
with each year I become more and more disabled. I am 72. That is old
age. All these constant shocks ruin my health. I don't have a permanent
home, and even if I did, I am unable to take care of myself without help.
That's how I've become an unwelcome weight on other people's shoulders. It's lucky that I can still manage to stand up on my own two feet, to
go outside into the yard, to walk around a bit. Often I am not well, but I
always manage to get back up on my feet.

I cannot even explain to you what I suffered when I was still living
in Utena and they rejected my request. All the people who I'd lived with
began tossing me out. Now my situation is the best that it could possibly
be. Each month I pay room and board, and I take whatever suits Genė
and Dovilė from the packages and I give it to them. And that's how I am
taken care of. Genė has a job with a lot of responsibilities. She is the
manager of a store. Her work is full of problems and unpleasantness. Her
wages are 65 rubles a week. She leaves the house at 9:00 am and returns
home at 9:00 pm.

Will this always be my situation in life? Times are changing; people are changing. My situation may change soon… The relatives whom
I'd lived with visited me and they were kind to me. Mrs. Vitkus and Janė
visited me several times. Now she's married. My uncles, the Žiulyses,
have also become more pleasant. Their daughter Milda is eager to get
that medical atlas and that woman wants those glasses I promised her.

It's been a long time since you've written to me. Do you still think
that you will hurt me? That's old news that does not have any bearing on
what is going on today, so forget about that "black sheep" business.
They rarely forget to mention Uncle in the newspapers, only now it's
been less frequent. That's the fashion these days. They practically kill
each other and then they brag about themselves… The Atheists have declared war on the Church, on religion, they slander the clergy.

I'm eager for your letters and for letters from all of you. They reju-
venate my soul. Lord! How much I could tell you if we were able to
meet!… Our newspapers write that there is massive unemployment in

Australia. Oh well, I've written all sorts of nonsense. I kiss you and Renzo both.

Mama

Kaunas, April 3, 1963

Dear Vida,

It's Easter now, a holiday of joy and spring. Unfortunately, there are dark clouds in my heart that do not let any rays of light shine through... God knows if that darkness will ever dissipate. Not too long ago I received a letter from Nijolė. Again the poor thing became ill and lost her baby. It is my deepest belief that her body is exhausted and that's why she cannot sustain a pregnancy. She needs rest and good food, but she is suffering over those exams *(at the time Nijolė was preparing for the specialist's exam in pathology).* In addition to all that there is her very stressful work. When I look at her wedding photograph I am horrified—her chest bones are popping out. Everyone is worried that her health wouldn't fall apart completely. I have very uneasy thoughts about her...

May 18th is Dovilė's name day. I'd like for you to send her a medallion with a nice chain and a few reproductions of famous artists' Madonnas. She is fourteen already. She is tall and slender. Her face and her figure is similar to Mindaugas's, may he rest in peace. She is strong; she does a lot of sports. This year she will complete the obligatory eight years of school. Recently there's been a fierce battle against religion. In the schools they force the children to be atheists. Dovilė also does not want to go to church. Well, I've filled up the entire page and I haven't written anything interesting. I kiss you.

Mama

April 8, 1963

Dear Nijolė,

Yesterday an individual came to see me and he recommended that you, Nijolė, take up my case with the General Secretary of the United Nations, and that you should explain the entire affair to him, making sure to mention that in my country I did everything that was necessary and required of me. The individual I'm speaking of was a guest in our country for a longer time and personally visited the Premier. They know each other well. Some are of the opinion that if such an individual were to get involved in our affairs, that they'd be able to help. Well, maybe someone else will have a better suggestion. In our opinion it would be very helpful; things couldn't get any worse.

I keep forgetting to tell you that you should send me a Lithuanian émigré newspaper, of course, one put out by the socialists or communists, anything else, *(as in a conservative newspaper)* will not get through... The newspapers here are terribly boring, but I read them anyway. That's how I am. I want to know what's going on in the world.

Yesterday someone sent you a page that was torn out of a magazine where, among other things, Uncle is slandered. Pass it on to Uncle and when you receive it, write to me. Milda received the book. She is thrilled and thanks you very much. I've received a letter from Vida written January 3rd. She wrote that she mailed me a package on the same day, but I haven't received it.

Here they sometimes play the songs "the little Italian" over the radio. His actual name is Roberto Loretti. Dovilė and I would like to know more about him. Could we get a photo of him? There are none here. We are enamored with his amazingly beautiful voice. I kiss you both.

Mama

Kaunas, April 28, 1963

Dear Algimantas,

I keep on wanting to visit you and the rest of you in my letters. I've written to Vida and Nijolė, now I just need to write to you. You must remember Father Gruodis. He is now living in the most destitute and miserable village in Lithuania. His situation is desperate, especially recently. You must help him. I've asked Nijolė and I'm asking you too to send Vida money so that she could buy him the food and clothing he needs. He's done so much good for our family. It is necessary that we help him in his hour of need. He must live where they've sent him... You must not forget people who have helped you.

Vida would very much like it if you were to visit her. You get vacations, and it wouldn't take that long for you to reach her by airplane. It would make her very happy. I kiss you many times.

Mama

Kaunas, May 12, 1963

Dear Nijolė,

Already two months have gone by since I received your last letter. I know that you don't have time to write, but when I don't receive a letter for a long time, I worry. I'm constantly concerned with your health, and I worry that you'd finally hurry up and finish those endless exams so that you could rest. Prayer has strengthened my health. I'm able to sleep now and my blood pressure has gone down. My head and my legs aren't doing well. It is summer now, so I walk around the yard and sit in the shade. I think of you all the time and I pray to Mary to watch over you. Maybe the Lord will grant me the happiness of seeing you again.

Milda came to me crying and asked me for 20 rubles. They found a cancerous tumor in her mother's throat *(Mrs. Žiulys)* and it's necessary to operate right away, so she needed money fast. Milda is in her second year of medical studies at the Kaunas University. She is very happy over the book you sent her; it helps her very much with her studies. She is 21 already, tall, stout, and a good girl, not someone who leans in the direction of today's way of life... If they really do find cancer there, it will be a tragedy for our entire family.

Although in our country they say that their medicine is the most advanced in the entire world and that our doctors have been able to revive many a patient whose pulse had stopped, notwithstanding all that, today a classmate of Dovilė's is being buried. She died of rheumatic heart disease.

On May 1st Petrė and Elizė came to visit me *(Uncle Karvelis's brother's daughters)*. They were very curious about Uncle and about Ugnė and were able to tell me a lot about their family. All of Uncle's brother's family send him their best wishes.

Soon in our country the price of food, footwear, wool fabric, and other things will increase... It looks as though life is going to get harder. A kilogram of butter costs 4 and a half rubles. That is very expensive. Wages are very low. You can call Lithuania a bottomless pit in terms of food exportation. There are more foreigners here than there are Lithuanians *(Russians brought in to colonize Lithuania)*. In the cities the population has doubled since before the war. Even though they discriminate against us destitute ones *(returnees from exile in Siberia who had no civil rights),* we are still better fed and better dressed than them. They try so hard to tear religious belief out of people's hearts, but there are still believers who remain among us.

Recently some of my old friends and some of my relatives have come to visit me. Their visits cheer me up and lift my spirits. I don't know if you receive all the letters I send you. In a few of my recent letters I'd asked you to send me a "liberal" Lithuanian newspaper, because no other kind would get through. I kiss you and Renzo both.

Mama

Kaunas, May 29, 1963

Dear Nijolė,

Vida is preparing to submit another request for me to leave for Australia. I live with hope and that gives me strength. Last Sunday I was in church for the first time in a year. I'll probably be going for the Pentecost too. Right now my health is stable and I'm not using any medication. I feel good in Kaunas.

They removed a benign tumor the size of an egg from Aunt Žiulys's thyroid. She sends you her greetings. Milda too. The Vitkuses visited me and brought me some food from their farm, although I didn't ask them too. Now they're living well. The Žiulyses and the Vitkuses have invited me to visit them, but I don't want to go anywhere anymore, just to you. In Kaunas my old friends can visit me, I knit a little, I read, I listen to the radio, especially when Loretti is singing, and then on television I watch all sorts of nonsense about religion, about the clergy, and about God himself. Everything is geared toward destruction, so that even one footstep would not remain. There are horrible lectures on this topic. People do everything they can just so that they can drink, sleep around, dress up.

In a few days Dovilė will be taking her exams from the required eight years of school. If she passes the exam she will move on to high school and will be in the ninth grade (there is a different educational system here in the USSR). After the exams are over she and her mother will be going to Palanga.

Genė's parents share a little house with their relatives in the same yard with strangers. This autumn those people are moving out and then Genė's parents and I will move into the two rooms and small kitchen they are vacating. Genė and Dovilė will remain here. That way we will all have a little bit more room.

Vida wrote that you could have gotten by without those exams. You haven't written anything about Ugnė. Elzė and Petrė found out from somewhere that she was married and that she was raising a son. I'd like her photograph very much. Uncle is often mentioned in the press.

In your last letter, I think, I wrote to you that you shouldn't bother looking for nylon with sequins, but people want it after all, especially white. This fabric sells for 15 rubles a meter here. It's easy to sell things that are very pretty and hard to get. There are people in our country who don't know themselves what it is they want. Although, they say that there is equality, only who knows from which end.

Okay, enough confusing you. I'll be waiting for your letter. I kiss you both.
Mama

Kaunas, July 16, 1963

Dear Nijolė,

Yesterday I mailed out a small package with gifts for you and Renzo on the occasion of your birthday. I put in that package amber beads, a woven sash to tie your hair (do you remember how you and Vida used to wear them in your hair?), and a short sash woven by me from yellow, green, and red yarn *(the colors of the Lithuanian national flag, which was banned by the Soviet government).* I've enclosed for Renzo a long, wide ethnic sash (they tie them over the shoulder of important dignitaries here), a neck tie, and an amber tie pin and amber cuff links. Genė put in a wallet and two small table cloths. Now it is very hard to find nice ethnic things with a good pattern. They don't make very many of them, and when they do they're terribly modernized…

I've received your huge package and its many contents. Everything disappeared right away. There was nothing left for me. They say: give it to us, they'll send you something else. Now it is summer and all the women want to dress up. I've also received a package from Vida. Dovilė would very much like to receive a white synthetic fur jacket, a hat, boots, wool fabric for a skirt, and a warm white scarf. If you can't find a jacket like that, send fabric and we'll have one made.

When you go on vacation make sure that you visit Uncle and wish him well from me. These days they write awful things about him in the newspapers. Also go and visit Ugne and give her my greetings. I want her photograph desperately. If you'll be in Italy, I'd like very much to get some beautiful Madonnas, no bigger than 15 centimeters. One I'd give to a certain person. You can send them through the mail. They treat them as art by famous painters. They don't allow other religious articles through. I'll end this now because my head is spinning. I kiss you.

Mama

Kaunas, August 4, 1963

Dear Vida,

On the occasion of your fortieth birthday I sent you, Algirdas, Juozas, and Marytė some gifts: for you there are amber beads, a sash, and two tablecloths. For Algirdas there is a neck tie and amber neck tie pin. For Juozas and Marytė I've enclosed books. These days there isn't anything nice around to buy. 40 years is the doorstep from youth to old age. Although it is not a pleasant step, it is unavoidable. I wish you, most importantly, good health and God's blessing, so that you would become worthy of His rewards and so that one day we would all be able to gather together in one place. There could be no better joy in this world. On the occasion of Rasa's birthday I'm also enclosing a gift in her letter. I kiss you all many many times.

Mama

Kaunas, September 2, 1963

Dear Vida,

Two weeks ago I wrote to you. I don't know if my little package managed to reach you in time for your birthday. I worry that Nijolė hasn't written in such a long time. She's probably already left for Europe, as she'd intended. I keep thinking about Uncle and Ugnė. Look what they do to the greatest patriots, to people who truly loved their country. They ridicule them. Of course, I think that our countrymen are very generous with the slander when it comes to Uncle... Poor Ugnė. How she did not want to leave Lithuania. It's really too bad that she lives so far away from you and Nijolė. Maybe Nijolė might be able to convince her to move to her country? I'd like to have her wedding photograph.

I burden you with expenses and requests. Perhaps Nijolė can take on Dovilė's affairs. I feel very sorry for her. She is just an orphan. Remember, that you two lost your father also. She is a pretty girl, tall, thin, lively, with a strong personality, and fast as lightening. Her shoe size is

38. She'd also need a scarf to go with her jacket. Genė's brother would like an electric shaver. I've lost my hair and so I can't go out without a headscarf. Send me several lightweight ones. You'd sent some very pretty ones with flower prints, but Genė took them both, one for her, one for her sister. I didn't get one and neither did Dovilė.

It's been seven years already since I've returned from Siberia. I've suffered much. Oh, how hard life was... Finally, I've grown used to everything, but I haven't given up hope of reaching you. Everything is stable in Kaunas, unless something else happens. I don't think I'll be returning to Utena or Panevėžys; I've had enough running around. In all respects, living here works out best for me. Genė is at work all day and all evening. Dovilė is in school all day, starting today. Here school children are kept busy all day long... No one has any free time. People are in the yoke all the time.

Well, I've filled an entire page. I kiss you all many many times.

Mama

Kaunas, November 1, 1963

Dear Nijolė,

I've been eager to receive your letter. I'm eager to find out about Ugnė and I'm waiting for her photograph. I'd also be interested in hearing about Uncle. Has God given you anything to look forward to?

Vida wrote that she has resubmitted her request for me to go to Australia and that she has written to four separate places. Maybe if she makes some noise it'll work? I wonder if it would be possible for her to talk to some of the ambassadors from the United Nations?

I myself peck around like a chicken. I don't spend my days in bed like I did before. My health is holding up. Otherwise, life is depressing. I'm not happy for a moment if I'm not working. All sorts of thoughts start spinning in my head. My arm is much better so I knit nonstop. Sometimes I sew this and that, to pass the time. I could weave some sashes and neck ties, but I can't buy any thread here.

Vida wrote that she sent Dovilė two books in English, but we haven't received them yet. Someone, I don't know who, sent her some magazines. I'd like for her to learn English. Some day she might have the opportunity to visit you. You'd recognize Mindaugas in her. On January 9th she will turn 15. In my last letter to you I asked that you send her a nice down blanket. Could it get here in time for her birthday? Your father, may God rest his soul, has a cousin in Utena. She can't hear very well. I read in the newspaper that there is this gadget that you can pin in your hair to transmit sounds and that it helps you with your hearing. When we started asking around where we could get one, we were told that we had to write a request to Moscow. That's an endless process and in the end you don't know if you'll get one. Can you get them in your country?

The Žiulyses send you their greetings. I kiss you both.

Mama

Kaunas, November 10, 1963

Dear Son,

After a long break, I am writing to you again. I've been waiting a long time for a letter from you, but I haven't received one... I don't even know what to think. I don't want to believe that you've forgotten me... I can't complain about my life. Thanks to you (you, Nijolė, and Vida) I am well taken care of, well fed, and dressed. I live with Genė. The years are passing by and I am heading into deep old age. What lies ahead when I will no longer be able to move and to take care of myself? I don't know... My greatest desire is to reach you and God alone knows if I'll ever attain this goal... My entire life right now is all about you... I think about you, I pray for you, and I talk to you in my thoughts. I am so happy when I receive a letter from you! My soul and my body are regenerated. Dear son, write and tell me about yourself. I am grateful to you for asking Vida to take care of my affairs. I'd like it very much if you could go visit Vida. She is separated from the wide world.

Here in the USSR the revolution celebrations have passed. On the one hand, the parade was lovely. Kaunas was decorated and people looked so happy. On the other hand, it is not a very pretty sight to see people standing on line just to buy bread. We live as though on a farm, we raise our own pig; we have our own vegetables, our own potatoes. Genė works in a store, so we don't need to stand on lines. You probably received the photograph of Genė and Dovilė that I sent you. Do you recognize Mindaugas in Dovilė? I kiss you and I'll be waiting for your letter.

Mama

Kaunas, November 24, 1963

Dear Vida,

A few days ago Vincė Kripaitienė and I visited the Vaitiekūnases. We visited with them for a few hours. We talked, but we were not able to get deep into conversation because they were absorbed with the loss of their pensions. I carefully approached the subject of your writing to me and asking me to visit Algirdas's parents. However, she asked that I do not tell Algirdas's father about that, because it is a sensitive topic. I did not find out why their pension was revoked. They were very reserved and fearful in an almost pathological manner and refused to trust us enough to open up to us. Knowing how things are these days, I don't see why they are so afraid and so private. When I was getting ready to leave I asked what I should write to you and your husband. They said to write that they were alive and well. I invited them to visit us over Christmas, but they said absolutely not. They mentioned that you rarely write to them. They were planning on chiding you about it. I could visit them more often, but they did not look like they were interested. They live their lives isolated from others. So, write to them more often, and since they're no longer receiving a pension, try to help them some more.

Since you are planning on sending a package in January, put in a light blue wool sweater for Genė's fifteen-year-old niece. Put in a nice nylon blouse for her mother and a sweater for him (he's tall). Send Dovilė two sweaters, a corset for me, scissors, plain soap and bath soap, scarves, socks. Enough of that for now. I kiss you all many many times.

Mama

Kaunas, December 2, 1963

Dear Vida,

Christmas is almost here. I don't know what words to use to send you all my greetings and wishes. Christmas brings us all great joy. I'm afraid to even to count how many Christmases have gone by bringing only sad longing... When I gather up all my strength I dare to seek out hope and with brave eyes see the flickering light of hope. I can't let hope die! And so I send you, Algirdas, and all your children, much much joy and the Lord's blessing. It would be very good if on Christmas Eve all of you could have your picture taken at the table. I'd like very much to see such a photograph. Probably Algirdukas will already be able to sit at the table either on his mother's or his father's lap. He might even be walking already.

Nijolė is expecting again. If only God gives her a healthy baby this time. This is her fourth pregnancy already. Maybe this time she won't overwork herself, now that her exams are over.

I am being tormented by a cough, just like every winter. Here people still decorate Christmas trees at home on Christmas Eve, but in the schools they decorate them on New Year's Eve. I kiss you all together and I'll be waiting for your letters and photographs.

Mama

P.S. We did not receive the English books you sent us. Could you check and see what might have happened to them.

1964

Kaunas, January 12, 1964

Dear Nijolė and Renzo,

I received your letter of December 19th on January 10th. It took three weeks to reach me. The mail might have been slow over the holidays. You cannot even imagine how happy I am that things are going well for you. When I don't receive letters from you for a long time, I think of you constantly, I even dream about you, I say the rosary and pray to Mary that she would watch over you and not let that tragedy repeat itself. *(The loss of Nijolė's and Renzo's babies).*

I've received an internal passport and am permitted to live wherever I want within the territory of the Soviet Union. But they will not rehabilitate me and therefore they will not return my property in Aleksotas. *(Under the Soviet law exiles to Siberia had to be rehabilitated for their alleged crimes against the government in order to enjoy basic privileges).* Not too long ago Uncle's brother returned from the East. He was treated in the hospital and now he's feeling better. His daughter and her family were also able to return. The cross that stood on the corner near Uncle's farm was found in the morning chopped down and cut apart in pieces. Your godchild, Genius Karsokas, will be returning this summer after serving in the Soviet army. He sends you his greetings. His parents are very poor and he doesn't have any clothes to wear. If you can, send him fabric to sew a suit, one that would be usable in the winter and in the summer, some undergarments, and a sweater. He is tall and thin.

The holidays have passed. I was in the Basilica for the first day of Christmas and for New Years. Aldona Marcinkutė came to visit me. Otherwise life is as usual. The young people pass their time doing sports, dancing, having fun—they are encouraged to do so by a wide variety of political leaders. They get married very young and they divorce quickly. In the schools they are trained to be atheists. The newspapers ridicule the Church and the clergy... In Lithuania people get enough to eat, but they drink vodka to excess—the old, the young, women, men, young girls, and even children. I can't imagine how they can afford it. The wages here are so low...

Do you ever see Alexander and his father? Pass on my greetings to him. Pass on my greetings to Mrs. Zaunienė and Lionė. Don't forget the medical journals for Milda. I kiss you both.

Mama

Kaunas, February 23, 1964

Dear Nijolė and Renzo,

I don't know if I'll be able to write you an adequate letter. I have so much to tell you. On February 16th we received a package from Vida with gifts for Dovilė, which took four months to reach us. Dovilė admired everything, and left happily wearing her new shoes to the skating rink. She came home with black and blues because she didn't know how to skate with figure skates and fell despite the fact that she is a good skater. The next day she went out not feeling well. The day before yesterday I received both your birthday greetings and Vida's, as though you'd planned it that way. I found Renzo's photograph in your letter. He is very good looking and has a pleasant smile. On the back of the photograph he signed his name in Lithuanian. I found a nice birthday card inside and a handkerchief that customs did not charge me a tax for. I am grateful to you both for remembering my birthday in such a pleasant manner. I'd like to get a nice photograph of you too. It's hard for me to look at your "skeleton." I'm sure you'll manage to gain some weight. Every morning when I wake up I look at Renzo's photograph and I kiss it. Vida also sent me a birthday card, and photographs of Juozas's first communion and photos of Vida and Andrius. Vida looks very good, except that she is a little too heavy. A few days ago I'd dreamed that I was reading letters from you and from Vida. Lately I dream of you often and think about you constantly, especially about you. I keep praying to the Virgin Mary to watch over you.

Today I received your package. It was so large that Dovilė and Genė could barely manage to carry it home from the post office. When I opened it my eyes lit up. There were so many fine and beautiful things inside. Dovilė is delighted and can't contain herself. Everything suits her perfectly. Her girlfriends are jealous of her and they call her the "American." What a beautiful scarf Renzo sent me. Give him a kiss from me, Nijolė.

That relative will send you the prescription for the hearing aid (it is being discussed by a commission of doctors). She desperately needs the hearing aid because she works in an office, has to talk on the phone often, and she can't hear. Life is difficult for her. Dovilė cannot find the words to express her gratitude for the beautiful gifts you've sent her. I kiss you.

Mama

Kaunas, March 22, 1964

Dear Nijolė,

Easter has come quickly this year and again I'm in that same mood... I don't know what to wish you and Renzo anymore. I think that the best thing would be to wish you good health and that your baby be born healthy and beautiful, and that he or she would inherit everything that is special about both of you. I'd like his or her name to be Christian, like Mary, which is the same in every language, and that the ethnic name be Rėda, which I believe does not change from one language to the next. Rėda was the princess of Pilėnai. She was intelligent and brave. She fought the crusaders until her son, Margeris, escaped imprisonment. They'd captured him while he was a small child. If you have a son, I'd like his name to be Konstantinas. He was the Caesar of Rome, and, I believe, the very first Christian. He placed one of the nails that had been used to nail Christ to the cross inside his crown. He gave the Christians their freedom and condemned death on the cross. Besides, Konstantinas was the name of your father. The second name should be Mindaugas. He was a king of Lithuania who made Moscow tremble. Mindaugas is also your brother's name. Of course, these are only my suggestions. The final decision is up to the parents. That God may bring him or her happily into this Godly world. Yesterday I received a letter from Grandfather *(Father*

Gruodis). He thanks you for your packages and your greetings and he will be offering holy mass and other masses up for you. I'll be waiting for news from you. Write even just a few words about how you are feeling. I kiss you both.

Mama

Kaunas, May 11, 1964

Dear Vida,

Yesterday I received the package with the gifts for Genė's sister. All the things in there were so pretty. As soon as she brought it home from the post office, the neighbors came running over to have a look, and soon our house was filled with noise and confusion. This package took three months to reach us. "Spurgutis" (Genė's sister's two month old baby) was soon dressed in the clothing you'd sent. Here people absolutely adore dressing up, partying, dancing. Otherwise, they complain that life is hard. All the packages I've received are treasured and beautiful, only I'm like some sort of a leech who keeps on sucking your blood. The worst of it is that when I sell the things you send me I don't get as much as you had to pay for it over there. That bothers me.

Right now my greatest concern is Nijolė's condition. Everything must be over by now, happily or unhappily. I'm eager to get news from her.

Because I'm weak right now, I've asked Mrs. Kripaitienė to check in on Mr. and Mrs. Vaitiekūnas, but she knocked and knocked and no one answered the door. We'll go there together after the Pentecost, maybe they'll let us in. That's enough for now. I'll be waiting for your letters and your photographs. I kiss you all.

Mama

Kaunas, May 17, 1964

Dear Nijolė,

Yesterday I received your letter and telegram. I am incredibly happy! When I took your letter into my hands not only did my hands begin shaking, but my entire body. When I opened the letter and read it and found that there was still no news, I calmed my nerves and stoically decided to wait patiently. A few hours later they delivered your telegram. May God give you the health to raise her. It would be much better if you could nurse her yourself. Will you be able to get a good caretaker for her? You'll probably want to go back to work. The Lucia is popular in Italy I think. *(The Lithuanian spelling for Lucia is Liucija. Mama would have referred to Lucia as Liucija.)* Rėda is a Lithuanian name, and so both names are special for you. Besides, your own sister's name was Liucija. *(Mindaugas's twin who died in infancy).* When you recover and when Lucia is a little older, have a photograph made. I'll be waiting. You did not write what day in May she was born. How much she weighed and if she looks like you or like Renzo. The best thing would be if she looked like both of you, but most importantly that she grows up healthy and intelligent. A few days ago Vida wrote that you've asked that she be the godmother. But she complains that she doesn't have anyone to leave her children with and that she doesn't have the money for the flight. I can't figure out how she and her husband get by financially. My expenses would not be that big if I could pay for things myself and my medical care weren't so expensive. I live from the packages you send me, although I have to hand everything out to everyone. It's a good thing that I get along well with the regional doctor. She visits me each week. She checks my blood pressure, the thickness of my blood, she sends a lab assistant to my home to do a cardiogram. All of that is expensive. This time the cardiogram showed a scar that was the result of a heart attack.

Often I think to myself that I'm some sort of a leech who sucks your blood. Maybe God will grant an end to all this nonsense soon... Maybe I will somehow reach you.

A few weeks ago Aldona Marcinkutė came to visit me with Laima Vitkauskaitė. *(Aldona and Laima were Nijolė and Vida's classmates in high school. Laima became an ophthalmologist.)* They stayed for three hours. It was pleasant to remember old times. People say nice things about Laima. I've heard that her ideology is different from that of her parents. I'll go to see her about my eyes.

Do you correspond with Algimantas? He writes to me for Christmas and Easter. He tells me that he often goes to stay at the youth camp *(Camp Dainava near Detroit)* and that he's done a lot of work there. It seems as though that youth camp is very dear to him, that it reminds him of his homeland. Even in the middle of winter, when there's no one there, he goes and wanders around. I'd like it very much if you invited him to be Lucia's godfather. You can have two sets of godparents you know.

Father's relative just cannot get that certificate for the problem with her ears. The doctors are afraid to give it to her... They all recognize that hearing loss is related to sclerosis and nervous disorders, but no one will tell her how much of her hearing she has lost. She really needs that hearing aid. I kiss the three of you. Greet Vincė for me.

Mama

Kaunas, May 18, 1964

Dear Vida,

Two weeks ago I received Nijolė's letter and telegram. She gave birth to a daughter, Lucia Rėda. I am so incredibly happy that everything went well. When I took the letter into my hands and later the telegram, not just my hands, but my entire body began to tremble. Some time ago I cried in my dreams. I was told that I would receive a great joy. And it has happened. Now the only thing left is for my affairs to take a turn for the better. How happy it would make me if you and Algirdas and Algimantas would go to the christening. Couldn't you get someone to take care of your children for two or three days? Nijolė ought to pay for your plane tickets. You paid her ticket when she came to Marytė's christening.

Whenever you send me packages always include polyester, wool, or silk scarves. Everybody took every last one out of my last package. There was one that was very pretty with black stripes, but Grandmother took it and I was left with nothing. You must send Milda some fur for her coat. As though they'd planned it, both Milda and Flora came to visit me at the same time. They wanted to read the letters from their god-mother, and in one of those letters you'd written that you'd sent a package to Flora. If you're sending to Flora, then you must send to Milda as well. They are both your goddaughters.

My health is much better, almost as good as it was before. You asked who takes care of me when I am sick? Genė's mother is here at home, and so she helps me. Otherwise I try to do whatever I possibly can for myself. Now all the danger has passed. Greet Mrs. Gudeliene for me. I kiss you all.

Mama

Kaunas, May 21, 1964

Dear Algimantas,

Today is May 21st, your birthday. 42 years ago on this day I held a tiny screaming baby in my arms and I couldn't fathom how a grown man could grow out of such a tiny little creature. I dreamed that when you grew up that you'd be a comfort and a support to your mother, and that you'd be a good citizen to your country, and a good man before God. I was not wrong. Although you live far from your homeland, you live in your mother's heart always. And I also can feel that your ties with God are close. On this special day I wish you a happy birthday and wish you everything that a mother's heart is able to wish: good health, joy, and the ability to remain a decent man before God and your homeland.

On the 15th of this month I received a letter from Nijolė, saying that she has successfully given birth to a daughter, Lucia-Rėda. I'd like very much for you to visit her on this occasion.

I wanted to send you a gift, but I'd been ill and haven't been able to go out and look for anything. I'd like to know what you'd like to get. I thank you for your support with my packages. I'll be waiting for a letter from you. I kiss you many many times.

Mama

Kaunas, July 19, 1964

Dear Nijolė,

I've missed you while waiting so long for a letter from you. I believe that Lucia brings you and Renzo great joy, but also a lot of worry. Has she gained a lot of weight? You'll exhaust yourself doing it all alone, and then you'll have to go back to work. Does Lucia eat well and sleep well? She's probably laughing and cooing already? She probably can't grasp anything yet, she's too young.

Here in the USSR expectant mothers are given 55 days vacation before the birth and 55 days after the birth, two weeks of paid vacation, and the right to take three months of unpaid vacation. Take good care of your health. You need your health right now more than ever before. No one will take the place of a mother for Lucia. They say that if you had to choose between the worst mother and the best aunt, that still it is better to take the mother.

In the USSR not very many women can raise their children themselves at home. Everyone is required to work because the father's wages alone could not support the family. From one year old babies are given over to nurseries and the mother picks them up in the evenings, after work. Many people are of the opinion that the nurseries do a good job taking care of the babies. It's true that the nurseries are clean and the food is good. Pigs grow well on a farm, but an infant is not a small animal, an infant needs a mother's love and not the arms of a stranger. I could say a lot on that topic, but I don't think it would be right for me to do that...

I'm eager to receive a letter from you with photographs. I worry that Lucia would not get sick and that you would not get exhausted. My health has gotten better again and my mood is much better, I have hope again... Did you receive the birth certificates? This time I sent them registered, so that you could check up on them.

Do you ever see Alexander and Kotrynėlė? I'd like to write her mother a letter, but I've lost the envelope with her address on it. Maybe Alexander's father might know the address? Greet Mrs. Vincė from me. Vida wrote to me that her husband died tragically. I hold onto my opinion that she will recover, that time will heal the wounds, and that she will live the remainder of her life happily. I kiss all three of you. Pat Lucia on the thigh for me.

Mama

Kaunas, July 21, 1964

Dear Vida,

Yesterday I received your package and it was ripped and disheveled. When I checked I found that everything you'd put in it had survived. I've sold most of it. Genė's brother-in-law is very happy with the electric shaver. Their child is doing well. They call him "the American" because he's dressed in the clothing you sent them, even though it's not American. They also call Dovilė "the American" because she dresses tastefully and well. When she wears the clothing you've sent from your country, people can't get over how nice they look. There's one blouse with fabulous designs on it. The beach bag that you sent is very interesting, and the towel is like a flag. Dovilė and her friends went swimming in the Nemunas River and they held up that towel so that it would blow in the wind. I almost forgot to tell you. Genė's brother-in-law broke the glasses you'd sent him. He asks that you send him a few more pairs, because, he says, they're very good quality. Maybe the things that I've ordered are more expensive than I can get for them. They are enough to cover my expenses, but I always must make it up to people for their help.

I'm thinking of going to visit the Vaitiekūnases together with Genė's brother-in-law. He'd bring me there; I'd introduce him. Maybe that would cheer them up. I feel sorry for them. I kiss you.

Mama

Kaunas, October 14, 1964

Dear Vida,

I waited a little while and I'm writing again. I've received a letter from Nijolė, one that I'd been waiting for a long time. First of all, she's afraid to leave Lucia with a stranger. Secondly, she did not receive the birth certificates I sent her, neither the ones I sent through regular mail nor the ones I sent through registered mail. I don't know what to think anymore. Now I've made four copies and I will send them all in various manners. You ought to receive one; mail it to Nijolė immediately. They tell us at the post office that international mail and packages do not get lost. I wrote to Nijolė and told her that she should not harm her own health while taking care of Liucija. Tell her that she shouldn't worry so much. As hard as it is to leave her baby with a stranger, she has no other choice when she has no relatives there to help her. She sent me photographs of Liucija. She looks beautiful. I kiss you all.

Mama

Kaunas, November 17, 1964

Dear Nijolė,

A week ago I received your letter with the invitation for me to go live with you. I went to my lawyer to see what he would advise. I'll gather together the necessary documents and will write a request for an external passport and an exit visa. It will not be complicated to put together the request because I already have all the copies and originals. But it takes time for the regional government to put together their papers. As soon as I submit my request, I will write and tell you. I've learned from my lawyer that you can't send birth certificates through the mail, that you must request them through your consulate in Moscow or through the Department of Foreign Affairs. It's too bad I didn't know that earlier, I wouldn't have wasted so much time. Some of the certificates are in the archives in Vilnius. I found my marriage certificate in the archives in Utena. The lawyer also told me that an actress had come to visit our country from your country (*most likely Rūta Lee Kilmonytė*) and that she brought her grandmother back to the United States with her. There was also a journalist who came here and sped up the process of getting his parents released. She advised that you ought to do the same. Of course, there's no reason for you to come here, but Renzo could come as a scientist with a scientific project or exchange, and of course, he'd have to bring proof that I am your mother. If I couldn't leave with him, at least he'd be able to make sure that I'd be released. Everybody recommends that you ought to get things moving through authority figures in our capital. Maybe now that the government has changed, it might be easier.

Don't worry so much about Lucia if she has a good nanny. You'll ruin your health over it. I haven't given up hope about coming, even if I won't be much help to you, at least its better to have a family member in the house during the day. I'll be waiting for a letter with Lucia's photographs. I kiss you three.

Mama

Kaunas, December 9, 1964

Dear Nijolė,

Christmas is near again, and the holidays have not brought any changes in my life. Always those same worries and those same hopes. May this be the last Christmas I pass in loneliness and longing... I've received a letter from Vida. They are all well. They are planning on expanding their house after the holidays. If she did not receive the birth certificate, then you should receive one mailed from Poland by a teacher who is going there. She'll let me know if she got it past the border, only we don't know if it will get through their border. I've learned from various sources that they don't allow official documents to be mailed. If they get through, it's only because they weren't noticed.

I've gathered together all my documents and one of these days soon I'll submit my request. I'm enclosing communion wafers from the

Vytautas Church. Send some to Uncle and Ugnė together with my greetings. I kiss all three of you.

Mama

(There was a post card enclosed with a picture of children feeding birds and squirrels. On the backside these words were written: Merry Christmas to you Liucija and a happy New Year. I wish you well and that you grow big and come to visit your grandmother. I kiss you many many times, you little rolly poly. Grandmother)

Kaunas, December 19, 1964

Dear Nijolė,

I haven't received any word from you and so I am writing again. I'm very curious as to whether you were able to receive even one of the birth certificates I sent you. I've sent them in various ways: through Vida, through Algimantas, Marytė, and through Poland. If you haven't received them, then you should get one through the Consulate in Moscow or through the Ministry of Foreign Affairs. My birthday is February 10, 1892. The date of my wedding was July 20, 1920. I handed in my request on December 15th. There are some people around who are of the opinion that those Jewish children, the ones who I hid during the German occupation and whose lives I saved, and the others who hid from the Nazis in my home, *(Bella Baroniene and her daughter Dina Baronaitė)* could help me now. These people recommended that I ask them to write a letter describing how I hid them and that I should include it along with my request. I think that Alexander's father would know how to write this kind of a document, he is a lawyer after all. I don't have Kotrynėlė's address or Dina's address. Mrs. Baronienė is dead already. He could help me put together and edit such a letter so that it would read as a request that I be released to join my children. He could send the letter directly to the passport office in Kaunas. The address is Laisvės Alėja Nr. 6 or he could send it to me and I would pass it on through my lawyer. *(Alexander's father, Dr. Samuel Gringauz, since*

1957 had been looking for ways to reach Nijolė, so that he could help Mama.)

I've already sent you a Christmas letter with a pretty card enclosed for Lucia. Right now she won't understand what it is, but when she grows up she'll have that first Christmas card from her grandmother. I'll be waiting for news from you. I kiss you many many times.

Mama

1965

Dear Nijolė,

Three days ago I received four letters from all of you (two were from you). That was a big dose of medicine for me. There's one person who tells me that you should appeal to the United Nations Committee for Human Rights and explain my situation to them. I'm beginning to have hope. The most important thing is that my affairs be discussed in the capital; from there they give the orders to our locals. Everything, in my opinion, is being hindered by my social standing. In this system a former capitalist is their greatest enemy.

From your letters, Nijolė, I gather that you have a lot of trust and enthusiastic hope for me. I'd recommend that you should not put too much hope into this because if it doesn't succeed you'll be very disappointed. I've already been through that a few times. If I would not succeed in leaving, my situation would be wretched. As long as I can remain on my feet, things aren't so bad, but if I were bedridden again, then that would be bad. Then I'd have to request to be placed in an old age home. You must do everything you can to get me out of here. I have not given up hope. I think that all the effort you've put in so far will make things happen. Only, I beg you to take care of yourself. If you become sick that would be bad for Lucia and for me.

I know of one family where the husband and children had left for the West and the wife had remained behind. His request was denied seven times. Only last year was she allowed to leave. He was an officer and a government official in the Zarasai region. His last name is Šlepetys. I don't know what city he lives in, only I heard him mentioned on your radio. *(Voice of America).* Our press mentions him often... Greet Mrs. Vincė and Lionė for me. I kiss all three of you.

Mama

Kaunas, February 7, 1965

Dear Nijolė,

Last night I dreamed of you and Vida, probably because I think about you all the time and I pray for you all the time. If only God grant that we meet again... These days in the newspapers and over the radio they're talking about how important leaders from your country and from my country will be exchanging visits. Maybe we could use this situation to help me somehow... For some reason a strong hope is reborn in me— only that we were not disappointed this time, like all the other times... Not many have been allowed to leave after they asked the first time; mostly people leave only after they've made many requests.

My health has stabilized. Of course, I'm not quick on my feet, but I won't be reaching you on foot... Recently a very old couple I know left for Australia to live with their daughter. They wrote that the flight took a day and a half, but it didn't make them sick. When my affairs take a positive turn, we'll have to get in touch with that international organization that takes care of people along the way, like Vida did. Well, it's still early for that.

Is Lucia running around already? She'll be nine months old soon. Children of that age often begin walking already. She might even be talking already? Ugnė learned how to walk and how to talk when she was eleven months old. A well-known pianist from your country is coming to visit our country. We'll hear him play on television. I kiss you all.

Mama

Kaunas, February 25, 1965
(A letter from Vincė Kripaitienė)

Dear Vida,

I thank you for the gifts. Everything is so nice and so pretty. I also would like to thank you for your letter with the Christmas greetings. The letter is very dear to me and very interesting. I could imagine your life completely.

Your Mama is doing fine. She energetically does battle with all her illnesses and with all of her other problems. Her high blood pressure is the hardest on her. Sometimes I'm afraid to take her out of the house because of her high blood pressure, but she doesn't give in and says she absolutely must go. Most of the time she returns in a better mood and in better health than when she first went out. Her wish to see the people who are dear to her and her hope gives her strength and the desire to live. And that hope, it seems, this time is greater than it has ever been before. Nijolė has found all sorts of means this time. But the surest means, in my opinion, would be for Nijolė's husband to travel here on some sort of a scientific project and to take care of Mama's affairs and then to take her back home with him. That has worked for others. The more opportunities, the bigger the hope. The problem is that the minute things go wrong it saps her strength and immediately her blood pressure rises. A new dose of medicine and new hope puts her on her feet again.

No matter how she is feeling, she keeps herself busy. Most of the time she knits. When she runs out of yarn, she unravels an old sweater and starts a new project. Her knitting is getting better and better. Each sweater she knits is prettier than the last.

Dovilė is a good girl; she is a good student, she's serious, and that brings comfort to her grandmother. Only that she wouldn't spoil her too much. She also gets along well with Genė. The worst is with Grandfather *(Genė's father)*. When he is sober he is not a problem, but when he gets drunk he becomes arrogant and says all sorts of terrible things. In general, he is a person who doesn't have much sympathy for others and doesn't understand much of anything. He does not even understand that it can be difficult for someone who has a heart condition to breath in his cigarette smoke. But your mother has learned how to accommodate herself to his tantrums. As long as she is well enough to walk, she doesn't need much from them.

In general your mother has many friends who visit her often, and so I think she is seldom bored. If she does have any unpleasantness at home, she can handle it by reminding herself that soon it will all end and that her new living accommodations will be much more comfortable. You will always remain a stranger among strangers. She rereads your letters constantly and she has practically memorized them by heart. Each letter she receives does her more good than a dose of medicine.

Right now people are getting the flu. It's the third week already that I haven't been out of the house and so I haven't visited your mother in all that time. A few times I've asked my husband to visit in my place because there were things to take care of with the new forms. I received a letter from her three days ago (we write to each other often) in which she complains that she isn't feeling well. It has been cold lately. This morning the temperature was 22 below Celsius, and so we've had to cut short our weekly meetings.

We don't know what direction our lives here will take. The future will show us.

I wish all of you, from the smallest to the biggest, all the best.

Vincė

Kaunas, March 10, 1965

Dear Vida,

Yesterday I received your letter. I'm making an exception in this letter for Milda. When you send Vincė her package, enclose some light-weight white fabric for Milda, something that would be suitable for a wedding dress or wedding suit, stockings, and some pretty white under-garments. Send some black fabric to sew a suit for her husband, shirts, and socks. Do this for me and use the money that Nijolė and Aligimantas sent to you.

Milda's fiancée is a medical student in the second year. He is 26, and has already served in the army. Here most often men marry when they are 18, before they go into the army, and then when they return they bring home a Russian woman with them. *(Under the Soviet system all young men were required to serve in the Soviet army for two years).* Girls also marry very young, but then divorce quickly. This is a huge topic and I couldn't possibly do it justice in this letter.

Because I don't have my own home and am forced to live in other people's homes, I am in an unpleasant situation. If God grants that I may see you again, then I will tell you about everything. It is impossible to write it all down. Do not be sad if God's will is otherwise and He calls me to Him. After all, I lived many years on this earth and I am in poor health... Well, I kiss all of you. I live with the hope of seeing you again.

Mama

Kaunas, March 30, 1965

Dear Vida,

I am writing this letter to tell you that my request for an exit visa has been denied. *(This was the fifth rejection).* This time around I'm not that upset over it, because I have bigger hopes. Also, last Sunday I received a letter from Nijolė with some real promises in it. Nijolė will write to you herself about it. Alexander and Kotrynėlė are helping to take care of my affairs.

Lately I had a check up, and I was told that my health had not deteriorated any further. All I need is peace and quiet, a good mood, and most of all, hope...

This year Dovilė is in second place as best student in her class. She could have been first, but she would have needed to study harder. At home, besides me, no one cares about learning. She is Mindaugas all over again. She is pretty and ambitious, doesn't socialize with just anyone, and doesn't run around like other girls. Yes, she does like to dress well, but she is neat and she is not lazy. We get along well and we often discuss serious subjects. I spoil Dovilė because she is an orphan. By dressing neatly and fashionably she gets more confidence, and that is very important. She orients herself well and is talented. Conditions are very bad right now, but she is able to tell good from bad and that will be her saving grace.

One doctor here is asking for a device to check blood pressure. I don't know if that costs a lot of money. And the nurse who injects my medicine has asked for a pretty dress for her two-year-old daughter. I kiss you all.

Mama

Kaunas, April 6, 1965

Dear Nijolė,

I received your letter a week ago. I read it holding my breath. Those children (I call them children only because I cannot imagine them all grown up) would be God's gift to me. The gift that would rescue me from this absurd reality. That would be the greatest joy in my life, although I do not have much longer to live. Please thank Alexander's father for all his care and concern over my well-being. Please also thank Alexander and Kotrynėlė from the very bottom of my heart. I cannot even find the words to thank them properly. Maybe someone will hear out the request of those poor children whose lives were in such danger? I'd like very much to receive a copy of the request they wrote, but in Lithuanian. I have no reason to believe that those letters would disappear along the way. My hope is much stronger now, knowing that such people are looking out for me. I believe that the good Lord will listen to the prayers of those children.

I gaze at Lucia's photograph and I cannot get enough. It seems to me that she will look like both her mother and her father. The most important thing is that she grow up healthy. A few days ago I received a letter from Vida. Milda is preparing for her wedding at the end of July. She asked Vida for wedding clothes, and Vida has already mailed them out to her. Vida is renovating her house right now and she is complaining over how much it costs and is wondering how they will get by. Algirdas sends many packages to his own parents. His parents have had their pensions revoked and his mother can no longer work. I kiss the three of you.

Mama

Kaunas, April 25, 1965

Dear Vida,

I've just finished reading your letter and I'm rushing to reply and tell you that nothing new has happened in my life besides my digestive troubles. It's been two months already that I've been tormented by my digestion. I've had to learn how to watch what I eat. A week has gone by in which I'm feeling alright. Otherwise I can't complain about life. I eat well, I have clothes on my back, thanks to you, children, and I'm not out on the street yet. My moral and spiritual life is floundering though. With those words I express the state of my soul. I could only open up my feelings to you, children, but in person. Only the hope of someday reaching you keeps me going. Mindaugas, may God rest his soul, was saved from prison as a prisoner of war with the help of Kotrynėlė's mother, Mrs. Baronienė and a few other Jews. I still hold onto the hope that my fate will somehow be determined by the fact that I saved those innocent children. Nijolė will explain to you how all of this is coming together.

(When Mindaugas was conscripted into the German army, he used his uniform to help save those children. Their handwritten accounts of how they were saved with Mindaugas's help are attached to the documents.)

Thank Mrs. Gudelienė for remembering me so fondly. Those three years we spent living together under the same roof while in the bloom of our youth have left an indelible impression on me. I've not received Nijolė's letter. I received Algimantas's Easter greeting on Easter morning. He wrote the same thing to me that he wrote to you. Does he send you money to help out with all of my expenses? He keeps writing that he spends every weekend in a Catholic atmosphere at a youth camp where he doesn't feel so lonely. It is a great joy to me that the three of you have not lost your faith. Here it is tragic how people have lost their faith.

Now I will change the subject to another topic—that of packages. I've not yet received your last package. This one will be for me exclusively, and for Dovilė. I will write to you again next Sunday. I kiss you all from the smallest to the biggest.

Mama

Kaunas, May 5, 1965

Dear Nijolė,

I've missed you, it's been so long since I've heard from you. I'd feel better if I'd at least just get a few words from you telling me that you are well. In a few days it will be a year since Liucija saw God's beautiful world for the first time. Is she walking and talking already? I think of her often and I see her face in my thoughts.

I am eager for news of my affairs. Who can tell if they're doing anything about it? I've not given up hope. Maybe the fact that I saved those innocent children will now influence my own fate? I was able to have Mindaugas, may he rest in peace, removed from the prison camp with the help of Jewish friends. I'd like to have Kotrynėlė's photograph. I kiss the three of you.

Mama

Kaunas, July 12, 1965

Dear Nijolė,

I've received your letter of June 24th, which I'd waited for with such anxiety. Now I want to write and explain to you how things are decided in our country, so that you would understand. I asked my lawyer, who is seeing to my affairs, and the affairs of many people like me, and who knows the situation. As far as she knows, these affairs are decided by a small committee of people. Whoever this committee decides to grant an exit visa, receives the exit visa. Moscow only confirms it. The committee does not add its own resolutions. Therefore, we know that all requests go through officials in the capital *(like those of Alexander and Kotrynėlė and others.)*

If those officials do not approve of a resolution, a request for an individual to be granted permission for an exit visa, then the request is sent on to our capital and left to the discretion of the commission. The decision is made based on their competency. Unless the officials in Moscow grant permission for an exit visa, there is little chance that the commission in our local capital can grant the exit visa. For example, a few years ago our country's leader visited your country and those people to whom he'd promised an exit visa, received the exit visa. There was an actress who came here *(Rūta Lee)* and she was able to receive an exit visa for her grandmother. And there was a journalist who came over here and was able to secure an exit visa for his parents.

You asked whether it would be possible for me to go see Chairman Paleckis. Yes, if there was a need, I would go. I couldn't do it alone, but I'm sure somebody would be able to help. To this day I haven't heard a word about my affairs. I think that I ought to get some sort of an answer soon.

I'm very happy that you are all well, and that Lucia is running around. I'll be waiting for photographs of Lucia and all of you.

Mama

Kaunas, July 25, 1965

Dear Nijolė,

I keep thinking about my affairs and always I think of something new to tell you. Remember, you wrote once that if it were necessary, that Renzo would come to Moscow and that he would bring along documents regarding my release. I thought about that from all angles and I've decided that Renzo really should not come here. I don't know if his coming here would help me, but I do know that it could do some harm. You'd be so worried about him until he returned. They could accuse him of spying, arrest him, and hold onto him. That happens often in our country. The only way he should come here is if he were to come with a group of tourists or some scientific exchange. According to our country's international agreements, citizens from your country can come here to participate in cultural events. Then, of course, there would be no danger, and he could speak to some officials about my affairs.

The last time I was hospitalized it was at the hospital on Jakštas Street. There was a doctor there, her name was Dr. Vainorienė, and she was rescued from the Nazis by Lithuanians, just like Alexander and Kotrynėlė. There's also a Dr. Šrafienė who had a similar experience and many more.

That person that Alexander and Kotrynėlė wrote to is dead already. To this day I haven't received any sort of announcement. Yesterday I received a letter from Vida. She is so worried over my health and all of my affairs, that I worry that she doesn't frighten you. My heartbeat is irregular, but don't worry about it. It is God's will. Without Him, we can do nothing. All of my responsibilities in this world have been completed, only your responsibilities are huge... If it is God's will that we never meet again in this world, then don't lose hope, we will meet again in the world of souls. And so we should remain strong and have hope.

Mama

Kaunas, August 28, 1965

Dear Nijolė,

I've received your letter and I understood everything. I'm afraid to be happy too soon because I've been disappointed so many times before. I've not given up hope though. Thank Alexander, his father, and Kotrynėlė for all their efforts on my behalf. I don't have anything more to thank them with, but God will make it up to them with His blessing. I often remember that time I met Alexander's father and mother, when they came to say good-bye to Alexander for the last time. I remember her moving words. I believe that the Lord will grant me the opportunity to see them again and to press them to my heart, now, all grown up. I think of them all the time and I feel a mother's love for them. After so many years meeting them again would be very emotional, but joyful. Ah, but the greatest joy of all will be to see all of you together again, to press you all to my heart, and to never let you go again. I believe that the bright sun will shine on our faces and dry the tears that have flowed down our cheeks all these years... Well, enough sad thoughts for now. I kiss you all.

Mama

Kaunas, August 31, 1965

Dear Vida,

I've just received your letter and I'm very upset over that my package has been tampered with. It's been four months since your last package. I'm waiting impatiently. Although according to the list you sent this package didn't contain that much, what it did contain was expensive and of good quality. I'm impatient for the sweaters, for the yarn, for everything that was in there. Dovilė is impatient to get the slacks. True, I have a little money saved, but I'm afraid to live without something in reserve. If I were given permission to leave, I'd have to take someone along to Moscow and that would double my expenses. And if I were to get sick, I'd need to be hospitalized, and then there would be the expense, even though medicine is supposedly free here. Now, I'll wait for your next package, because I don't expect to ever see this one. I'll repeat once more what I'd like to receive: Sweaters, bathing suits, and so on. Don't send food. My digestion is not as bad as it was before. The infections have healed and I've learned how to regulate my diet. I cannot drink that delicious coffee you used to send because it causes my heart to race, it makes my heart beat like a bird trapped in a cage. When I'm not upset, my heart does better. Mood is important, and getting a good night's sleep. I don't buy anything myself nor do I cook. I pay Genė's mother and she cooks for the entire family. And if I need anything special, Dovilė runs around town until she finds it for me. Vincė also would not be doing so bad, if she had some peace and quiet. Right now she's knitting herself a suit from the yarn you've mailed her.

That's enough for now. I must write to Nijolė today as well. I kiss you all and I'll be waiting for your letters.

Mama

Kaunas, September 3, 1965

Dear Nijolė,

I'm writing to you again on the same old topic. I want to illuminate you on how affairs like ours are managed in this country. You need to constantly stay on top of things, because these things are never rushed. I am convinced that we will still need to try several more times before it works out. I am very curious how you know that the request written by the children, which was handed over to Paleckis, was received positively? Up until now I haven't received a single scrap of paper about it. Miss Narkeliūnaitė must already be in Lithuania. Will she really be visiting me, and most importantly, will she really talk with our officials? You ought to know that these things are not done lightly in our country. I'm waiting and waiting, but we'll see. I kiss you all.

Mama

Kaunas, September 5, 1965

Dear Nijolė,

I've begun writing to you almost every other day. I keep thinking of something new I must tell you. I read the newspapers every day, but there still is no mention of Miss. Narkeliūnaitė's visit. I don't know if she'll visit me for real. *(The journalist Salomėja Narkeliūnaitė traveled to Lithuania at that time. She promised that she would visit Mama.)*
I've heard that Ugnė is moving to New York. If that's true, then that's a good move. *(Ugnė came to New York to further her studies at Columbia University and to earn a Master's degree.)* There are many Lithuanians there and that's important for Christopher to be able to learn his native language. She will probably also feel better among her own people. Poor Uncle. They keep writing all sorts of nonsense about him in the press.
I live with hope still and I have reason to believe that I won't be disappointed. I understand how this country works... You've probably

received my letters in which I've explained how things work here. I'm curious to know more about Ugnė. Pass on my greetings to Mrs. Zaunienė and to Lionė. I kiss the three of you.

Mama

Kaunas, September 20, 1965

Dear Nijolė,

I've just returned home from the basilica and I'm rushing to write you a letter. Today I prayed for the first time with the rosary beads you sent me, and I offered up a mass in thanks to the people who are helping me right now. This night I lay and tried to think of ways to write to you and express how thankful I am to the guest from your country. You will not believe the positive impression she has made on me. When I saw her, I was shocked, she took my breath away and tears came to my eyes. Although you'd written to me that she'd come to visit me, there was no way I could imagine how that would happen. I think that I was impolite to her, that I was cold, and that I didn't know how to properly receive such a guest... She calmed me down and told me not to cry, she told me to smile, not to be sad. She filmed me. She photographed me. I smiled through my tears. She promised to do everything she could to help me. I answered her most important questions. It would not have been helpful for me to tell her too much and we didn't have the time for it either. What I couldn't say in words, I said with my tears. I believe that she understood me.

After a few days had passed since her visit, I was able to calm down and to stop my tears. First of all, you must thank Mr. M. *(Mr. Micaras, who passed on Alexander's and Kotrynėlė's letter to Chairman Paleckis)* and Miss N. *(Narkeliūnaitė)* for her concern and the sacrifices she has made for me.

Writing this letter my eyes fill with tears again... I've regained hope where I'd had none. When I begin to think, what am I guilty of, when one of my relatives is their enemy? I lived under a different form of governance... I don't have any education, I'm only self-educated, I've been a widow for thirty-two years, left with four small children, and two grandmothers, having lived through the horrors of war and having seen all of it. I understand all of it because I am 74. I am a human being who has a mind and who is capable of understanding all sorts of situations and who knows what to value. I've never been involved in any sorts of politics nor was I ever a member of an organization. Alone I had to provide for a family of seven. I knew nothing but work and worry. During the German occupation I hid two Jewish children, and for that my entire family could have been shot, as we all knew from all the official announcements. These children were brought to me when the German soldiers, using dogs, were tearing children out of the arms of their mothers. I had to keep them hidden in my house and that cost me my peace of mind. But they remained alive and today they are professionals and they are raising families of their own. Besides these children, there were many other Jews, who were in danger, and who also spent hours, days, nights, hiding in my house under my protection. I shared my bread with them. My situation was difficult. I had to support a family of seven while supporting them.

Therefore, when I think it all over, when I reflect on it, I am upset to think that our own countrymen are the kind of people (I don't know how to even say the words that describe them) who are maybe intellectually deformed and while living comfortably themselves cannot and will not accept responsibility. They do not understand other people at all and they close their eyes to them, so that they would not see their hardship and their sorrow.

The permission to obtain an exit visa is determined by a handful of our own Lithuanians. They shout: everything for the people. Man is friend to man, a buddy, a companion. Those are beautiful words on paper, but in real life they are ready to drown you in a spoonful of water. People are enemies to the people, a wolf, a beast, when you must have anything to do with them.

In my ripe old age I may find myself in the position were I will have to go knocking on the door of an institution for the elderly. There will be no one to take care of me. I have a great hope that the people from your country will save me from that fate. Keep up your contacts with them. I think that I will have to submit one more request to our country's leaders. I'd like to ask you to read them this letter of mine. I cannot say out loud in words what I've put into this letter.
Mama

Kaunas, October 3, 1965

Dear Nijolė,

Today it is still Sunday. Those words, spoken by that precious guest, keep ringing in my ears, "Don't cry, don't be sad, we'll do everything we can..." And I feel so good, so happy, so hopeful... But then the dark clouds return and you end up in an uncertain situation. I torment myself this way, waiting and waiting... I dreamed of you worried; I thought that maybe my letters upset you? I want to tell you everything, everything that weighs on my heart, so that you would understand my situation. After all, it all started during Stalin's times, when no one cared whether you were guilty or not-guilty. All they cared about was whether they disliked one of your relatives. The entire family had to answer for it if they did. I've analyzed my life and am trying to find what I could have done to be considered guilty by them. Of course, they don't like my family, but that was during Stalin's reign. Now they've rejected him; they've even removed him from his grave. It would then follow, that everything that he had damned, ought to now be redeemed...

That's our nation's fate. Now we're scattered over the entire earth. I think and I think. I think that it would be a good thing if all of our countrymen were to return to their dear homeland and that they would live together like true citizens of their own country, and that they'd all love each other like family, and that they'd put aside all their quarrels, fights, disputes over politics and ideology, and that first and foremost they would feel inside themselves that they are all Lithuanians. In my thoughts I round them all up into one big embrace. They are all that dear to me. Our homeland is so beautiful, so rich, and it feels so good to live here... That's my view on life, on my homeland, and on my nation...

Unfortunately, I am too weak, too old, but my heart and my mind are young, and are pushing to reach you... I'm very eager for your letter. I'm very interested in what kind of an impression my dear guest will bring back to you? I'll finish this letter by asking you to pass on my greetings to my dear guest, and to tell her that I believe in her words, and in her actions. I kiss all three of you and I'll be waiting for dear news from you.

Mama

Kaunas, October 11, 1965

Dear Vida,

Yesterday I had a good opportunity to travel to Vilnius to visit the Mother of God at the Gates of Dawn (Petrė Karvelytė drove me in her car), but I did not have the opportunity to visit the basilica after all because before we left I suddenly had a lot of trouble with my digestion and only now have I been able to get up out of bed and write to you. For an entire month I was so happy that I was getting better, but something in the food caused a huge revolution in my body. For two days I did nothing but drink water. So what can I do if it is my fate to suffer not just spiritually, but also physically? God alone knows if anything will come of all this worry. I can still hear that whisper in my ear, "Don't cry, don't be sad, we'll do everything we can." Oh, how I treasure these words! It seems if only I could, I'd hug that treasured guest of mine to my heart and hold her there, so that she could whisper to me over and over again, "don't cry, don't be sad."

That so-called free medical care, that I seem to need so much of, is very expensive. Sometimes I'd like to just go across town, visit a friend or two, and put myself in a good mood. But I can't do that alone. Vincė alone helps me, but she has her own problems, and her health is poor. And so I end up sitting in the same place all day listening to all sorts of nonsense over the radio, especially about perverted monks, slandered priests, and so on. Rarely can I see a decent film that is not propagandistic. That's why I curl up in bed and daydream. That's how time crawls along as I await my final end. Nobody here has any use for me and everyone would only be too happy to see me go. Although, now the Žiulys family is inviting me to stay with them, I don't want to go stay with them, nor do I want to return to the Vitkuses. If there no longer will be any possibility for me to live here, then I will go to an institution for the elderly. What can you do? People live there too. I get along well with Dovilė; we understand each other. Genė has a good heart, but you need to have more than that.

And now let's take care of business. The people here are wild. City people, but especially people in Kaunas, want all sorts of fancy things. Although wages are low, everyone here is used to stealing, but they don't value the things that they steal, they want to buy what is most beautiful or modern; they like to dress well, drink, party. Salesgirls swindle as they can by cheating people out of kopek here, a kopek there. They really want corsets for large and for average figures, men's and women's sweaters, scarves, and so on. Do you sometimes find left-over yarn in the stores? If you do, I could knit mittens out of it. I've learned how to knit mittens with patterns, and that keeps me busy. I cannot live without work. I've written you all sorts of nonsense, but that is my fate. Forgive me. I kiss you all, the big ones and the little ones.

Mama

Kaunas, October 17, 1965

Dear Nijolė,

A few days ago I received your letter and all the great hope that it contained. It's as though rays of sunshine have broken through thick clouds. Some sort of inner intuition is telling me to prepare for my journey. I begin thinking about what I should bring with me, and then suddenly the thought enters my head—no, it can't be! And then I hear that dear guest's words in my ears again, "Don't cry, don't be sad, we'll do everything we can." All this time, when those dark waves overtake me, those words come back to me and bring me hope, "Don't cry, don't be sad..."

I cried when my guest filmed me and photographed me, and you cried when you saw the pictures of me crying—and so we both cried. Perhaps God will feel pity for us, for my tears and your tears, and will bring us together again.

I'll have enough money for the trip to Moscow. Genė and Dovilė are preparing to accompany me. I want to remind you once more that these kinds of things take time here, and so it is hard for me to say when I will reach you. The most important thing will be to receive the letter announcing whether I'd been granted an exit visa. Maybe we will need to make one more request, to remind them, so that it wouldn't take too long.

However it all works out, I am in the mood to plan this trip. I felt it when I received your last letter. Pass on my greeting to my dear guest (I can't call her by any other name). I kiss the three of you all together. I can see in my mind how Lucia plays and can hear her coos. I'll be waiting for her photograph.

Mama

Kaunas, October 18, 1965

Dear Vida,

Today I am writing letters to all three of you. A few days ago I received a letter from Nijolė with the dear hope of seeing you, which I still can hardly believe. That hope, which up until now had been covered by thick clouds, has shone through, and an inner voice inside of me keeps telling me to prepare for the trip, but then sometimes the dark thoughts come back and darken everything. Maybe God will take pity on our tears and our suffering and will allow us to be all together and happy at least at the end of my life.

I keep forgetting to tell you that you should include a leather belt in your package for Dovilė and some pretty fabric, and that you should put in some fabric that we could sew a blouse from. They sell blouses with short sleeves here, but I need one with long sleeves.

I still cannot imagine how all of this will turn out. It seems as though it were impossible, unreal, but then my dear guest's words come back to me, "Don't cry, don't be sad, we'll do everything we can." Those words reinvigorate me. There's nothing more that I could write about myself. My thoughts keep revolving around the same thing. I'm getting ready to go and visit with your husband's parents and to tell them the good news.

You haven't written to me yet and told me whether you received my birthday greeting—the postcard with the puppies and kittens. I kiss you all.

Mama

Kaunas, October 21, 1965

Dear Nijolė,

In this letter I want to tell you about the state of my health, keeping my trip in mind. I don't have any news yet, but since your last letter something inside of me has changed. The darkness in me has been enlightened because of hope. Even though I still don't know anything for sure, my intuition tells me to prepare for my trip. And I'm thinking about my trip. Because my health is so fragile, I am worried about the journey (they say that if you prepare yourself for the worst, things will work out for the best). That's why I'd like to describe all the details for you. You wrote in your last letter that you would meet me. That is fine. There will be someone to take me to Moscow, but on the trip from Moscow to you I will be alone. This is where I worry. You wrote that I shouldn't take anything with me. I do have to take a few articles of clothing with me, after all (I only own a few pieces of necessary clothing). My wardrobe is suited to my figure and my age, so if I didn't bring it with me I'd have to go out and buy new clothes right away. I can't have everything sewn to my specifications. I'd look like a monkey. I can't really carry anything or even lift anything. I walk by myself only out here in the yard where I can grab onto the fence, otherwise, out on the street or in a larger room, I must hold onto someone's arm. I get dizzy easily and then I fall. Besides, I walk very slowly and easily become short of breath. When I finish a course of medicine, I can usually breathe easier for a while. I will do that as I prepare for the trip. In one of your letters you wrote that you have a person who can accompany me. I'd need someone to accompany me from Moscow to you. You must take care of that. Send my regards to my dear guest. Her words ring still in my ears, "Don't cry, don't be sad…" I kiss you all.

Mama

Kaunas, November 1, 1965

Dear Vida,

Today is All Saints Day and also All Souls Day. I've offered up mass for all the dead in our family. Remember them, Vida, yourself. I don't know what to write to you. Nijolė's last letter has given me so much bright hope that I'm even afraid of what would happen if that hope were to be extinguished. I daydream and I dream about one and the same. I'm waiting and waiting for that letter. God only knows if it will happen for real this time... If only I don't be disappointed... If only at least this one time all this nonsense would end at last.

The summer was cold in Lithuania and now is over completely. All of the leaves have fallen off the trees. In Australia the leaves must never fall from the trees, and you probably never have to light the stove. How is Rasa doing? Did she win her contest? How is Juozas and Marytė? Andrius is probably already in kindergarten. And Algirdukas must be talking already. When he turns four, you should send him to preschool. Rasa must be able to help you during vacations. How are your finances? Your debts? How is Mrs. Gudelienė doing? Send her my regards.

And now about business, again. Dovilė would like some clips for her hair. When she goes out without a hat her hair flies in all directions. She says that our hair clips don't work. She'd also like some combs. We also need pins with heads—we need them for sewing. Put in a lot. Don't forget the scarves and bathing suits. And I'll finish here. I kiss you all many times.

Mama

Kaunas, November 28, 1965

Dear Nijolė,

I know that you are as eager to hear from me as I am to hear from the Police Station, but I still don't have any word. When I handed in my documents, I was told it would take three months. I don't think they'll answer me any sooner than that. The committee's decision is sent on to

Moscow for approval, and it takes time. They don't hurry. If that high official *(Chairman Paleckis)* promised an answer when he took the request, and if the answer was positive, and then he passed it on to the committee, then we should receive a positive answer.

I don't know if you've received all the letters I've written since my dear guest visited me. In those letters I explained to you how these things are taken care of in our country. I've written about everything, thinking that because you are young, you might not understand it all, and how it affects me and my life.

For now I have nothing else to tell you about besides prophetic dreams, hope, and as yet unfulfilled daydreams. That dear guest's words keep on giving me hope and keep reinvigorating me. I've heard that right now most people who ask are granted permission to leave. Even during the reign of the harshest tsars, there had been moments of amnesty. Our country is celebrating an anniversary this year. I'll finish this boring letter of mine. I kiss you all many times and I'll be waiting for a letter from you, one that confirms this hope.

Mama

Kaunas, November 28, 1965

Dear Vida,

When you tear open this letter you'll think that it will contain an answer. Unfortunately, not yet. When I'd hand in my requests, I'd usually need to wait about three months, because the committee must send their decision on to Moscow for approval, and until the papers go back and forth, it takes that much time. It doesn't matter if I must wait longer this time, as long as the answer is a good one. Probably Miss Narkeliūnaitė must already have a promise from Chairman Paleckis if Nijolė is that convinced that it will really happen.

Waiting is hard, but what can you do if that's our fate, just as long as the outcome is good... I kiss you all and I'll be waiting for your letters.

Mama

Kaunas, December 8, 1965

Dear Nijolė,

Today, at my lawyer's advice, I submitted a letter asking why it is taking so long to receive an answer. I asked that I be granted an exit visa once they'd reviewed my documents. Of course, the lawyer formulated the letter and I signed it. Many people who don't receive an answer write those kinds of letters. My lawyer recommended that you too write such a letter and that Alexander and Kotrynėlė do it too since their words are also on your request. Perhaps Mr. M. and Miss N. could also submit letters because they submitted their requests. They submitted the request directly into the hands of Chairman Paleckis, and so they may ask him about it. The letter must be written in Russian. The lawyer advised that I most definitely do it, because in her opinion, they might be waiting for my reply or perhaps they need some more documentation. It's been more than three months already without an answer, and so it's time to start bothering them. Everyone does it. Often requests for exit visas get lost in the paperwork and lie there until someone calls attention to them. Other people go and ask in person. Maybe that might help. That's how things are here. I kiss you and I haven't given up hope.

Mama

Kaunas, December 8, 1965

Dear ones,

Christmas and the New Year are almost here. We had expected to celebrate these holidays together. Unfortunately, fate has disappointed us. What can you do? It does not depend on us, it is not for everyone to know joy in this life... And so, I wipe away a sad tear and send you my heartfelt greetings for the holidays. May this be the last holiday that we spend separated in foreign lands. I've enclosed Communion wafers, so that our souls might be joined on Christmas evening. I'm also enclosing a postcard for each of you, suited to your age and occupations.

I've not yet received any news about my departure. Today I've sent a letter asking why it is taking so long. I will write to Nijolė and ask her to write a letter as well. I'm anxious to receive the packages because I've begun wasting my reserves, and I need money to get to Moscow. I try not to spend anything in vain, but the expenses keep coming and coming. For me to remain without a kopek is the same thing as going and knocking on the door of the institution for the elderly and asking for a bed.

November has been cold here. At night it's been minus 19 degrees outside. But now in December the temperature is above the freezing point and it is raining and sleeting. That's enough for now, enough of what's weighing on my heart. Finishing this letter I'd like to wish you a Merry Christmas again, and kiss you all warmly.

Mama

1966

Kaunas, January 12, 1966

Dear Nijolė,

   Yesterday I received long awaited letters from all three of you. This is the second time that's happened. First of all, I'll start with my affairs. On the 8th of this month I received a letter from the Ministry of Foreign Affairs telling me that my last request has expired and is no longer valid. The time limit ended in December and now I must submit a new one no sooner than March. I must absolutely submit that request. Even if I were to receive an exit visa through the request made to Chairman Paleckis, I would still need to have submitted an official request registered with the police. There was no mention of the request made to Paleckis in the letter. What has happened is clear to me—those letters were handed to him in person, and so they are either still with him, or if they were handed over to the appropriate agency, they are lying around somewhere being ignored. You absolutely must bother them about it because that's how things are done around here. In a word, I could tell you a few jokes about this, but I'd rather not do that in a letter... Here bureaucracy and papers rule. I've already given you a few examples of this. I'm sure that you must have figured this out for yourself by now. It's a very good thing that Miss N. and Mrs. T. wrote to them. The Ministry of Foreign Affairs will either tell you the same thing they told me or they won't answer you at all, because they'd written to me.

   Now the first thing you must do is to send me an invitation again, which is necessary for me to file another request, and make sure you write and tell your Consulate in Moscow that you've sent me another invitation. They will send you the appropriate documents to attach to my request. Do that as soon as you can so that I could resubmit my request in March. It takes three months for them to respond to a request. When the request is submitted, if necessary, I will go and see them myself about it. Therefore, I ask of you, take care of my invitation as quickly as you can.

So much about that. I'm grateful to Miss N. and Mrs. T. for taking such care to help me with my affairs. I cannot think of my dear guest without breaking into tears. Her words are still with me, "Don't cry, don't be sad..." Those words give me hope, give me strength, and the energy to keep going... For some reason I think that I will reach you by August, unless a miracle happens... In our country words flow like water, only actions take a very long time. Well, what can you do? As long as everything works out in the end, it doesn't matter how long it takes. This time I am firmly convinced that the miracle we've been waiting for for so long will take place... Especially when such people are helping me... I fear that I no longer will be able to thank my friends for all they've done for me. The Lord God will reward them for their good efforts.

You wrote that you've decorated my room and that you've bought me furniture. Don't make such a fuss over me and don't go to such expense either. I'm accustomed to a hard life (I live in a corner right now) and it's enough for me. If only that I'm able to reach you; I don't need anything else.

I look at Lucia's photograph and I am amazed at how fast she has grown. Thank God that the Lord has blessed you. May everything go well this time. It is not good to raise just one child in a family. Usually that child is sad, lonely, and most of the time he grows up to be selfish, an egotist. If God gives you another daughter, I'd recommend the name "Gema." She was an Italian, and when she was 21 she was recognized as a saint. The name is easy to pronounce in Lithuanian, and I think in Italian as well. For her Lithuanian name I would choose "Jūratė." I think that would also be easy to pronounce in Italian. And if you were to have a boy, I'd suggest "Tomas"—I think it's the same in Italian. As a Lithuanian name I'd suggest "Vytautas" because it is a historic name. Though, in the end, choosing a name is a parent's job. I don't sleep at night, but instead I pray the rosary and offer up the third part for all of you. I heard during a homily that it is especially important for parents to pray for their children. They say that prayer is powerful. Pray can break down stone walls and melt ice. I pray the way I know how to pray, and it is good enough, as long as I feel strong enough and I don't let go of hope... My health is stable, but just barely. I have good days and I have bad days. If only I could have peace and quiet.

It seems as though I've written everything in this letter that was important. I'll be waiting for news from you. Genė and Dovilė thank you for your greetings. They all send you and your entire family their regards. Pass on my best regards to Vincė and Lionė. Pass on my greetings to Mrs. Šodienė and Muska. I kiss the three of you many many times and I'll be waiting for your letter.

Mama

Kaunas, January 13, 1966

Dear Vida,

Two weeks ago I received letters from all three of you at once. That's the second time that's happened to me. My affairs have still not been resolved. Nijolė wrote that Miss N. and Mrs. T. sent letters of inquiry asking why they haven't yet released me. I've also written and sent a letter of inquiry. I still need to put in an official request through the regional police office because Nijolė's invitation expired in December and is no longer valid. I've asked Nijolė to mail me an updated invitation, which I will submit with my request. Those are the rules and the protocol. I am sure that this time they will grant me the exit visa, but it is taking longer than all of you had thought it would.

You asked whether Dovilė has taken her exams? In our country everyone passes the exams notwithstanding how well they've studied, but then when they take the exams to enter the university the students who do not pass are not invited to study at the university. Of course, there are other ways of getting into the university... Dovilė is a strong student, so there is no question of whether she will pass her exams or not. Her favorite subject is Physics, and then comes Chemistry; although she is also good with languages. Genė and Dovilė thank you for your greetings. They send their greetings to your family. I will finish now. I am convinced that this year everything will work out. I kiss you.

Mama

Kaunas, January 14, 1966

Dear Nijolė,

A few days ago I wrote you a long letter and I thought that I'd told you everything, but when I looked over the details of my affairs, I realized that there was more I needed to tell you. Yesterday Vincė Kripaitienė came to see me. We talked about everything in great detail and we came to the conclusion that I should personally go and see Chairman Paleckis and the Ministry of Foreign Affairs and ask them where those requests are, which had been personally hand delivered him. We've decided to send Mr. Kripaitis to go and see him on my behalf. He knows how to handle these kind of things. When the Kripaitises had to get documentation that they had been unjustly deported to Siberia they wrote ten requests to the Vilnius Supreme Soviet and to Mr. Khrushchev himself. When they didn't receive a response, they went to see one of their good friends in Vilnius who intervened and went to the Ministry and asked where those ten requests were and why hadn't any of them been answered. At the Ministry they searched for them in their archives and they found them misfiled. If they hadn't inquired, those requests would have lain there for who knows how long. Only once they'd gotten things moving and had gone one more time to the Ministry, were they able to solve their affairs and receive a response.

In your letter you mentioned their hearts. They have no hearts. All that they care about are their personal bellies, which are stuffed to satisfaction, and anything else is nothing but words on paper for them. They don't care that some old lady somewhere is suffering. It would only be better for them if she keeled over and died quicker. It is a very good thing that Miss. N. and Mrs. T. wrote those letters of inquiry. It's also a very good thing that you wrote and that Alexander's father wrote. You wrote to the very Ministry that makes the decisions on these questions.

Mr. Kripaitis has promised me he will do this for me. First he must ask for three days leave from his workplace, and then I must write him a power of attorney document. You, Nijolė, must write that letter of invitation and send it to me as soon as you can, so that I can resubmit my request in March. Even if they were to grant me permission to obtain an exit visa through Chairman Paleckis, I'd still have to go through all the formalities. They wrote to me and told me that our last request from

1961 has expired and that it is no longer valid. That one had been submitted in Utena and it was according to the letter of invitation from Algimantas. Two requests were submitted in Kaunas—one under Vida's invitation, and one under your invitation. And so you see how "careful" they are about keeping records. Whatever they come across, that's what they answer. I happen to know that the letter of invitation from 1964 has also expired, but they didn't mention that one, but then they didn't mention the letters of invitation from last June and September either. Either those two are lying around somewhere in Chairman Paleckis's office or they have been passed on to the appropriate office and got lost there. That's why we must inquire and get them to look into it.

Send me one of the photographs that Miss N. made. One of your Father's relatives has asked me for my photograph, but I have none to give her, besides my passport photo. Dear Nijolė and dear Renzo, don't make such a fuss over me and don't go to any expense decorating a room for me. I'm accustomed to hard living and I don't need much. All that I need is to lay my weary head down besides yours. Take care of your health, so that the tragedy that occurred with your first babies doesn't happen again. I'll write to Grandfather *(Father Gruodis)* about you. His prayers will help your baby's birth go easily. Oh! If only I could get there in time for the baby's birth! I kiss you three and I'll be waiting for when that hour will come when I will press the three of you to my heart.

Mama

Kaunas, January 17, 1966
(By telegram)

I've received permission. I'll see you in three months. Mama

Kaunas, January 17, 1966

Dear Nijolė,

Today I received the permission to receive an exit visa and to be able to travel to you. I believe that this Easter we will all celebrate together.

Pass on my most heartfelt gratitude, everything that could possibly fit in my heart, everything that I could never possibly put into words, to Mrs. M. Miss. N. and Mrs. T., and to Alexander's father, and to Alexander and Kotrynėlė. I will never be able to repay them all or thank them enough. The Lord God himself will make it up to them. You, Nijolė, for all of your suffering and for all of your sacrifice for the sake of your poor mother will be repaid through the Lord God through your children. That's how I will finish this short letter. Your country's Consulate in Moscow has been informed. I think that you'll be able to work out all the details with him. I kiss you, Renzo, Lucia. May God bless you.
Mama

Kaunas, January 17, 1966

Dear Vida,

Today I've received permission to be able to go to you. I believe that this Easter we will all celebrate together. I thank you and Algirdas for all the good you have done for me. I don't think that I will be capable of thanking you enough and of repaying you—that the Lord will do through your children.

Vida, you were planning on sending two packages in January, do it. If they don't get here before I must leave, Genė will receive them. I will borrow money from her right now for the trip, and I could repay her through the packages. I've had to spend some of the money that I'd saved for my trip. I'll have to borrow from her, and that's why I need the packages. I'll finish this letter now because I'm getting dizzy from the good news. I kiss you all many many times.
Mama

Kaunas, January 18, 1966

Dear Nijolė,

I'm writing you the third letter in a row. My lawyer has written a letter for me in my name to your country's Consulate in Moscow, asking him to execute my paperwork as quickly as possible. She told me that sometimes the Consulate can hold up the visa process for three to four months. She advised that I should write to you and ask that you write a letter, asking the Consulate to move quickly with my affairs. The Consulate had told me earlier that as the mother of an American citizen, I do not have to wait in line for a visa. Tomorrow I am going to see the regional police. I am bringing the forms and the photographs for my visa. I no longer have any more business with my country's officials. I will no longer have to write anymore requests. Now the only thing left for me to do is to write to your Consulate in Moscow and to worry about my health, so that I'd have the energy to make the trip. Through all these troubles my health had taken a turn for the worse, but now I feel incredibly calm. Genė and Dovilė will travel to Moscow with me. So then maybe God will help me reach you safely. Our reunion is not that far away. This is the miracle we'd been waiting for so many years... Those few remaining months of waiting will fly by as if in a dream. Oh, that the Lord may grant me the strength I need! I kiss the three of you.

Mama

Kaunas, January 30, 1966

Dear Nijolė,

Yesterday I received your letter and I was so happy that my telegram reached you before my emotional letter. I wrote that letter crying bitter tears and I'm sure that you cried too when you read it. After that letter I wrote two more that I'm sure you've also received by now. You'll find everything that I needed to say at the time in those letters. In my telegram I wrote that we'd see each other in three months. I took the average because my lawyer told me that usually the American Consulate takes from about two to four months to finalize all the documents. My exit visa was with the regional police, but they did not send it to me directly, they send it along with all of my paperwork to the Ministry of Foreign Affairs. The police told me that I no longer need to work with them, that now all of my paperwork will come through the Consulate. My lawyer wrote the Consulate a letter, telling them that they should rush my paperwork through the system because I haven't seen my children in over twenty years, I am old, and I want to be reunited with them as quickly as possible. The police warned me that I might have to spend as many as ten days in Moscow. I will be writing quite a bit to the Consulate. I will also need to have my lungs x-rayed, a blood test, and proof of immunizations against small pox. I will have to do all that when they send me the appropriate forms.

Right now I have a very unpleasant case of bronchitis, which almost developed into pneumonia. But the danger has passed, only I was worried that when I had my lungs x-rayed that there would be scars. A nurse, who lives close by, comes over and helps me take my medications according to the doctor's orders. And so you see, I am preparing myself for the trip on all fronts. That's it in terms of my physical health, and now about my spiritual health.

I'd been resolved to visit Mary of the Gates of Dawn, but because of all sorts of different reasons, I was not able to do it. Therefore, I've made my offering to Mary of the Vytautas Church in Kaunas. On February 2nd mass will be held for my intention. On February 11th Grandfather *(Father Gruodis)* will hold Holy Mass for your intention and my intention: for me to have a successful journey and for you to have a successful delivery. There is a priest who comes to visit me—someone who'd shared my fate in Siberia. We were exiled together in the same cattle car and we lived in the same place. He will also support me with his prayers. Your Aunt Veronika, may she rest in peace, has a second cousin in Utena. She has been praying for me to find my way back to you. I have another similar cousin in Rokiškis. She is a very good person. She has a university degree in chemistry and works in a textile factory as a lab supervisor. She is a very good and devout person. She is also remembering me in her prayers. And so you see, I have some very good people who are supportive of me.

Genė and Dovilė will accompany me to Moscow. I asked them first and they are only too glad to do it. If Mrs. Tysliavienė could accompany me on the flight from Moscow, I'd be very happy, because I don't feel confidant about making the flight alone in my condition. And now for my finances. I've had to spend a portion of my savings for this trip. One of the last three packages I'd received had been greatly tampered with. I will have to borrow money from Genė for the trip to Moscow, but she will get her money back when the package in her name arrives.

Now about Kotrynėlė. She asked in her letter how she could help me. I wrote and told her that I don't need anything, that my children take care of me. If she can, it would be nice for her to send something to Dovilė to thank Mindaugas, her father, for what he did for her. He helped Mrs. Baronienė bring her and Alexander out of the ghetto and to me. He did it at great personal risk. I wanted to somehow show Dovilė what kind of a man her father was—she knows him only from his photograph. Kotrynėlė could do something for her in memory of her father. If it is difficult for Kotrynėlė to understand my letter, which I wrote in Russian, then you should describe Dovilė to her. I'll finish for now because I'm getting dizzy. I kiss the three of you.

Mama

Kaunas, February 6, 1966

Dear Nijolė,

Today is Sunday, my day for writing letters. This time my hand is shaking as I write this letter because I'm being tormented by a cough. I still have bronchitis. Thank God, I can feel its getting better.

I haven't received any documents yet. One month is either direction is not that important. I must improve my health. Time is flying by quickly. Everything will happen as decided. If only I'd get over this bronchitis. Everything else is not that terrible; the most important thing is that in my soul I am calm; my worries have dissipated.

In my last letter I did not mention Lucia because I was tired from writing such a long letter. Aldona had come to visit and she showed me Lucia's photograph. She was sticking out her tongue in such a silly, devilish manner. You, Nijolė, should not allow Lucia to stick out her tongue. Children get used to doing that and then when they are three it's hard to get them out of the habit. It looks to me as though her nanny is not paying attention. Otherwise, she is a chubby girl. When Vida brings over her Algirdukas, they'll have a good time together. I'm asking you to please take good care of yourself so that nothing bad happens. I'm also worried about Vida. I tried to talk her out of getting involved with such a huge renovation. It has exhausted her.

There's not much time left until we all see each other again and are able to talk over everything in person. In the spring the birds will fly back to the homeland, but I will be flying away from the homeland. That is our family's fate. Springtime is the most beautiful time in our homeland and I will have to leave it behind. I will have to leave behind those dear pretty birds that sing to me from the fence beside my window. I'll see you soon! I kiss the three of you many many times.

Mama

Kaunas, February 11, 1966

Dear Vida,

Yesterday I received the letter from you that I'd been waiting for such a long time. You asked me when I'd receive notice of the date that I may leave. The regional police are no longer involved. My exit visa has already been sent to Moscow and I've been told that now I must wait for word from the Consulate in Moscow. My leaving is entirely dependent on them. My exit visa will be given to me in Moscow along with my passport. I don't know why it takes this long. Although one month here or there is not going to make that much of a difference. The most important thing is that my daydream has come true. Genė and Dovilė will come to Moscow with me. And if Mrs. Tysliavienė or anyone else can accompany me from Moscow, well, then that would be the greatest happiness. I no longer trust my own abilities.

You wrote that Algirdas and the children are disappointed that I am not coming to live with you. You are all equally dear to me and I would like to hug you all together at once and press you all to my heart. What can you do that the distances that separate you are so great? Thank God for the wonderful thing He has done for us. When I get there we can discuss how I will live—when and where. You're afraid that I'll be disappointed in you and in my new surroundings. Dear Lord, how could I ever answer that in a letter? I will tell you everything when I see you.

Thank the Lord that all that hardship over sending those packages is now over for you. Of course, you must not forget Dovilė. Now I ask the Lord for only one thing—the health and strength to reach you. I think only about the trip ahead of me and of the great joy I will feel when I see you again. I kiss you all many many times.

Mama

Kaunas, March 1, 1966

Dear Nijolė,

Although there is nothing new to tell you, I just wanted to write to you anyway. It has been already a month since I received the permission to join you. Soon March will pass. I've made two copies each of all the documents that I will need to bring to Moscow in order to receive my passport. Right now there is nothing but peace in my soul as I think only about my trip. I've written letters to all my relatives and friends. I keep thinking about Lucia and what it will be like when we meet and can gaze at each other eye to eye. I am a gray-haired old lady and she is a baby. But old ladies and babies know how to talk to each other—I'm sure we will too. And Vida is planning to bring Algirdukas along with her. I'm curious whether they'll fight. Well, I kiss the three of you many many times.

Mama

Kaunas, March 8, 1966

Dear Nijolė,

I wrote to you three days ago. Today I have a reason to write to you, to explain how I will receive my passport. Like I wrote to you earlier, my documents to receive a passport have been mailed to the Ministry of Foreign Affairs in Moscow. Your Consulate will need to send them my exit visa and then they will prepare my passport. Then the Consulate will inform me of what I must do and when I should arrive in Moscow.

A few days ago I received a reply to the letter I'd send to the Consulate on January 17. The Consulate answered that they still had not received my exit visa or my passport from the Ministry of Foreign Affairs. As soon as they receive it, they will contact me and tell what needs to be done. Now it's clear why it takes a few months until you can leave. The Consulate took six weeks to answer my letter. Business is conducted very slowly at the Consulate and at the Ministry. They have stacks of work and all of that takes time. My local police told me that I probably will be able to leave in April and that I should wait for a letter from the Consulate. That is good for me. All my winter illnesses will have a chance to pass and in the springtime I'll get stronger. Thank God, that awful bronchitis is gone, although I still cough in the mornings. I can breathe easier now.

Now I think only about my trip. As soon as I receive my letter from the Consulate, I will send you a telegram. I have two strong women who will help me get to Moscow. They ought to let them lead me to the airplane. They say that you must climb stairs up into the airplane; maybe they'll let them help me up the stairs. God's Image will help me make the trip. Trust in Him. I will not wait for Mrs. Tysliavienė, even though it would be much easier to travel together with her. Someone might still turn up who can help me make it through those three hours to Paris. As soon as I receive letter from the Consulate, I will leave. Putting off the trip would only make me nervous and then there would be the risk that my health would decline in the meantime.

Well, stay healthy. Until we meet again! I kiss the three of you many times.
Mama

Kaunas, March 17, 1966

Dear Vida,

Right now many Jews are leaving our country. Although they have their own Consulate, all of their exit paperwork must go through the Ministry of Foreign Affairs in Moscow. That is the agreement with Israel. They are leaving with their entire families and that is why the Ministry has such a backlog of paperwork. That's what my lawyer told me. She has promised to help me with my affairs up until the very end. My doctor is now on maternity leave, but she still comes to check my health. And so, that's how I'm getting myself ready. Let us have patience to wait. I kiss you all.

Mama

Kaunas, March 19, 1966

Dear Vida,

I wrote you only a few days ago, but then I got distracted and I forgot to write and tell you what I needed to tell you. You see, here in my neighborhood one widow's children, a five-year-old boy and a nine-year-old girl wandered quite far away from their home and they both drowned in a stream. There was a lot of confusion and noise here yesterday. Yesterday they brought them home from the Medical Institute and they held the wake at home. All sorts of curious people showed up and they started to give the mother a hard time (you see, she liked to drink). However, on the day that the children drowned, she hadn't been drinking. Don't be shocked about how I'm writing to you about this mother's habit. Right now around here alcoholism is rampant. Not only do men drink, but women too, and young people, and even children.

Because I was so upset over those children I forgot to tell you in my letter that I did not receive the package you sent by airmail. It's been a month already. As soon as I receive my letter from the Consulate I will send a telegram to Nijolė so that she can write to the Consulate and ask them not to hold up my paperwork for too long. May the Lord grant that we meet again successfully and that He may grant me just a few more years to live in your company. Pray that God may grant me the strength to undertake such a long and arduous journey.

Mama

Kaunas, March 28, 1966

Dear Vida,

You wrote that it will be sad for me to say goodbye to Genė and Dovilė. I will not be sad to say goodbye to anyone besides to my native land and to the family's plot in our cemetery where I'd always expected to lay my old bones to rest beside the people who were so dear to me. I believe that it must be painful for you and for all the Lithuanians over there who've lost their homeland without ever having done any wrong. What can you do when small countries have always been bullied by larger countries. Maybe the Lord God will compensate the small countries for all their suffering. Over here some people must wait and wait. We've waited ten years already and we're still waiting. But, the end of all that waiting is now in sight. I look to that end with all my strength and all my thoughts.
    Your husband's father came to visit. That's enough for now.

Mama

Kaunas, April 4, 1966

Dear Nijolė,

This time I am late writing to you. I am still waiting for news from the Consulate. And so Easter is just a few days away and my letter will not make it in time with my Easter greetings. That is our fate, to wait and to wait and to wait, but this final waiting is not one of tears, but one that brings hope. What can you do? Everyone who receives permission to leave must wait up to three or four months. No one is about to make any exceptions for me. After all, there is much less time left to wait. My health is getting better, and everyday I go out into the yard (actually, out onto a narrow path) and I walk around and build up my stamina. I live only in my daydreams of my trip and my meeting with you... This time I do not have appropriate cards for the holiday; my mind is on other things. Does Lucia like postcards with pictures of birds and animals on them? I will read to her when I get there. I'd like to end this letter by sending you my Easter greetings. I kiss the three of you many times. I'll see you very soon.

Mama

Kaunas, April 15, 1966

Dear Nijolė,

I've just received a letter from your country's Consulate in Moscow informing me that the Ministry of Foreign Affairs has passed on my exit visa and my passport. Any kind of news always excites me. When the postman brought the letter, which I recognized immediately from the envelope, my entire body began shaking so violently that I was barely able to sign for it. The letter had been insured. I read it quickly and I'm writing to you immediately. Now I must write to the Consulate and request that they issue me a visa to America. I have all the other necessary documents prepared (the birth certificates, photographs, and ID); now the only thing I need to do is to have my lungs x-rayed, take a blood test, and receive my immunizations. Then I will have to let them know that everything is in order. Then all I will have to do is wait for the letter announcing the date that I should be in Moscow and be ready to leave the country. The letters from the Consulate come directly to my house and usually take seven to eight days through registered mail. I think that it will probably be early May when I fly to Moscow. In this letter they tell me that the ticket to Moscow will cost me 400 rubles.

So, the signals are here that the trip that you and I have been waiting for so long will now take place. My health is getting much better and so I don't think that I will have any difficulties along the way. I kiss the three of you for now.

Mama

Kaunas, April 16, 1966

Dear Nijolė,

I wrote to you yesterday and now I am writing to you once again. I believe that you will understand my letter and my telegram. Today I wrote to the Consulate and informed them that I have all the necessary documents in hand and that I'll be waiting for notice when to leave for Moscow. They told me that I will need to spend ten days in Moscow. It will probably take a month before I receive notice when to go to Moscow. It seems as though I will only be reaching you at the end of May. Write to the Consulate and ask them not to draw things out this long. I kiss the three of you and I'll see you soon.

Mama

Kaunas, May 1, 1966

Dear Nijolė,

Today is May 1st. Unfortunately, I had no way of getting to Church because there is no way to get across the Aleksotas Bridge because of the parade. Today mass was held for deceased mothers, tomorrow they will be held for living mothers.

My letter has already reached the Consulate because I've already received my receipt with their signature on it. Every day I wait for news of when I must fly to Moscow. As soon as I receive news, I'll send you a telegram. I will send one from Moscow as well. I believe that the Lord God will guide me. There are people who have paved my way to you with their prayers and their tears.

A few days ago I went to visit Cipkutė. *(Father Stankevičius, Vida and Nijolė's religion teacher at the Aušra Gymnasium for girls.)* You cannot even imagine how happy he was to be able to send you his greetings through me. He gave me a card and some gifts to bring to you: a large chunk of amber and some small pieces, two woven sashes, and a few ties. I don't know if I'll be allowed to bring it out of the country.

The poor man has suffered much. He remembers all the girls from your class.

I'll tell all about everything when we meet. Just one moment more, one moment more and we will be together again! It seems as though it is so close... With my soul's eyes I can see all of you... I kiss you.

Goodbye for now!

Mama

This was the last letter Mama wrote from Lithuania. From then on we received word through the American Ambassador in Moscow, Foy D. Kohler. Congressman Kersten and Congressional leader John W. McCormack acted as intermediaries. On May 20th Mama was presented with her immigration visa to the United States. A few days later, on May 24th, once she'd organized her trip; she flew to Paris where she was met by Vida, Uncle Karvelis, and Mr. Edvardas Turauskas (an old friend from Voronez).

Vida accompanied Mama from Paris on the flight to New York. She arrived in New York on May 25th. In New York, at the John F. Kennedy airport, she was met by Renzo, Algimantas, and me (Nijolė.)

Afterword

When the plane landed, Mama was wheeled out in a wheel chair. I barely recognized her when I saw her. She looked old and shriveled to me, like a very ancient woman. And now, when 33 years have passed since Mama's death on August 29, 1970, I cannot think of that long dreamed of meeting without crying, a meeting that took place after 22 years separation. God helped her to fulfill her greatest wish and she lived four more years in the heart of our family and was able to participate joyfully in the lives of her granddaughters, Lucia and Laura. Unfortunately, she never had the opportunity to meet Vida's children, all of whom lived in Australia.

Dr. Nijolė Bražėnaitė-Paronetto

How Mama's Release Really Happened

All of my efforts and all of the efforts by all of the people mentioned in Mama's letters on her behalf did not result in her being allowed to leave Lithuania. Already in 1956 when Mama had returned from Siberia Congressman Charles J. Kersten was the first American to take an interest in pulling Mama out of the grips of the Soviet Union. Through Congressman Kersten's efforts Richard Nixon, vice president at the time, became involved in Mama's case. In 1959 while on a visit to the Soviet Union, Nixon presented a list of names of Lithuanians who'd been exiled to Siberia, and requested that they be granted permission to reunite with their families in the West. Mama's name was on that list. In addition, in October 1959 the aide to the Secretary of State, Roderic O'Connor and the chief of protocol, Wiley Buchanan Jr. handed Khrushchev my written request that Mama be released from the Soviet Union. Also Dr. Samuel Gringauz, whose son Alexander together with Sarah Shilingovsky had been saved by Mama during the Nazi occupation, put much effort into obtaining Mama's release.

Only Salomėja Narkeliūnaitė, a well-known Lithuanian-American journalist, was able to open up the doors for Mama to be released to the West. She did it by bribing the commission in Vilnius who decided, with Moscow's approval, who would be given permission to receive an exit visa. According to her, the commission would not release Mama because I am the widow of the partisan leader Juozas Lukša-Daumantas. When Salomėja Narkeliūnaitė asked the commission why they would not give Mama the permission to leave the Soviet Union, they shot back: "What do you think? That we're going to release that bandit's wife's mother?" Salomėja Narkeliūnaitė answered them by explaining that Mama did not even know that her daughter was that "bandit's wife." She asked why Mama had to suffer for that. In the end she put down the $1000 bribe and that settled everything.

Dr. Nijolė Bražėnaitė-Paronetto

Appendix

Konstancija Bražėnienė's Medals of Honor

In 1985, fifteen years after her death, Konstancija Bražėnienė was awarded the Yad Vashem Medal of the Righteous of the Nations of the World along with an honorary certificate for her rescue of Alexander Gringauz and Sarah Shilingovsky. Valdas Amdamkus, President of Lithuania, awarded her posthumously the Life Savior's Cross in 2000.

Item 1: The certificates that accompanied the Vashem Medal of the Righteous of the Nations of the World and Life Savior's Cross.

Photo 1: Konstancija Bražėnienė with Alexander Gringauz and Sarah Shilingovsky in New York, 1967.

Item 2: Sarah Shilingovsky's (Capelovitch) description of her rescue from the Kaunas ghetto.

Item 3: Alexander Gringauz's description of his rescue from the Kaunas ghetto.

Item 4: Typed version of Sarah Shilingovsky's handwritten letter.

Item 5: Dina Baronaitė-Steinberg's description of her rescue from the Kaunas ghetto.

Item 6: The letters of Congressman Charles J. Kersten, Roderico L. O'Connor, Dr. Samuel Gringauz, Vice-President Richard Nixon, Chief of Protocol Wiley T. Buchanen. These individuals wrote these letters on the behalf of Konstancija Bražėnienė between 1956 and 1959.

Item 7: The letters of Walter J. Stoessal Jr., Charge d'Affairs, the American Embassy in Moscow and Congressman Charles J. Kersten, 1965.

Item 1: The certificates that accompanied the Vashem Medal of the Righteous of the Nations of the World and Life Savior's Cross.

Item 2: Sarah Shilingovsky's (Capelovitch) description of her rescue from the Kaunas ghetto.

CAPELOVITCH SARAH PH.D

Neurodevelopmental Therapist
4 Pinsker St. Rehovot, Israel   76308

קפלוביץ שרה PH.D

פיזיותרפיסטית ניורו-התפתחותית
רח' פינסקר 4, רחובות 76308

Tel: +972 (0)8 9476539 :טל
Fax: + 972 (0)8 9362286 :טל
e-mail: cape_sarah@hotmail.com

30. 1. 2002

Dear Nejole,

A book should be written how a 5 year old (not quite 5) little girl is saved by a Lithuanian family while her family and a whole community of Jews are being massacared around. Dates I know not, and a book I have not written yet, it is difficult to reach into that hell - hole which is memory! A few things shine bright - the loving care of your dear mother is one, the other a bit blurred by a dark cold night, fear, tears, shivers - is a man. The man wore a uniform, he had black tall boots. The man picked me up, he covered me, because when I looked back to see the bridge and the river that I crossed - I could not see it anymore... He brought me to your mothers house and left. Sometime later, he came again, he brought my mother out of the ghetto to see me for a few minutes at dawn, before she was shipped off

THE RESCUE

On a dreary, dark, cold morning in October, 1943 a bundled up 9-year old boy stood inside the main gate of the Kovno (Kaunas) Ghetto. He was tucked into a phalanx of men, maybe eight abreast, and what seemed twenty or more men long. It was one of the many brigades which leave the Ghetto every morning under heavy guard to do labor on road and airport construction, and then return in the evening. After what seemed to the boy an interminably long march through the city, the man on his right took the boys' hand, pulled him from the brigade on to sidewalk and quickly entered a doorway to a house. "Wait here inside" he said, "someone will come soon to get you". The man left quickly to rejoin the brigade.

The door had a glass window through which the boy was   able to observe the   comings and goings on the street. The brigade soon vanished. Pedestrians were walking on both sides of the street. He could also see horses pulling wagons. The scene was interspersed with motor vehicles, most trucks and occasional cars. Many of the vehicles had Nazi insignia on their doors and hoods.

The boy waited constantly peering out through the glass portion of the door. Shortly he noticed a solitary "German" soldier carrying a rifle on his shoulder beginning to cross the street diagonally towards the door. The boy was suddenly gripped with fear. He wanted to run but the second door behind him leading into the house was locked. The soldier quickly entered the small alcove, looked down on him and asked: "Are you Alexander"? The boy nodded. "Come with me". He took the boy by the hand and they briskly crossed the street. They didn't speak again for the longest time. As the boy's fear subsided he suddenly blurt out "Where are you taking me"? "To my mother's house", the soldier said curtly. Nothing further was said until they reached their destination.

They entered the house; an elderly woman came out to greet them. She smiled stretching her hands out towards the boy. "This is my mother", the soldier said. The boy felt safe.

The boy was Alexander Gringauz
The soldier – Mindaugas Brazenas

Item 4: Typed version of Sarah Shilingovsky's handwritten letter.

CAPELOVITCH SARAH PH.D

Neurodevelopmental Therapist
4 Pinsker St. Rehovot, Israel 76308

30. 1. 2002

Dear Nijole,

A book should be written how a 5 year old (not quite 5) little girl is saved by Lithuanian famil7y while her family and whole community of Jews are being massacrated. Dates I know not, and a book I have not written yet, it is difficult to reach into that hell-hole, which is memory!. A few things shine bright – the loving care of your dear mother is one, the other a bit blurred by a dark cold night, fear, tears, shivers - is a man. The man wore a uniform, he had black tall boots. The man picked me up, he covered me, because when I looked back to see the bridge and the river that I crossed – I could not see it anymore... He brought me to your mother's house and left. Sometime late, he came again, he brought my mother out of the ghetto to see me for a few minutes at dawn, before she was shipped off to Schtuthoff – a death camp for Jewish women. Your mother called him Mindaugas, I am pretty sure it was the same young man that picked me up at the foot of the "funiculaire" – at the foot of the hill. I know now, that the children of ghetto Kaunas were gathered and extermninated just after that.

I am here, I have two lovely daughters, two beautiful grandchildren, a loving husband.

The family of Konstanca Brazeniene (I apologize if I misspelled the name of that dear woman) – provided a life line of love and care amidst a world of hate and annihilation.

All my love to you and yours,

Sarah – or as named by your family - Katrinele

Item 5: Dina Baronaitė-Steinberg's description of her rescue from the Kaunas ghetto.

In memory of Konstancija Bražėnienė and her acts of heroism saving Jews during World War Two in Lithuania.

Dina Baronaitė-Steinberg was born in 1922 in Kaunas and lived in Kaunas until December, 1944. This is her story:

During World War Two my family lived in Kaunas, on Ukmergė Street 34. My father, Benjamin Baronas, an accountant, worked in a bank and also managed the estate of the widow, Mrs. Bražėnienė, most especially the management and rental of her property on Laisvės Alėja.

When the war began my father and his brother, Daniel, were arrested and later killed because they were Jews. My mother, Bela, and I had to go to the ghetto in Vilijampolė. Mrs. Bražėnienė, who lived in Aleksotas, and who my mother and I had never personally met, made it known to my mother that she was prepared to help us. At the time we were preparing for our trip to Vilijampolė together with our neighbors, Mrs. Shilingovsky and her four-year-old daughter Sarah. We lived in the ghetto from 1941 – 1944 and the entire time we maintained contact with Mrs. Bražėnienė. When the Jewish work brigade would be marched to the Aleksotas airport to work, my mother would sometimes slip away and go see Mrs. Bražėnienė. In October 1943 my mother made plans with Mrs. Bražėnienė to have Sarah and Alexander brought to her. In this way these two children were saved. Mrs. Bražėnienė had falsified documents made for me, stating that I was a Lithuanian girl, so that I could escape the ghetto. In October 1943 I succeeded in slipping out of the ghetto. I was on my way to the home of Mrs. Bražėnienė to pick up the documents that she had prepared when I was intercepted by the Gestapo and placed in prison on Mickevičius Street in Kaunas. If I had been able to reach the home of Mrs. Bražėnienė safely, my mother and I both would have had a safe place to hide there.

I was returned to the Kaunas ghetto from the prison. On June 14 – 15, 1944 the ghetto commandant announced that all of the ghetto's occupants would be sent to forced labor in Germany. A day before the ghetto was liquidated I slipped through the barbed wire that surrounded the ghetto and tried to reach Mrs. Bražėnienė once again. However, I could not cross the Vilijampolė Bridge because soldiers were checking people's documents at the entrance to the bridge. My mother managed to escape from the train used to liquidate the ghetto to Germany and did reach Mrs. Bražėnienė safely. She hid in the home of Mrs. Bražėnienė safely for three weeks until the Germans withdrew from Kaunas.

Risking her life and the lives of her family, Mrs. Bražėnienė saved the lives of the Jews I've mentioned in this statement. In her name a tree is planted in the Jad Vashem Garden of the World's Righteous. May her loving memory live on in our hearts.

Dina Steinberg
June 30, 1992,
Savyon, Israel

Item 6: The letters of Congressman Charles J. Kersten, Roderico L. O'Connor, Dr. Samuel Gringauz, Vice-President Richard Nixon, Chief of Protocol Wiley T. Buchanen. These individuals wrote these letters on the behalf of Konstancija Braženienė between 1956 and 1959.

<u>AIRMAIL</u>   May 23rd, 1959

The Honorable Richard M. Nixon
Vice President of the United States
Senate Office Building
Washington, D. C.
                        RE: <u>KONSTANCIJA BRAZENIENE</u> (LITHUANIA)

Dear Dick:

About two years ago, at my request, you asked our Moscow
Consulate to assist the immigration to the US of the above
Lithuanian mother to be re-united with her daughter who is
now a permanent US resident living in New York.

On February 28th, 1958, I am informed, our Moscow Consulate
granted the mother a permanent US immigration visa.   In
October of 1958 the Soviet authorities refused her exit.

The case is a very worthy one, Dick.   Typically heart-breaking.
If, when you are in Moscow, you could make known to a top Soviet
your wishes in the matter and an exit permit were given this
poor mother, many prayers of thanksgiving would be said by the
daughter, Dr. Nijole Brazenas, Mt. Sinai Hospital, New York,---
and by a host of her friends.

I am told that when Stevenson and Mrs. Roosevelt were in Moscow
they effected a release in several such compassionate cases.
As I told my Baltic friends in New York, what S. and Mrs. R. can
do, Dick Nixon can do twice as well because he has a bigger heart.

The mother's name and address are: <u>Konstancija Brazeniene, 67 yrs,</u>
<u>Lithuania, Utenos Rajonas, Utenas Pastas, Kolchozas "Naujoji Vaga."</u>
About 3-4 years ago she was permitted to return to Lithuania from
a lumber camp on an island in Lake Baikal, Siberia.

The daughter, Dr. Brazenas, married one who was probably the most
heroic Lithuanian underground leader when he made his way thru the
Iron Curtain into Germany in 1948.   He was parachuted back into
the Communist orbit in 1950 by US plane and shortly thereafter met
death at the hands of the Communists.

Mary Kizis, in charge of the American-Lithuanian Center in NY is
very much interested in this case, too.

Might you help?   Best Regards.   Asevvvx.

                                (Charles J. Kersten)

DEPARTMENT OF STATE
WASHINGTON

In reply refer to
VO 150 Brazeniene, Konstancija   August 24, 1956

Dear Mr. Vice President:

    I refer to your memorandum of August 1, 1956 with which you enclosed the
attached letter from a former Member of Congress, The Honorable Charles J. Kersten,
regarding his interest in the desire of Doctor Nijole Brazenas, presently at Met-
ropolitan Hospital in New York City, to bring her mother, Mrs. Konstancija Brazeniene,
to the United States from the Soviet Union.

    It is noted that Doctor Brazenas is not a citizen of the United States but that
her brother, Mr. Algimantas Brazenas of Detroit is a citizen and can sponsor his
mother, I would suggest that he file a petition for her on Form I-133 xxipxipx
with the Immigration and Naturalization Service, Department of Justice, 3770 East
Jefferson Avenue, Detroit. This will serve to accord her a second preference-status
within the quota of her country of birth, presumably Lithuania. At the moment second
preference numbers are available under the Lithuanian quota.

    When Mr. Brazenas' approved petition is received from the Immigration and Na-
turalization Service, we will send it at once to the American Embassy at Moscow.
Upon its receipt there, the Embassy will inform Mrs. Brazeniene of her immigration status
and what documents it will be necessary for her to present in support of her visa
application. She will also be informed where she should apply for the necessary permission to leave the Soviet Union.

    No persons living in the Soviet Union or Soviet administered territories can
legally leave with Soviet exit permits. The Soviet authorities have repeatedly indi-
cated that the issuance of such documents is a matter over which they exercise ex-
clusive jurisdiction. Although the Department has on a number of occasions, one
very recent, made representations to the Soviet Government regarding the general problem of close relatives of American citizens desirous of joining members of their
families in the United States, it is felt that any attempt to intercede on an individual basis in behalf of Mrs. Brazeniene at this time would tend to hamper rather
than help her in her efforts to obtain permission from the Soviet authorities to
leave. In recent months there has been a slight increase in the number of close relatives of United States citizens who have been permitted to leave. It is interesting
to note in this connection that none of them have been cases in which our Government
made representations.

    In the thought that it might possibly strengthen Mrs. Brazeniene's application
for a Soviet exit permit, her son may wish to consider writing her a non-political letter that she can present to the Soviet authorities expressing his desire to have her
join him in the United States for permanent residence and suggesting that she make
application for a Soviet exit permit. If such permit is granted she should communicate
immediately with the American Embassy at Moscow, which will extend all appropriate assistance to her in applying for an immigrant visa for entry into the United States.

Mr. Brazenas might also prepare and mail directly to the Embassy an affidavit of support for his mother since the Embassy will need evidence to show that her support will be assured in the United States in determining her eligibility to receive a visa. Subdivision 7 of the enclosed Departmental leaflet contains general suggestions for the preparation of an affidavit of support.

In order that the consular officer conserned may know of the steps contemplated in this case and Mr. Kersten's interest in having everything possible done to facilitate the emigration of Mrs. Brazeniene, I have sent the Embassy a copy of his letter as well as of my letter to you.

Sincerely yours,

Roderic L. O'Connor
Acting Assistant Secretary

Enclosures:

1. VO-General Leaflet
2. From Mr. Kersten
   July 12, 1956

Item 6: The letters of Congressman Charles J. Kersten, Roderico L. O'Connor, Dr. Samuel Gringauz, Vice-President Richard Nixon, Chief of Protocol Wiley T. Buchanen. These individuals wrote these letters on the behalf of Konstancija Bražėnienė between 1956 and 1959.

DR. SAMUEL GRINGAUZ
NEW YORK N. Y.
MONUMENT 2-1800

447 Fort Washington Ave
Apt 63

Lietuvos Konsului
New York.

Vasario mėn 19d, 1957

Gerbiamasis Tamsta!

Turiu garbės prašyti Tamstą padėti man sužinoti panelės medic. daktaro Noelės Bražinaitės antrašą. Pan. Bražinaitės motina padėjo pagelbėjo mano sūnui Wasiui persekiojimo laikais. Jos tėvas buvo Kauno Miesto Savivaldybės architektas. Po karo pan. studijavo Austrijoje ir emigravo Amerikon.

Prieš porą dienų gavau žinią iš Izraelio, kad ponia Bražinienė buvo deportuota iš Lietuvos ir prašė pagalbos. Kadangi gautoje žinioje nebuvo pažymėtas ponios Bražinienės antrašas, darau pastangų sužinoti ponios Bražinienės antrašą ir būčiau Tamstai labai dėkingas jeigu galėtumėi man jį suteikti.

Reiškiant pagarbos
Sam. Gringauz
Buv. Klaipėdos Advokatas.

Item 6: The letters of Congressman Charles J. Kersten, Roderico L. O'Connor, Dr. Samuel Gringauz, Vice-President Richard Nixon, Chief of Protocol Wiley T. Buchanen. These individuals wrote these letters on the behalf of Konstancija Bražėnienė between 1956 and 1959.

OFFICE OF THE VICE PRESIDENT

WASHINGTON

June 10, 1959

Dear Dr. Brazenas:

This is just a note to thank you for your letter of June 4 concerning your desire to have your mother come to the United States. Charles Kersten also wrote me about your situation.

I have the most sympathetic interest in this entire problem, as a large number of people have written who have members of their family separated from them and living in the Soviet Union. It is my intention to take this matter up with the Communist authorities and, while I do not know what their attitude will be on specific individuals nor what the general world situation will be during my visit, I can assure you that I will do everything possible to be of assistance.

With all best wishes,

Sincerely,

Richard Nixon

Nijole V. Brazenas, M.D.
105 West 72nd Street
New York 23, New York

Item 6: The letters of Congressman Charles J. Kersten, Roderico L. O'Connor, Dr. Samuel Gringauz, Vice-President Richard Nixon, Chief of Protocol Wiley T. Buchanen. These individuals wrote these letters on the behalf of Konstancija Bražėnienė between 1956 and 1959.

DEPARTMENT OF STATE
WASHINGTON

October 22, 1959

Dear Dr. Brazenas:

    I received your letter which you sent to me at the President's Guest House. In the presence of Chairman Khrushchev I gave it to one of his assistants. They said it would receive attention.

        Sincerely yours,

        Wiley T. Buchanan, Jr.
          Chief of Protocol

Nijole V. Brazenas, M.D.,
   2044 Cropsey Avenue,
      Brooklyn 14,
        New York.

Item 7: The letters of Walter J. Stoessal Jr., Charge d'Affairs, the American Embassy in Moscow and Congressman Charles J. Kersten, 1965.

EMBASSY
OF THE
UNITED STATES OF AMERICA

American Embassy, Moscow,
Department of State,
Washington, D. C. 20521.
June 9, 1965

Dear Mr. Speaker:

In the absence of Ambassador Kohler, I am replying to your letter of May 25, 1965 regarding the immigrant case of Mrs. Konstancija BRAZENIENE, mother of Dr. Nijole Brasenas PARONETTO, 11 Riverside Drive, New York.

Mrs. Brazeniene last reapplied for Soviet exit documentation in December 1964. The Embassy subsequently notified the USSR Ministry of Foreign Affairs of her application and requested the Ministry's favorable consideration. The Embassy, however, has received no information regarding the outcome of her latest application.

It is important to keep in mind that many of the limited number of persons who have been fortunate enough to secure Soviet exit documents have been successful only after repeated applications extending over a number of years. In the event the application is refused, the Embassy understands OVIR's, depending on the locality, will accept new applications six months to one year from the date of the refusal.

Please be assured that Mrs. Brazeniene will be given every consideration consistent with the applicable laws and regulations of the United States if Soviet authorities grant her exit permission.

Sincerely yours,

Walter J. Stoessel Jr.
Charge d'Affaires a.i.

The Honorable
John W. McCormack,
U. S. House of Representatives,
Washington, D. C. 20515.

Item 7: The letters of Walter J. Stoessal Jr., Charge d'Affairs, the American Embassy in Moscow and Congressman Charles J. Kersten, 1965.

KERSTEN & McKINNON
ATTORNEYS AT LAW

CHARLES J. KERSTEN
ARLO MC KINNON
J. P. MC KINNON
E. CAMPION KERSTEN
GEORGE F. KERSTEN
. KERSTEN

MILWAUKEE OFFICES

231 W. WISCONSIN AVE.
MILWAUKEE, WIS. 53203
271 - 0054

June 18, 1965

Nijole V. Brazenas, M.D.
11 Riverside Drive
New York, New York 10023

Dear Nijole:

I received a letter from Speaker John McCormack in this morning's mail with an enclosed letter from the American Embassy in Moscow, copies of both of which are herewith enclosed.

With best regards to you and Renzo.

As ever,

Charles J. Kersten

CJK:smr

Enclosures